THE SILENT PARTNER

THE SILENT PARTNER
West Germany and Arms Control

Barry M. Blechman and
Cathleen S. Fisher

with

Jeffrey Boutwell
Clay Clemens and
Stephen F. Szabo

AN INSTITUTE FOR DEFENSE ANALYSES BOOK

BALLINGER PUBLISHING COMPANY
Cambridge, Massachusetts
A Subsidiary of Harper & Row, Publishers, Inc.

International Standard Book Numbers: 0-88730-316-1 (CL)
0-88730-320-X (PB)

Library of Congress Catalog Card Number: 88-6174

Printed in the United States of America

LIBRARY OF CONGRESS
Library of Congress Cataloging-in-Publication Data

Blechman, Barry M.
The silent partner : West Germany and arms control / Barry M. Blechman and Cathleen S. Fisher : with Jeffrey Boutwell, Clay Clemens, and Stephen F. Szabo.
    p. cm.
"An Institute for Defense Analyses book."
Includes index.
ISBN 0-88730-316-1.   ISBN 0-88730-320-X (pbk.)
1. Nuclear arms control—Germany (West)   2. Security, International.
I. Fisher, Cathleen S.   II. Boutwell, Jeffrey D.   III. Title
JX1974.7.B58 1988
327.1′74′0943—dc 19   88-6174
                                                            CIP

CONTENTS

LIST OF FIGURES

LIST OF TABLES

FOREWORD

Soviet General Secretary Mikhail Gorbachev appears to have made arms control initiatives a central element in his European policy, with dramatic effects on European perceptions of the two great powers, the threat of war, and the possibilities of significant cutbacks in military forces. Conclusion of the Stockholm Agreement on Confidence and Security Building Measures in 1986 and the 1987 U.S.-Soviet Treaty on Intermediate-range Nuclear Missiles are the first tangible results. Budget pressures in all NATO countries, as well as within the Warsaw Pact, the convening in 1988 of European talks on conventional forces, and the proposals for major reductions in conventional forces already put forward by the Warsaw Pact guarantee that arms control negotiations will remain central among European security issues for some time to come.

Mr. Gorbachev no doubt has many reasons for the high priority he accords to arms control. Domestic political and economic factors are important parts of his motivation. It also seems clear, however, that the potentially negative impact of arms control initiatives on political harmony within the Federal Republic of Germany and, most importantly, on Bonn's relations with its allies in NATO—particularly with the United States—are key considerations in Gorbachev's arms control offensive. The intermediate-range missile negotiations have already had divisive political effects within West Germany, causing heated controversy within the ruling party coalition, straining U.S.-FRG ties, and embarrassing Chancellor Helmut Kohl. Moreover, the preparations within NATO for the talks on conventional arms have revealed differences in perspective between West Germany and several of the allies, differences which if not resolved effectively could have serious long-term consequences for the Alliance.

Arms Control Issues and Processes in the Federal Republic of Germany provides a comprehensive factual base for understanding West German attitudes on arms control issues, the role these questions play in the German political system, and the complex military and political considerations that determine Bonn's positions on these matters. It also provides a road map for understanding the FRG's decisionmaking system, identifying the key organizations and individuals who play a part in the decision process, and laying out the formal and informal arrangements through which arms control decisions are made.

This book is a modified version of a report prepared for IDA in 1987. The primary authors, Barry Blechman and Cathleen Fisher, thank Robbin Laird and Victor Utgoff for their advice and assistance in the project. The opinions expressed in this book are those of the listed authors and are not necessarily endorsed by the Institute for Defense Analyses.

W.Y. Smith
President
Institute for Defense Analyses

1 OVERVIEW

Geopolitics, history, and events since World War II have rooted the Federal Republic of Germany (FRG) firmly in the West; however, the same factors have given Bonn a substantial interest in developing good relations with its eastern neighbors. As a significant but nonnuclear member of NATO, the FRG's relationship with the United States and other allies is the cornerstone of its security policy. This special dependency, of course, has enhanced West German security, but has tied Bonn's security inextricably to American and Soviet policies, and to the general climate of East-West relations.

West German arms control policy, as part of its broader security policy, is no exception. The arms control policy of the Federal Republic is shaped by a continuing interplay between domestic considerations and changes in the international context, both in the East and the West. This persistent tension between the internal and the external, and between Bonn's *Westpolitik* and *Ostpolitik*, is a necessary background for understanding the FRG's arms control policy.

In a very real sense, Bonn's arms control policy is "hostage" to Germany's commitment to a close relationship with the United States and to NATO. Initially, the arms control process was seen solely as part of the superpowers' relationship, to be left in the hands of the United States. As the process expanded to include multilateral forums, however, and became more institutionalized, the FRG was compelled to develop both the capacity and the decisionmaking procedures to address arms control matters. The development of a more independent decisionmaking capacity is likely to continue in the future, particularly if Bonn becomes increasingly dissatisfied with what it perceives as an American predilection toward unilateralism.

Over time, moreover, arms control has come to be linked in the West German public's mind with an ongoing process of détente, or *Ostpolitik*.

On the whole, West Germans are inclined to give a positive assessment of the relative benefits and costs of the détente of the 1970s, particularly with regard to the value of improvements in inter-German relations. Accordingly, West German politicians and government decisionmakers tend to embrace a hazy notion of détente and arms control as serving German interests, or at least offering reassurance to an *Angst*-laden public.

This general orientation notwithstanding, specific arms control policy decisions may be explained on the basis of governmental decisionmaking processes and the views of specific officials. In the Federal Republic, real power is lodged solely in the executive branch, and on arms control issues, the voice of the Foreign Minister and his deputies is decisive. The Federal Republic's constitution and other legal documents, a long history of powerful bureaucracies, and the structure of Bonn's parliamentary system of government effectively guarantee the executive's predominance; legislative organs play only secondary roles. The Bundestag may provide a setting for public debate, but it cannot determine executive decisions, or even influence them directly, as can the U.S. Congress; opposition parties can only seek to educate the public on alternative views (and the talents of their security experts), in order to influence future elections and to prepare for a return to power. National political parties do channel information on public attitudes to government officials, however.

The future evolution of West German arms control policy will depend similarly on both domestic and international developments. National elections in January 1987 returned the center-right coalition to power, but by a substantially smaller margin than had been expected, given West Germany's then-favorable economic prospects. The election also resulted in a shift of weight within the coalition between the Christian Democratic and Christian Social Union (CDU/CSU) and the small Free Democratic Party (FDP). The gains of the FDP were widely interpreted as a vote of confidence in the foreign policy leadership of Foreign Minister Hans-Dietrich Genscher. Thus domestic factors favor continuity in FRG arms control policy. However, future policy decisions will depend also on developments in the international context, in particular the course of Soviet-American, Soviet-German, and German-American relations.

This study explores the sources of West German arms control policies and the processes through which they are determined. In this overview, we review the key actors in the process, both within and outside the government, and discuss the sources of their beliefs and the specific positions they tend to prefer. The concluding section projects rough outlines of FRG arms control policies in light of the January 1987 electoral outcome under alternative international scenarios.

The "Special Analyses" which follow include more detailed descriptions of the preferred arms control policies (and the sources of such views) of each of the major political parties in the FRG (CDU/CSU, SPD [Social Democratic Party], FDP, and Greens), an assessment of West German public attitudes toward arms control, and a detailed description of the decisionmaking process within the West German government. Short biographies of key actors are included in the Appendix.

DECISIONMAKING PROCESSES AND ACTORS

Arms control policy in the Federal Republic in large measure bears the stamp of executive actors. The Basic Law and related legal documents assign primary responsibility for the conduct of foreign policy, which has been interpreted to include arms control negotiations, to the Foreign Office. By the same token, the Basic Law's right of concurrence (*Mitzeichnungsrecht*) guarantees the Ministry of Defense (MoD) an input into the policy process. The long-standing tradition of professional civil service and the one-sided balance of power inherent in a parliamentary system further cement the predominance of executive agencies. Consequently, although the Bundestag as an institution, all national political parties, and other nongovernmental actors may attempt to channel their views to relevant decisionmakers, only the parties that govern can tap directly into bureaucratic sources of expertise and power. Opposition parties and nongovernmental actors may serve to inform government officials of new ideas and changes in public attitudes, but in general they can play only secondary roles.

Interagency coordination and conflict resolution are persistent problems in the decisionmaking process within the executive branch. Coordination among executive agencies is complicated by the generally decentralized character of the Bonn bureaucracy and the autonomy enjoyed by division heads. Within the executive branch, conflict often has developed between the Foreign Office and the Ministry of Defense, or between one or the other and the Chancellor's Office. The Foreign Minister has been a member of the minority party in the governing coalition for almost two decades; this has tended to reinforce institutional conflicts. Indeed, in general, coalition politics and the competing aims and agendas of the governing parties are an important source of friction and conflict.

A further complication derives from the Federal Republic's membership in NATO and its close relations with the United States. As already noted, domestic decisionmaking processes are never insulated from the influence of American attitudes. Within NATO, a complex structure of consultative bodies and procedures has evolved to handle arms control issues; many opportunities for bilateral exchanges exist as well. In theory, such channels can function as a "two-way street" to influence arms control policy either in Bonn or in Washington. In practice, NATO and bilateral channels provide more constraint than opportunity for decisionmakers in Bonn.

In the future, multilateral forums will constitute an increasingly important counterweight against American predominance in the arms control process. The Conference on Security and Cooperation in Europe (CSCE) process has spawned a multitude of mechanisms to coordinate with Bonn's European allies in NATO and members of the European Community (European Political Cooperation). These have been supplemented since 1982 with frequent bilateral Franco-German consultations on a range of security matters.

WEST GERMAN ATTITUDES ON ARMS CONTROL

A variety of domestic and international factors influence the attitudes of all actors in the West German decisionmaking process. Geopolitical realities and the division of the German nation constrain all policymakers. The lessons of German history, ideological traditions, and the perceived benefits of *Ostpolitik* and détente shape perceptions of security needs and policies. Additionally, such internal factors as political and sociological changes may alter perceptions of security needs and the role of arms control. The net impact of these variables is a set of broadly shared attitudes and concerns.

Geopolitical Factors

All actors in the policy process share an awareness of West Germany's geopolitical situation. The fact that Germany is divided creates a perception of special security needs. Close relations with the West, above all with the United States, are seen by a majority as indispensable to West German security; at the same time, the FRG has special interests in maintaining good relations with the East. The result is an underlying tension between policy components, sometimes more apparent than not, which poses problems for all West German leaders, regardless of party. In the 1950s, this tension took the form of a domestic debate over rearmament which, the SPD argued, would cement the division of Germany and eliminate any hope of reunification in the short run. A more recent example was the controversy over the deployment of intermediate-range nuclear forces (INF); critics of the NATO dual-track decision argued that deployment would threaten the gains of the inter-German détente of the 1970s. The CDU, which otherwise supported the decision, thus took parallel actions to prevent a deterioration in Bonn's relations with Eastern Europe and inter-German relations as the missiles were being deployed, granting trade credits to East Germany to coincide with the beginning of deployments. The division of Germany and Bonn's special interest in an East-West climate conducive to inter-German dialogue do not necessarily mean that a desire to continue *Ostpolitik* will override all other security considerations. But it will mean that any party in power will be at least concerned about the atmospherics of East-West relations.

The border running between East and West Germany obviously divides NATO and Warsaw Pact countries as well. This "frontline" position contributes to an acute sense of vulnerability; even the public's only dim awareness of the presence of large numbers of Allied troops and weapons on West German soil heightens the sense of being the "most exposed" member of the alliance. This "frontline" position influences attitudes toward arms control in a number of sometimes contradictory ways. For many West Germans, it underscores the importance of the American connection, and creates concern lest any specific arms control agreement be "decoupling," or introduce tensions to the relationship. This concern was reflected in the Kohl government's critical reaction to the arms control agreements discussed at the November 1986 Reykjavik summit, and in the reaction of CDU/CSU conservatives to the proposal in spring 1987 to remove all intermediate nuclear forces from the FRG. Similarly, Gorbachev's offer in March 1987 to delink an agreement on intermediate-range nuclear forces from negotiations on strategic defenses led Kohl, Dregger, and other figures in the CDU to caution the West against concluding an agreement on INF unless measures were taken to address imbalances in shorter range systems and conventional weapons.

The general sense of exposure and vulnerability among members of the German electorate also may prevent any party, once in office, from implementing the more extreme aspects of its program. It is not certain, for example, that even an SPD majority government could proceed decisively with arms control policies that caused difficulties within the alliance and thus were perceived to run counter to the majority's pro-NATO sentiments. On the other hand, a latent *Angst*, surfacing primarily during times of increasing international tension, causes even CDU governments to press hard for progress in arms control, if only for its reassurance effects. In this sense, the arms control process itself may be more important to many West Germans than the specific terms of particular agreements. Many West Germans share the view that as long as the superpowers are talking, things cannot be all bad. Such attitudes are rooted fundamentally in basic feelings of insecurity due to West Germany's geopolitical place in Europe.

Historical Factors

No matter what their party affiliation, all West German arms control actors share a common historical legacy that may influence attitudes on security and nuclear weapons in the broadest sense. The experience of combat, devastation, and occupation during World War II undoubtedly continues to affect views on the role of force and the relative efficacy of military defense and détente. The impact of the war was most evident in the first decade of the Federal Republic's existence. Resistance, first, to rearmament and, subsequently, to the deployment of U.S. nuclear weapons in Germany, drew strength from antimilitarist sentiment. Civil-military relations, though generally good, can still be a point of contention. Though many of the West German leaders now in power were not directly exposed to war and its aftermath, there are sufficient reminders of the past. While younger West Germans may not feel the deep aversion to the use of force that was typical of the immediate post-war period, they are likely to be at least ambivalent, all the more so when the issue concerns the use of nuclear weapons. The German electorate's recognition of the implications of any war, conventional or nuclear, for West Germany is linked importantly to their perception of the relative utility of arms control for West German security.

The German ideological tradition continues to influence the policies of the political parties toward arms control. In its most basic form, an ideology may color a party's entire outlook on security. The Social Democrats' historical tradition of antimilitarism and internationalism was doubtless a factor in the party's opposition to rearmament in the 1950s. In one sense, the SPD's rejection of INF deployments in the 1980s, as well as its current departures from NATO's existing policies, are a return to normalcy—a revival of older SPD notions about security and German interests.

Similarly, the CDU/CSU's attitudes toward arms control are rooted in a strong tradition of anti-Communism. Among conservative West Germans, anti-Communism retains its potency, magnifying perceptions of a persistent Soviet threat and underscoring the importance of military readiness. Any departure from tried-and-true *Westpolitik*, any venture that is seen to lead to neutralism or "Finlandization" is rejected. Anti-Communism feeds the sense of primacy afforded the American connection. As a result of this more or less latent ideological underpinning, the CDU/CSU views arms control as an uncertain variable, and is particularly uneasy about the possible decoupling effects of many actual or prospective arms control agreements, including SALT I and II and the separate agreement that will bring about the total elimination of intermediate nuclear missiles from Europe.

Internal ideological disputes may affect the priority that parties assign to military defense and détente, or arms control, as well. The Social Democratic Party, for example, has suffered from internal tension between its doctrinaire socialist and reformist social democratic factions. While such ideological disputes are primarily a response to domestic political and social changes, they sometimes have spilled over into security issues. For example, the emergence of the Greens as a national political force in the late 1970s threatened to steal voters away from the SPD's left wing. Internal wrangling over whether to move the party leftward in response to changing social conditions led to the emergence of a counterelite (*Gegenelite*) that challenged Helmut Schmidt's leadership of the party. Eventually, this *Gegenelite* also began to explore alternative security conceptions, such as the "security partnership" with the East, as means of regaining the support of these defectors.

A third, more recent historical experience was the successful *Ostpolitik* in the 1970s. For many West Germans and, above all, for West Berliners, the Soviet-American and inter-German rapprochement of the early 1970s was not merely an ephemeral phase of East-West good feeling, but resulted in concrete, visible improvements. Few would deny, for example, that the security of West Berlin was well served by the 1971 Quadripartite Agreement. Today, West Germans may disagree about the cost of further improvements in East-West relations, but few would favor a return to the hostile truce of the 1950s and 1960s.

This generally positive assessment of the détente period causes West Germans to view the arms control process more favorably than do most Americans; there was not a widespread sense of disillusionment about the process of détente in Bonn, as in Washington. In fact, both the FDP and the SPD currently proclaim hopes for a new phase of détente. Many, though certainly not all West Germans have come to view arms control as part-and-parcel of détente and support it as such.

Internal Changes

Domestic sociological and political changes may cause shifts in attitudes toward security and arms control. Two recent outgrowths of the INF debates, the "securitization" of West German politics and the revival of the German national question, have fostered a new-found sense of legitimacy for specific "German interests" and may lend security issues a lasting salience on the nation's political agenda.

Following the extensive mobilization of antinuclear groups in the early 1980s, some analysts suggested that security policy-making in the Federal Republic had been "democratized." But the controversy over the NATO dual-track decision, in fact, has not changed the process of arms control decisionmaking in the manner implied. There is little evidence that new channels for popular influence have been opened or new means created to check the predominance of executive agencies. Existing mechanisms for legislative input have not been exploited to their fullest due to persistent constraints on resources and know-how and the inherent limitations of a parliamentary system. Security policy-making, in this sense, has not been "democratized."

The true impact of the INF debates may be the lasting "securitization" of politics in the Federal Republic. Elections may continue to turn on economic issues—growth, unemployment, and tax reform—but security issues have greater saliency than before. Public acceptability has become a more important criterion of arms control decisionmaking. West German leaders have become more attuned to any policy's perceived impact on the overall *process* of arms control, though public understanding of, and interest in, negotiating positions remains sketchy and therefore of less significance. Within the Foreign Office, more careful attention may be paid to the various barometers of public opinion—party resolutions and platforms, or Bundestag debates on security and arms control policy—to determine the likely public reaction to any specific policy position. The Chancellor's Office, ever concerned for the impact of policy decisions on the chancellor's popularity and on support for the government, seeks to ensure that a repeat of the INF debate does not occur. An ongoing arms control process is desirable if only to reassure Germans that the East-West dialogue continues.

"Securitization" of the decisionmaking process has been reinforced by the revival of interest in the German question. The latter is no longer posed primarily in terms of reunification, but has taken on a number of forms. Whether the talk is of German identity, or a shared "community of fate" between the GDR and FRG, a common element is a new-found confidence in the legitimacy of what are perceived as specifically German interests. This may help to explain the SPD's slogan in the 1983 elections: "Im Deutschen Interesse" ("in the German interest"). Four years later, the SPD, from the more conservative Helmut Schmidt to spokesmen of the party's leftwing, called for the "self-affirmation" (*Selbstbehauptung*) of Europe. The CDU/CSU, once an ardent opponent of *Ostpolitik*, in essence has continued the social-liberal policies with only cosmetic rhetorical changes. The concern for protecting the inter-German dialogue from escalating tensions between the superpowers translated into conciliatory policies to parallel the beginning of INF deployments, including a one billion DM trade credit deal with East Germany facilitated by Franz Josef Strauss. For the FDP, German national interests tend to be cast in the guise of a renewed enthusiasm for the European "pillar" of NATO, or talk of the Europeans taking a more independent and united role in arms control vis-à-vis the United States. The common theme running through each party's policies is a readiness to press what are perceived as special German interests.

If it proves a lasting trend, the "securitization" of politics and discussion of German identity and interests may cause West German governments to become stronger advocates of positions perceived to be in the German national interest, even when such positions diverge from American or NATO policies to a degree. In some instances, this may mean pressuring the United States to conclude arms control negotiations or, conversely, to ensure that West German interests are safeguarded in specific Soviet-American arms control agreements; in others, it may mean an emphasis on new forms of European consultation and cooperation, with the goal of devising independent positions on arms control. The most direct link between arms control issues and the inter-German dialogue, however, would be official arms control negotiations between the Federal Republic and the GDR. The Social Democratic Party and the East German ruling Socialist Unity Party have already completed the outlines of draft treaties to ban chemical weapons in Central Europe and to create a corridor free of tactical nuclear weapons along the interbloc border. While the Liberal Party (FDP) has excluded the possibility of a separate arms control dialogue with East Germany, Foreign Minister Genscher does favor consultations between the two Germanies within existing multilateral arms control negotiating forums. Moreover, former Special Commissioner Friedrich Ruth met on occasion with his East German counterpart to discuss arms control issues.

General Concerns and Attitudes

The factors discussed above shape the attitudes of all actors in the arms control decisionmaking process, as well as public concerns. A number of broadly shared views are discernible, not all of them mutually compatible:

1. *Support for the process of arms control.* Whether out of pragmatism or conviction, a majority of West Germans support the arms control process, as broadly defined. In the case of the CDU/CSU, support may be most closely related to an awareness that an arms control dialogue dampens public feelings of vulnerability. It may also be seen as a way to sustain a consensus behind what the CDU/CSU perceives as the vital component of West German security—the American nuclear guarantee and the NATO connection. In contrast, the Social Democrats perceive the arms control process as an integral component of détente, a necessary concomitant of successful *Ostpolitik*. Similarly, the FDP is committed to the arms control process for its intrinsic merits and, increasingly, for its utility in the push for greater European independence and autonomy in the security field. In each case, concerns may arise regarding particular provisions of a negotiated agreement, but support for the process is a view shared generally by all parties.

2. *Fear of decoupling.* West German defense experts and CDU/CSU party leaders believe that arms control agreements, if poorly conceived, undermine the credibility of the American nuclear guarantee.

The fear that reductions in arms could "decouple" U.S. strategic forces from the FRG may help to explain why some CDU/CSU leaders initially supported the United States' so-called "zero-option" proposal, made in 1982, to remove all INF. After the 1986 Reykjavik summit, however, and again in March 1987 with Mikhail Gorbachev's initiative to conclude an INF regime separate from other strategic issues, CDU/CSU leaders became alarmed that such an agreement appeared within reach. While CDU/CSU leaders may reject the military utility of nuclear weapons, they recognize that American weapons deployed in West Germany are stark symbols of the U.S. commitment to the FRG's defense.

3. *Importance of public opinion.* Public attitudes on arms control matter when it comes to the formulation of arms control policy. Increasingly, any West German government feels great pressure to appear to be promoting the arms control *process* and advancing German interests. Simultaneously, however, public attitudes may check any government from taking extreme positions or attempting radical departures. The INF debate has *not* broken the consensus on foreign and defense policy. Admittedly, it is no longer tabu to question the terms of existing West German security arrangements, but there is still a generally shared sense that détente and *Ostpolitik* are not sufficient to guarantee national security, as seen in the fairly unwavering support for NATO. The public thus embraces membership in NATO and, in a broad sense, support for its existing policies, but also demands *Ostpolitik*, détente, and arms control, even though all elements may not be compatible at all times. This contradiction compels all parties at least to pay lip service to all components. Thus, the CDU/CSU may see military defense and the American connection as overarchingly important, but it feels compelled to support, at least rhetorically, the arms control process. The SPD suggests far-reaching changes in NATO military policies, but insists on its continued allegiance to NATO and support for cooperation with the U.S.

The Parties and Arms Control

The partisans of the FRG's several political parties exhibit divergent attitudes on arms control. Moreover, the more politically active portion of the population, represented by actual party members and leaders, is split into factions within each party. Party positions on arms control are rooted fundamentally in ideological traditions, but also reflect alternate views of the German-American relationship and the requirements of West German security.

Positions on arms control within the *CDU/CSU* can be grouped broadly into "Gaullist" and "Atlanticist" factions. This internal split can be traced back to the late Adenauer era and is rooted fundamentally in different views of how much the FRG ultimately can or should depend on the United States for its security. Generally speaking, the Gaullists are skeptical of the durability of the American guarantee and, consequently, have striven to reduce European (including German) reliance on the United States.

Latter-day Gaullists, such as Franz Josef Strauss, Alfred Dregger, and Juergen Todenhoefer, are adamant about the primacy of military defense, skeptical of the real gains possible through arms control, and relatively unconcerned about the reassurance effect of negotiations. In general, the Gaullists tend to be strongly anti-Communist and adopt more uncompromising stances. The Gaullists have been highly critical of the CDU/CSU *Fraktion*'s "Genscherists," who have supported a continued policy of détente and arms control.

The "Atlanticists" take the view that the establishment of a bipolar international structure is irreversible, and as a result, Europe and the FRG cannot afford to adopt policies that could alienate the United States. Dominating the leadership of the CDU, the Atlanticists, including Chancellor Kohl and Volker Ruehe, are apt to support policies compatible with U.S. policies. They are concerned lest arms control agreements or, conversely, disputes between Bonn and Washington over arms control threaten the U.S. defense connection. At the same time, the Atlanticists recognize the domestic reassurance value of arms control.

At any one time, the official CDU/CSU stance on arms control reflects a compromise between these two factions. The party claims that it can represent West German interests in arms control more effectively because of its closer ties and more harmonious relations with Washington. Generally, the CDU/CSU emphasizes the notion that Bonn must first be a reliable partner if it is to have any influence over American arms control policy. Loyalty and reliability, the CDU argues, will cement the American interest in coupling its security to West Germany's. In this view, moreover, a cohesive NATO will have enhanced bargaining power relative to the Warsaw Pact. The FDP's insistence on a more independent European voice or the SPD's advocacy of radical departures from U.S. policies, the

CDU/CSU maintains, can only cause friction and weaken the Western arms control position.

Under certain conditions, the necessity of its two factions to compromise may force the CDU/CSU to adopt untenable or contradictory positions, or even to reverse itself on specific arms control issues. There is an inherent tension in the party's arms control policy between efforts to further the process of arms control and positions that in the CDU/CSU view, would undermine the American-German defense connection. In the case of INF, for example, the party, in an appeal to the popular desire for a continuing arms control dialogue, initially endorsed the so-called "zero-option," but later made it clear that it preferred an agreement that would leave some intermediate-range missiles in place. Similarly, the CDU/CSU supports German participation in the Strategic Defense Initiative, but has also argued that participation guarantees Bonn a channel to influence the evolution of SDI and a means to ensure continued adherence to the ABM treaty. In the end, as long as it remains in office, the party will support whatever position ultimately is adopted by the U.S. Government on both issues, although it may articulate certain nuanced differences in reasoning.

The *SPD* is far more seriously divided over security issues. In the late 1970s, partly in response to the Greens' challenge, a younger, more militant left wing gained strength within the party. The faction's growth was fueled by a series of developments at the domestic and international levels: a deterioration of East-West relations, a growing dissatisfaction with the SPD government's support of NATO and U.S. policy, the neutron bomb controversy, and, finally, the 1979 NATO dual-track decision.

The SPD is divided between a moderate faction and its left wing. The moderate faction, including such figures as former chancellor Helmut Schmidt, former defense and finance minister Hans Apel, and Richard Löwenthal, an older party moderate and member of the party's Commission for Basic Values, argues for a centrist course, a continued commitment to existing NATO policies, including reliance on nuclear weapons for certain deterrent purposes. In the 1980s, and particularly after the party left the government, this faction waned significantly in strength, and is now in the minority. Helmut Schmidt declined to run for reelection to the Bundestag in 1987. Both the SPD executive committee and presidium are now dominated by the left wing.

The party's left faction is further divided between an old guard of moderate left leaders and a younger, more militant group. The "old guard"—Willy Brandt, Egon Bahr, and Herbert Wehner—has been instrumental in introducing the concept of "security partnership" to the SPD program, but continues to assert the party's commitment to NATO. The SPD's younger, more doctrinaire wing features such figures as Saar premier Oskar Lafontaine and SPD presidium member Erhard Eppler, and incorporates a group of security experts including Karsten Voigt, Erwin Horn, and Andreas von Buelow. Though not all these experts agree on the degree of reform that is required, they share a highly critical view of NATO and U.S. policy and advocate important changes in Bonn's security and arms control policies.

Specifically, the SPD advocates a more forceful and independent representation of West German interests in arms control. The underlying assumption of many of its proposed changes in defense organization and security policy is that détente and arms control must be given more weight within Bonn's overall policy. Thus, while the SPD has asserted its continued allegiance to NATO and has dismissed unilateral measures, it also has argued that the Europeans must have more independent influence within the alliance. The SPD has advanced a number of ideas that could enhance the importance of arms control: a major reorganization of arms control decisionmaking, including the creation of an arms control office as part of the Chancellor's Office; and the continuation on an official level of an inter-German arms control dialogue now being carried out by the SPD and East German Socialist Unity Party. In general, the SPD's program is one of greater independence vis-à-vis the Americans and pursuit of what it perceives as divergent European and/or German interests.

In the *FDP*, there are no apparent factional divisions over foreign policy. Reflecting the guidance of Hans-Dietrich Genscher, the party unites behind a policy of "continuity and predictability," of steadfast support of NATO's Harmel formula of defense and détente. The internal divisions of the FDP over economic policy and civil liberties have no influence on the party's arms control stance.

The FDP's positions on arms control fall between those of the two major parties. The Liberals have reaffirmed their commitment to the alliance, but insist that the Europeans have a special responsibility for security and must play a more autonomous role in East-West relations and arms control. Consequently, the FDP places emphasis on multilateral negotiations. The European framework may also be designed to pursue specifically German objectives, but is less liable to arouse suspicion in Washington or other European capitals than a direct approach. Genscher supports an inter-German dialogue as long as it is carried on within the context of ongoing multilateral negotiations. In general, the FDP attempts to strike a balance

between automatic acquiescence to American views and defiant independence or unilateralism.

Of all West German parties, the *Greens* hold the most radical positions
on arms control and security. Rooted in its commitment to the principle
of nonviolence, the party advocates an "active peace policy" to replace
the FRG's current military commitment to NATO. Arms control plays
little or no role in this view, because it has failed, along with all
conventional notions of security, to bring mankind closer to a demilitarized, disarmed world. The Greens propose a number of radical measures,
including withdrawal from NATO, unilateral disarmament measures, and
the eventual dismantling of the Bundeswehr.

Though generally viewed as utopian and thoroughly impractical, the
Greens' program nevertheless may have a marginal impact on the future
evolution of West German arms control policy. The Greens' pronouncements on security vent more generally shared reservations about the
presence of nuclear weapons in West Germany and appeal to underlying
sentiments of pacifism and antimilitarism. Further, there is an explicit
linkage between German security and the fundamental issues of autonomy
and national interests. Last, the Greens' radical program is a constant
reminder to voters in the SPD's leftwing who may be dissatisfied with the
Social Democrats that another alternative exists, a factor certain to figure
into the SPD's calculations in choosing the party's new leaders, a point
discussed below in greater detail.

FUTURE DIRECTIONS IN WEST GERMAN ARMS CONTROL POLICY

In the near term, domestic factors will shape Bonn's arms control policy.
The center-right coalition's victory in the January 1987 national elections
determined the important players and likely sources of conflict in the
decisionmaking process. The return of the CDU/CSU-FDP government to
power and Genscher's return to the Foreign Office will be strong forces
for continuity in West German arms control policy; however, such
continuity may come at the price of coalition unity and strength. For the
losing parties, the electoral outcome will influence their future internal
evolution and, thus, indirectly, longer term positions on arms control
policy.

Impact of the 1987 Elections

By January 1987, the outcome of the West German national elections
seemed a foregone conclusion. Chancellor Kohl had made a seemingly

miraculous political recovery; all economic indicators were positive; and the SPD was widely viewed as too divided and weak to offer a viable alternative. A return of the governing coalition was a certainty, and the only question was by how large a margin. The only spark to the otherwise dull campaign were occasional spats between the FDP and the CSU over the future of foreign policy and internal security measures. As expected, security issues played a minimal role in the campaign.

As a result of the election, the governing coalition was returned to power, but with a shift within the coalition in favor of the FDP. The CDU/CSU registered significant losses (over four percentage points), while the Free Democrats garnered 9.1 percent of the second party vote, an increase of 2.1 points from its weak performance in 1983. The SPD won 37 percent of the vote, somewhat better than had been predicted, but it lost votes to the smaller Green party, which managed to increase its share of the vote to 8.3 percent (from 5.6 percent in 1983). In one sense, the real victors in the election were the two smaller parties, and above all, Genscher's Liberals.

Once again, the small FDP defied the gloomy prognoses regarding the party's future. Following the shift of coalition partners in November 1982, the FDP had suffered significant membership and leadership losses in all parts of the country and stood in general disfavor for bringing down the social-liberal coalition. The FDP's subsequent elimination from a number of *Land* parliaments and the European parliament provoked speculation that the party would not long survive on the national level.

The FDP's campaign strategy and the indirect help of the party's ardent opponent, Franz Josef Strauss, triggered the party's rebound. The FDP has long relied on the support of West Germans who see the party as a "corrective" to government, and a counterweight to either conservative or radical elements of the larger coalition party. During the 1987 campaign, the FDP emphasized the importance of this role and claimed that its return to the Bundestag was vital to guarantee continuity and moderation in West German foreign policy. The FDP attempted to link the party's role to the policies and the person of Hans-Dietrich Genscher. Though it refrained from stating this explicitly, the FDP made it clear that if the party were returned to power, Hans-Dietrich Genscher naturally would continue as Foreign Minister.

The recurrent conflicts between the FDP and the CSU provided the only point of interest in an otherwise dull campaign. True to form, the attacks of the CSU's Franz Josef Strauss against the FDP's Genscher led many CDU/CSU supporters to cast their second party vote for the FDP, not only enabling the party to clear the 5 percent hurdle, but to return to power in a strengthened position. As in the past, voters appeared uneasy with the prospect of one large party governing alone, and particularly with the greater role that Strauss would play in such a government. Beyond these general concerns, the FDP's gains imply an affirmation of the Genscher course in foreign policy.

The relative redistribution of weight within the coalition will affect the process and substance of Bonn's arms control policy. With his tenure as Foreign Minister secured, and backed by a personal electoral victory, Genscher will have added authority to determine the broad outlines and special emphases of arms control policy. The power of other competitors, such as the Chancellor's Office, will be eclipsed. With Genscher in charge of the key post in the arms control decisionmaking process, and the position of CSU and CDU conservatives visibly weakened, Genscher's policy of continuity is virtually guaranteed.

Continuity in arms control policy, however, may exact a high price in terms of coalition unity and governmental strength, as seen in a series of disputes in 1987 over Bonn's INF policy. The proposal to eliminate all categories of INF—the "double zero option"—and the issue of Pershing 1a modernization caused rifts not only between the FDP and CSU, a predictable development, but between the CDU and CSU as well. The need to reconcile intracoalitional differences likely delayed the government's response in both cases, contributing to a general impression of indecision and weakness at the national level. The relative redistribution of influence within the coalition in favor of the FDP will strongly favor continuity in arms control policy, but will exacerbate existing ideological and policy differences between the coalition partners.

The election results will affect the future evolution of the opposition parties as well. The SPD must select a new generation of leaders and resolve its internal divisions. Both will affect the party's positions on security and arms control. The Greens' future evolution will have an indirect impact on arms control policy. Its more secure existence at the national level will exercise a leftward pull on the SPD and force the Social Democrats to define their party's relationship to the Greens.

In charting the future course of the party, the SPD must take into consideration indications of longer term sociological and political changes. Ideological roots aside, if the SPD is to return to government, it must adapt its program to the realities of electoral arithmetic. The 1987 national elections and subsequent contests at the regional level revealed that politics in the Federal Republic is changing. Both major *Volksparteien* lost votes to the smaller parties, indicating a breakdown in traditional party commitments and an increasing tendency to shift allegiances. There was a high incidence of "ticket-splitting" but no pattern dominated nation-wide. Last, national and regional elections proved that the Green party is a more permanent political force than its critics had been willing to grant. The party's strong overall showing in 1987, and its ability to capture 20 percent of the large pool of first-time voters, suggest that the Greens have not lost the ability to appeal to younger Germans. In sum, the traditional lines of division between the parties has clearly broken down, and a new addition to the ranks must be considered on a permanent basis.

Though the SPD knew that victory was very unlikely, the elections were nevertheless crucial to the party's internal development. At the Nuremberg party congress in August 1986, the SPD was able to put dissension and internal rifts aside and unite behind its moderate candidate, Johannes Rau. This unity, however, proved more illusion than reality. The party remained split between a radical leftwing and a minority moderate faction, the latter including much of its trade union support. Brandt and Rau's decision to nudge the party toward the center was a calculated bet; according to the polls, the SPD had to compete for the center if it were to have a chance of returning to power. The crucial question for the party, however, was whether it could gain more votes in the center than it would lose on its leftwing. Given the current political constellation, voters may choose to split their ballots, using their second vote to shore up the Greens. (This is the practice from which the FDP has long benefitted.) And this, in fact, is precisely what happened. Post-election analyses indicate that the SPD's second vote losses were often the Greens' gains.

To the party's left wing, the 1987 election results seemed a refutation of the SPD's centerward course, proof that the party must shift to the left. On the other hand, Rau did not do as badly as might have been expected. More importantly, he made a strong showing in his native *Land* of North-Rhine Westphalia, not only the most populous state in the FRG but also the home of over one-third of all SPD members. Long-term trends in voting patterns and preferences are not clearly discernible, making the problems of leadership succession and party program all the more difficult for the SPD.

For the next four years in opposition, the SPD will be absorbed by internal matters, above all the selection of successors to top leadership positions. Brandt stepped down as party chairman in March 1987. The immediate appointment of Hans-Jochen Vogel as his successor may constitute solely a "transition" to a member of the "Enkel" ("grandchild'') generation, such as favorite son Oskar Lafontaine, Gerhard Schroeder, or another candidate of the same generation. Alternatively, Vogel may remain as chairman with one of the younger figures picking up the gauntlet as chancellor candidate, thus providing a basis for continued juggling between left-wing and moderate factions. Immediately following the elections, before Brandt's actual resignation, Lafontaine called for a rapid resolution of the leadership question, suggesting a desire to move the party decisively to the left. Many left-wing and even moderate figures were quick to rally round this call. There are signs of support for Vogel, however, and many party members remain uneasy about Lafontaine's stance on West German membership in NATO. (Lafontaine first advocated the withdrawal of West German forces from NATO's integrated command; he has modified this stance, and has suggested that France might return to NATO under a European commander of Supreme Headquarters Allied Powers Europe [SHAPE].) Ultimate resolution of this party division remains uncertain, and will probably remain ambiguous in the near term.

The SPD must clarify its relationship to the Greens as well. As chancellor candidate, Rau remained fundamentally opposed to any form of cooperation with the Greens. Following the elections, SPD leaders, including Brandt and Vogel, stated that the party must reconsider this position. Specifically, cooperation with the Greens on the national level might be possible if the Greens were to make concessions in two areas: the recognition of the state's right to a monopoly on the use of force; and, second, its position on NATO and security issues. In this vein, SPD security expert Karsten Voigt has attempted to engage the Greens in a substantive exchange of views on security policy, but without much apparent success.

The Greens have their own internal divisions to contend with. The battle between "realos" and "fundis" continues, turning on the broader issues of participation and responsibility in government, and the role of extraparliamentary versus parliamentary activity. The "fundis" retain majority control of the party's executive committee and are represented on the parliamentary group's executive committee; and the "realos" predominate at the grass-roots level and constitute a majority of the *Bundestag* caucus.

Even if the "realos" ultimately do triumph and the Greens become a more conventional political party, they still may not concede on security issues, making the prospects for any cooperation with the SPD at the national level exceedingly slim. The Greens have deep pacifist roots and close ties to the West German peace movement. They reject membership in NATO on principle, along with any form of "bloc thinking." Otto Schily, one of the party's better known "realos" and most competent politicians, has said that the party's absolutist demands on security policy are not "operative" policy. But this is probably not a position taken by the majority. Unless the party can resolve these internal divisions, any form of cooperation with the SPD would be inconceivable in the near term. The only experiment in an SPD/Green coalition to date, the coalition between Hesse SPD premier Holger Boerner and the Greens, collapsed in February 1987, hardly an encouraging sign. Even if the Greens were to move toward the center or the SPD to the left, the creation of a "red-green coalition" at the national level would be highly problematic.

Alternative Scenarios

The future evolution of West German arms control policy also will depend on developments at the international level. As we have discussed, the attitudes of all actors in the arms control decisionmaking process are shaped partly by external factors, in particular Soviet and American policies and the general state of East-West relations.

In periods of relative calm, the West German government is not faced with the task of choosing between its commitments to détente and to NATO and bilateral cooperation with the United States; there are no readily apparent tradeoffs. *Ostpolitik* and inter-German cooperation can continue apace, in tune with developments in the larger international context, and the public's *Angst* is greatly alleviated. Conversely, in times of escalating U.S.-Soviet tensions and arms control stalemate, the public fears that such tradeoffs between *Ostpolitik* and close relations with the United States may become necessary, and management of the domestic debate accordingly becomes more difficult. A deterioration in U.S.-Soviet relations, particularly when accompanied by signs of Soviet aggression (Afghanistan in 1979 or the fear of Soviet interference in Poland in the early 1980s) may stir up feelings of vulnerability and insecurity in the West German electorate; the need for arms control as reassurance grows commensurately. Moreover, the West German government perceives a greater sense of urgency to appear effective in promoting West German interests vis-à-vis those of the United States.

The government in Bonn will have to consider the broad international context in determining its arms control policy. Developments in Soviet-American, German-American, or German-Soviet relations particularly will affect Bonn's stance on arms control. In speculating upon the likely policies of the Bonn government, we thus must also consider alternative international prospects:

- an improvement in U.S.-Soviet relations, accompanied by progress toward major arms control agreements;

- a deterioration in U.S.-Soviet relations, including a prolonged stalemate or actual breakdown in negotiations and increasing tension between the superpowers;

- perceptions of the German-American relationship; and

- an improvement in German-Soviet relations.

In a climate of stable or improving U.S.-Soviet relations, the center-right coalition's arms control policies would be likely to continue along current lines, but fissures in the coalition would become more apparent. The key actors in the decisionmaking process, particularly Foreign Minister Genscher, would remain unchanged. In light of the strengthened position of the FDP in the coalition, and proven public support for progress in arms control, radical departures or a new conservative agenda would be highly unlikely. In such circumstances, the CSU and the right wing of the CDU would step up pressure on Kohl to ensure that any prospective agreement would not be decoupling, such as occurred in 1987 as the INF agreement began to take shape. Special German interests, such as the need to negotiate an agreement on shorter range nuclear forces, or the treatment of Pershing 1a missiles, were expressed directly to U.S. decisionmakers through private and public channels. Other members of the CDU, who favor an agreement, would be bolstered by the general East-West climate; CDU moderates would no longer be isolated within the party. The pressure from the right also would be counterbalanced by strong FDP support for arms control agreements. With the Liberals in firm control of the Foreign Office, Genscher could press quietly ahead on his plan to enrich European consultative procedures and to improve Bonn's relations with Moscow and East Berlin.

If there is any change in Bonn's overall arms control policy, it is likely to be a new emphasis on negotiations to reduce conventional forces. Genscher has been a strong proponent of the new forum for conventional arms control, to run parallel to the bloc-to-bloc negotiations in Vienna. The new talks will be a part of the CSCE process. Genscher may see the latter as offering the Europeans and, of course, the Germans the best opportunity of developing greater independence from the Americans in arms control. In the same vein, Genscher has used the broader European context of the CSCE as a vehicle to secure French participation. As if to express the new importance of the Bonn-Paris axis in European arms control, foreign ministers Genscher and Dumas made a joint appearance in January 1986 at the Stockholm Conference on Confidence- and Security-Building Measures and Disarmament in Europe. Such initiatives can be expected to continue and to intensify.

A rapidly improving climate of East-West relations, however, would expose the center-right coalition to new strains and stresses. The debate over Bonn's response to successive INF initiatives revealed deep fissures in the coalition over security issues; differences have emerged as well over economic issues (tax reform) and civil liberties. A series of new Soviet proposals, for example in the area of conventional force reductions, would rekindle the defense debate within the coalition. If coupled with major differences in other policy areas, or a conservative refusal to approve further compromises, the center-right coalition might collapse.

A prolonged period of Soviet-American tensions, similarly, could pose serious problems for a CDU/CSU, FDP government and would likely exacerbate existing divisions within the coalition—above all, between the FDP and the CSU. During the 1987 election campaign, CDU/CSU conservatives criticized the FDP and Kohl for too much "continuity" in foreign policy. Immediately after the elections, Franz Josef Strauss stated that the coalition negotiations would have to clarify and define the meaning of a "second phase of détente." As seen in the intracoalitional disputes over an INF agreement, deep divisions remain. The conflict over INF policy arose under conditions of improving Soviet-American relations. If Genscher continued his present course in the context of U.S./Soviet tensions, or sought to propel the arms control process by taking independent German or European initiatives, attacks from the right wing would intensify. Genscher is fully committed to a policy of improving ties with the East; on this point, he would have the solid backing of his entire party and a dramatic failure of U.S./Soviet arms control negotiations would simply fuel this determination. Support from the CDU, however, would become problematical. The CDU/CSU, FDP coalition would confront pressure from without as well, as the domestic need for reassurance would increase, all the more so if inter-German relations deteriorated parallel to escalating Soviet-American tensions.

If severe enough, these internal and external tensions could break the coalition. A midterm collapse would be even more likely if the deterioration in U.S.-Soviet relations were accompanied by an economic downturn or a series of events similar to those in the late 1970s and early 1980s. If Kohl's popularity or support for the government declined considerably, and it was apparent that the CDU/CSU was headed for a downfall, the FDP leadership might assert its autonomy by pursuing independent arms control initiatives, the surest means of giving the Liberals a separate profile and ensuring that the FDP did not go down with a sinking ship. Genscher is fully capable of airing his disagreements with government policy. Considerations of party survival would warrant such a course, and it is one for which there is considerable precedent.

Developments in German-American relations will be crucial to Bonn's arms control policy as well. If U.S. isolationism grows, for example through congressional initiatives to withdraw American forces from the FRG, or through clumsy handling of strategic defense issues or the ABM treaty, tensions between Bonn and Washington would be exacerbated. There would be a greater sense that Germans cannot permit their security to remain hostage to the whims of the United States, and that Bonn has the legitimate right to choose a separate course, to defend special German interests. This feeling has already emerged with regard to Western antiterrorism strategies. The decline in the credibility of American leadership on this issue may spill over into other areas as well. In such circumstances, criticism would be voiced by the left, but could be fed by the Gaullist wing of the CDU as well. American policies and actions could thus be instrumental in creating a sort of unholy alliance between Kohl's critics on the left and right, putting greater pressure on the Kohl government to appear a forceful advocate of German interests.

Perceptions of Soviet leadership and the evolution of Soviet-German relations will be another important factor. Genscher has stated that the West must be willing to give Soviet leader Gorbachev's views a fair hearing. In his perspective, new Soviet proposals and initiatives must be considered seriously. Disagreements between Bonn and Washington over the appropriate response to Soviet overtures would spur Genscher to seek the support of Bonn's European allies as a counterweight to American views. Genscher has also indicated his interest in a new phase of relations between Bonn and Moscow, to be fueled by greater economic and technological cooperation between the two countries.

LONG-TERM PROSPECTS FOR ARMS CONTROL

In the long term, the evolution of West German arms control policy will be affected by broader political and societal changes in the FRG. Two such changes are considered below: the polarization of German politics on security issues; and a lasting shift in the attitudes of the younger generation.

An understanding of the meaning of the INF debate is crucial to an assessment of future directions in West German arms control policy. It is possible that the controversy over the NATO dual-track decision and subsequent political activities was an idiosyncratic matter, an outgrowth of the special conditions of the time: the congruence of the NATO decision with an economic downturn and escalating East-West tensions due to, among other factors, the Soviet invasion of Afghanistan and the military crackdown in Poland. Moreover, there have been subsequent indications on both ends of the political spectrum of a movement toward a centrist consensus on security issues, one incorporating both close support of the U.S. security link and détente and arms control. Over the past four years, the CDU/CSU, despite occasional criticism from its conservative wing, has made efforts to appeal to supporters of détente and arms control, including the rather visible arrangement of several loans and credits to East Germany, and the East German leader Erich Honecker's historic visit in September 1987 to the Federal Republic. The SPD, in its electoral campaign, attempted to set aside security issues and to unify the party behind a moderate candidate with a relatively moderate program.

Nevertheless, more recent events suggest that the previous trend toward further polarization is not to be dismissed so lightly. The CDU's response to developments at the Reykjavik summit, above all Kohl's visible expressions of concern over the shape of possible arms control deals, and the CSU's virulent opposition to an INF agreement, suggest that the conservative constituency in the CDU/CSU causes Kohl considerable worry, the reassurance value of arms control notwithstanding. National election results offer further indications of polarization. For the most part, ticket-splitting occurred within the two blocs, between the CDU/CSU and the FDP, and between the SPD and the Greens. At the same time, the left wing of the SPD continues to press the party leadership to abandon the preelection moderate course.

Given the right set of conditions, a further move toward polarization could have serious consequences for Bonn's position on security issues. The center-right government has sought to maintain a cautious balance between support for détente and arms control and support for the U.S.-German defense link. As long as external events support this effort, the government will have little difficulty in staying the course, but this requires an unusually favorable set of circumstances over the long term: sustained economic growth, low or no inflation, no sudden or sustained flare-ups in U.S.-Soviet relations or, conversely, signs of deals negotiated with undue consideration of European security interests, or the emergence of U.S.-generated problems within the alliance, such as initiatives for U.S. troop withdrawals. Under adverse circumstances, the balance may be impossible to maintain. If the trend toward polarization continued, criticism both from the left and the right would make it difficult for the Bonn government to avoid the tradeoffs between *Westpolitik* and *Ostpolitik* that it has hitherto been able to avoid.

Under these circumstances, the precise impact of polarization would depend largely on whether the belief in special German interests is a lasting trend. The evidence on this point is more clear. The new attention to specifically German interests has found expression in each political party, albeit in a different form, and is not limited to members of the "successor generation" in the FRG. The willingness to defend special German interests is seen in the vocal criticism of CDU/CSU conservatives of any arms control agreement that would harm what they perceive as vital West German security interests, and in the Genscher demand for a more united and independent European voice in arms control and security matters. It is seen most clearly in the ongoing arms control dialogue between the SPD and the East German Socialist Unity Party, but the continuing efforts by the conservative ruling coalition to foster closer political, economic, and human relations between East and West Germany reflect similar attitudes and political imperatives. Even under the best of circumstances, there will be pressure on the Bonn government for greater independence in arms control issues, presumably in the guise of increased European cooperation. Under adverse conditions, this sense of Bonn's obligation and right to protect its own interests could lead, at best, to greater tension in U.S.-German relations and, possibly, to independent West German initiatives in arms control and East-West political relations.

CONCLUSION

The arms control decisionmaking process of the Federal Republic reflects the continuous interaction between internal and external factors in the formulation of Bonn's security policies. Arms control policy is caught between West Germans' commitment to a special bilateral relationship with the United States and their interest in good relations with the East, above all with the GDR. Progress in arms control depends ultimately on the U.S. commitment, an external factor. At the same time, West Germans increasingly view arms control as part of a European détente process that should be more independent of the great powers' behavior.

This common thread of internal/external tensions runs through all aspects of West German arms control policy. The decisionmaking process has a clearly domestic component: conflict among executive agencies, public debate in the Bundestag, the impact of domestic changes such as the "securitization" of politics, and the resurfacing of the German question. But bilateral channels also exist and ensure input from the United States.

Similarly, the broader factors that shape the attitudes of all actors and public views are internal and external. Thus, some things are unique to the German experience—division, the experience of war, the rewards of *Ostpolitik*. Others are part of the broader international context: Soviet and U.S. policies, East-West relations, the progress (or lack thereof) in arms control negotiations.

The future evolution of arms control policy likewise will depend not only on election outcomes or coalition strife, but on developments at the international level as well. Whatever coalition is in office, the policies of the West German government will be strongly affected by the evolution of Soviet-American relations.

If the INF debates have had any lasting impact, it is the new importance of domestic interests in the security policymaking process. Unquestioning support for NATO has broken down. The splits within the SPD and the defense policy alternatives put forward by the party are evidence that national interests, and new domestic perceptions of security needs, are given more weight. This evolution is certain to continue.

Change in arms control policy, nevertheless, is likely to be incremental. Geopolitically or historically derived feelings of insecurity and vulnerability persist. A majority of West Germans continue to support membership in NATO. But attitudes can and do change. Indeed, the growth of support for détente or *Ostpolitik* and the arms control process occurred gradually yet undeniably. Taking a longer term view, increasing polarization on security issues, a slow but evident erosion of support for NATO, a different perspective on the prospects or benefits of security alternatives, and, above all, a new-found sense of the legitimacy of questioning current arrangements and their service of German national interests are likely to influence West German security and arms control policies.

2 ARMS CONTROL DECISIONMAKING IN THE FEDERAL REPUBLIC

The West German arms control decisionmaking process is complex, fragmented, and decentralized. The Foreign Office is assigned primary responsibility for arms control policy, but other ministries and executive agencies, as well as nongovernmental actors play a part in the process. The constitutional right of concurrence (*Mitzeichnungsrecht*) guarantees the Ministry of Defense (MoD) an important input into decisions; the Chancellor's Office, the Cabinet, and the Federal Security Council (BSR) play secondary roles. While the legislature's official influence is marginal, parties and other nongovernmental actors may convey information about public attitudes on arms control to decisionmakers, thus constituting a subtle form of participation.

Additional inputs into FRG decisionmaking enter through U.S.-German bilateral channels. The Federal Republic is firmly embedded in the NATO and European frameworks; like all aspects of its security policy, West German arms control policy is linked inextricably to U.S. and Allied policies. Formal consultative structures, informal mechanisms, and, within the NATO context, working contacts between American and German military personnel may serve to convey American military views on arms control with special emphasis.

The diffusion of responsibility for arms control decisions and the profusion of actors make the problems of coordination and bureaucratic conflict-resolution critical. In interagency struggles for influence over arms control policy, leadership personalities and bureaucratic skills matter. The formal predominance of the Foreign Office may be diluted through the consensus and coalition-building processes implicit in German governmental decisionmaking.

The current arms control decisionmaking process in Bonn has evolved over time and has been influenced by developments in other nations (for example, the creation of the U.S. Arms Control and Disarmament Agency), progress (or the lack thereof) in international negotiations, key personalities, and social and political change at the national level. The recent security debates in West Germany may not have truly "democratized" decisionmaking, as some analysts have argued, but there are indications, conversely, that German politics may have been "securitized." In other words, security issues have come to matter a great deal in domestic West German politics. As a consequence, public attitudes on arms control are considered seriously when the government of the FRG formulates arms control policy; this trend is likely to continue. Moreover, the simultaneous reemergence of the "German question" has highlighted what are perceived to be special German security interests.

The combined impact of the various forces injecting political considerations into West German arms control decisionmaking could have a number of consequences. It could lead to increased pressures on Bonn, both from within political parties and through outside channels, to advance perceived "special" West German interests more forcefully. It also could lead to a more active role for the Bundestag in decisionmaking, with both Bundestag committees and political parties taking part in the formulation of arms control positions. These pressures might also lead to greater emphasis on developing European consultative processes which could facilitate the formation of broadly supported, and distinctly European, positions on arms control. Finally, the greater saliency of arms control in West German politics could result in a push for major reorganization of the federal decisionmaking process to increase the importance of arms control considerations within the federal bureaucracy.

EXECUTIVE AGENCIES

Arms control decisionmaking in the Federal Republic is the formal prerogative of executive agencies; within the executive, the weight of each relevant institution has been shaped by constitutional and legal principles, the traditions of the German civil service, and coalition politics. The Basic Law formally bestows primary responsibility for arms control upon the Foreign Office, but guarantees as well a role for the Ministry of Defense, the Chancellor's Office, and the Cabinet. The legal division of responsibility combines with German bureaucratic traditions to create a decentralized process of policy formulation. Working level operations are vital;

executive agency coordination is achieved through a matrix system of extensive horizontal communication and contacts between departments and ministries. The exigencies of coalition politics exert great pressure on executive agencies to exercise restraint and to resolve conflict at the lowest possible level.

Though the formal institutional framework favors the Foreign Office in arms control policy, the personalities and capabilities of individual actors in key posts can shift the relative balance of decisionmaking power. Given a forceful leader, other executive agencies, particularly MoD or the Chancellor's Office, can play a far greater role.

The Foreign Office

Primary responsibility for the conduct of international relations, including arms control, is housed in the Foreign Office. Its central authority is based on three legal provisions: Article 65 of the Basic Law (*Grundgesetz*) establishes the principle of departmental autonomy (*Ressortsprinzip*), which gives the foreign minister broad discretionary powers over the affairs of the ministry, and limits the chancellor's interference in ministry affairs to ensuring that foreign policy is compatible with "general policy guidelines."[1] Article 73 of the Basic Law and Paragraph 11 of the rules of procedure (*Geschaeftsordnung*) assign the Foreign Office all responsibility for international relations. In operational terms, these three principles mean that the Foreign Office initiates preparatory work on arms control and reserves the right to make final policy decisions. Strictly interpreted, the *Ressortsprinzip* may also block the efforts of any other executive agency—including the Chancellor's Office—to coordinate work on arms control policy.[2]

Within the Foreign Office, operations are divided along the traditional hierarchical lines of German bureaucracy (see Figure 2–1). In general, the minister, his deputies and secretaries, the commissioner on arms control, and working level officers take the most active part in arms control decisions. The foreign minister is doubtless the most broadly influential actor in the process, but his direct involvement may be limited to determining the general orientation of arms control policy. The secretaries' main function is to aid the minister; they ensure that his guidelines are carried out at lower levels in the bureaucracy. The special commissioner occupies a pivotal position in the ministry; he has access to the minister and political leadership, but is also in touch with working level operations in division 2a. The commissioner may thus play a more or less active role in the process, depending upon the person and his relationship to the foreign minister. Working level officers are responsible for interagency coordination, conflict resolution, and implementation of policy on a day-to-day basis.

Political leadership comprises the foreign minister, two deputy ministers, and two permanent state secretaries. Two deputy ministers serve as aides to the minister; they are recruited largely on the basis of political affiliation. They are usually skilled political actors, and act as liaison between the Foreign Office and such political bodies as the parties, parliamentary party groups (*Fraktionen*), and the Federal Council (*Bundesrat*). The two permanent secretaries have been drawn traditionally from the senior civil service, but are selected increasingly on the basis of political criteria as well. The permanent secretaries may be more active in the formulation and discussion of substantive policies with division heads or desk officers. The ministerial staff is largely a personal task force of the minister; its members are selected by the minister, and leave office when his term comes to an end.[3]

The direct involvement of the minister and his secretaries in policy-making is limited by the sheer volume of work; time and energy must necessarily be allocated selectively. Moreover, West German bureaucratic policy-making tends to be decentralized; most work is accomplished at the desk (*Referat*) level. Senior officials and political leaders apparently are informed but are seldom actively involved in the routine processes of decisionmaking.[4]

The degree of political level participation, however, also depends on the foreign minister's personality and particular interests. The current foreign minister, Hans-Dietrich Genscher, in office since 1974 and representing the junior coalition partner, has displayed a long-term personal and professional commitment to a continuing East-West dialogue, of which arms control negotiations are an integral part. Moreover, the political fortunes of his party, the FDP, may be linked to its ability to portray itself as the voice of experience and moderation in foreign policy matters. Consequently, Genscher takes a more active interest in arms control and security decisions than another foreign minister might assume.

At *the intermediate level*, the planning staff of the Foreign Office is only sporadically involved in specific issues and then mostly at the behest of the foreign minister. Established in 1963 and patterned in part after the U.S. model, the planning staff is composed of approximately twelve civil servants.[5] In the past, only one to two officials have usually been involved in arms control matters.

Also at *the intermediate level*, political divisions 2 and 2a are charged with primary responsibility for arms control and disarmament decision-making. The creation of division 2a in 1981 was a result of a series of initiatives since 1977 to upgrade arms control policy within the Foreign Office.[6] The head of division 2a is also the commissioner of the federal government on questions of arms control and disarmament. The commissioner has been granted ambassadorial rank, an indication of the post's importance.[7]

The federal government's commissioner on arms control and disarmament is the central actor within the Foreign Office, linking the executive political leadership with working level operations. As division head and special ambassador, the person occupying the post enjoys a signficant degree of latitude to interpret his or her role and to determine the scope and nature of the post's activities. Among the more important of the commissioner's duties are the maintenance of regular contacts with allies, nonnuclear states, and international organizations; participation in the decisive directors' conferences within the Foreign Office (see below); under certain circumstances, participation in cabinet meetings with the chancellor; and discussions with the Foreign Affairs Committee and Subcommittee for Disarmament and Arms Control of the Bundestag. Additionally, the commissioner may engage in public education and information programs on arms control and disarmament through a variety of press channels, and can also maintain regular contacts with a number of private German international organizations working in the arms control field.[8] The commissioner thus has access to political leaders, as well as contacts with all other potentially influential actors.

Dr. Friedrich Ruth, commissioner for arms control from 1977 to December 1986, exploited the post's potential successfully. Cast in the mold of the traditional civil servant, Ambassador Ruth operated out of the public eye, but within the Foreign Office, his influence over arms control policy was decisive. He worked closely and successfully with Foreign Minister Genscher for years, implying that the two shared the same orientation toward arms control issues. In the view of one observer, any FRG arms control position presented either through bilateral or multilateral channels bore the stamp of Ruth's office. Another individual in the same position, but with less interest in assuming an active role or lacking Ruth's expertise, might reduce the importance of the position. Similarly, another foreign minister, less inclined to delegate responsibility to the commissioner, might deny the commissioner's post any real influence.[9]

At the working level, responsibilities within division 2a are further divided into four desks. Desk 220 is responsible for global disarmament and arms control (including the START and INF negotiations); desk 221 handles security, disarmament, and arms control in Europe (including MBFR and CSCE); desk 222, nuclear nonproliferation and verification, and the prohibition of biological and chemical weapons; desk 223; disarmament within the context of the United Nations. These four desks routinely coordinate with two desks in division 2, which is responsible for all decisions regarding NATO or East-West relations. Within division 2, desk 201 deals with NATO and defense matters; desk 212 is responsible for East-West relations and assigned primary authority in the CSCE process.[10]

Working level operations are affected significantly by limits on personnel. Currently, there are only eighteen to twenty officers of diplomat rank in division 2a. Moreover, desk officers are concerned primarily with day-to-day operational matters. Their tasks include, for example, preparing the foreign minister or the commissioner for meetings of the Federal Security Council, NATO consultations, and bilateral meetings, and responding to specific Allied arms control initiatives. Desk officers usually have only very limited time to devote to conceptual studies or innovation; their work tends to be responsive. To carry out their tasks, officers in division 2a must work closely with desk 201 (division 2) and MoD officers.[11]

A further constraint at the working level is the limited number of sources available to desk officers for information on arms control. Diplomats normally do not have technical expertise, and the Foreign Office's analytical capabilities are reduced further by the demands of operational matters. In addition, expertise is lost whenever desk officers, who are usually career civil servants, are rotated, on the average once every three or four years.[12] Funds to support outside research are minimal. The primary source of outside expertise is the Research Institute of the Foundation for Science and Policy (SWP, Ebenhausen). The Office for Studies and Exercises of the Bundeswehr (Bensberg) or the German Foreign Policy Association (DGAP, Cologne) may provide additional background research.[13] The functions of these institutions are discussed further below.

The Ministry of Defense

A fundamental organizing principle of the Basic Law, the right of concurrence (*Mitzeichnungsrecht*), gives the Ministry of Defense a voice in the decisionmaking process. The concurrence principle guarantees MoD the right to advise the Foreign Office and to contribute ideas and suggestions at all levels.

Similar to the Foreign Office, arms control decisionmaking in the Ministry of Defense follows strict hierarchical lines (see Figure 2–1).

At *the political level*, the defense minister exercises primary political control over all defense decisionmaking and, like the foreign minister, is guaranteed relative autonomy in defense matters by the *Ressortsprinzip*. The minister is assisted by a parliamentary secretary and three state secretaries.[14]

The inspector general performs both political and military functions. He is the highest ranking military officer and is chosen by the minister of defense with the chancellor's concurrence. The inspector general is also linked directly to the government and political leaders. He is chief military advisor to the government, the German representative to NATO's Military Committee, and is a nonvoting member of the Federal Security Council. Within MoD, the inspector general reports directly to the minister, but he may also be called upon by the chancellor, Cabinet, or Defense Committee of the Bundestag to provide expert or advisory opinion. As commander of the Armed Forces Staff (*Fuehrungsstab Streitkraefte* [FueS]) he relies largely on division II, which is responsible for all politico-military affairs.[15]

In general, the planning staff of the Ministry of Defense plays only a minor role in arms control decisionmaking. The staff is headed by a civilian and reports directly to the minister and his state secretaries. Its tasks include speech writing for the ministry's political leadership and preparation of MoD's annual defense *White Paper*. The planning staff lacks an analytical capability, however, and cannot have a substantive impact on arms control policy. It may play a small conceptual role, acting as a coordinating agent upon demand of the Armed Forces Staff.

The role of the planning staff, however, may vary depending on the personality and leadership style of the defense minister. Under former Defense Minister Helmut Schmidt, the planning staff played an important role in arms control policy formulation and development, providing

Figure 2–1. Institutional Structure for Arms Control Decisionmaking.

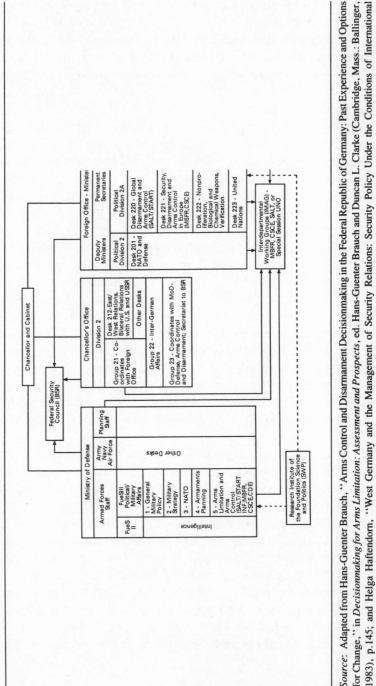

Source: Adapted from Hans-Guenter Brauch, "Arms Control and Disarmament Decisionmaking in the Federal Republic of Germany: Past Experience and Options for Change," in *Decisionmaking for Arms Limitation: Assessment and Prospects,* ed. Hans-Guenter Brauch and Duncan L. Clarke (Cambridge, Mass.: Ballinger, 1983), p.145; and Helga Haftendorn, "West Germany and the Management of Security Relations: Security Policy Under the Conditions of International Interdependence," in *The Foreign Policy of West Germany: Formation and Contents,* ed. Ekkehart Krippendorff and Volker Rittberger, *German Political Studies,* Vol. 4 (London and Beverly Hills, Calif.: Sage, 1980), p. 14.

moreover a counterweight to the military influence within the ministry.[16] At that time, the planning staff was headed by Theo Sommer, a prominent journalist and associate of Schmidt's. Sommer's successor was Hans-Georg Wieck, a career diplomat who served as ambassador to Moscow and until recently as Bonn's permanent representative to NATO. Under Defense Ministers Georg Leber and Hans Apel, the planning staff was headed by Walter Stuetzle, who is credited with the writing of Schmidt's now famous 1977 speech at the International Institute for Strategic Studies, which led eventually to NATO's dual-track decision. The post is currently held by Hans Ruehle, former research director at the Konard Adenauer Foundation and close associate of Defense Minister Manfred Woerner.

At *the intermediate level*, the Armed Forces Staff is the most important MoD policy-making body. It links the minister, his state secretaries, and the inspector general with division heads and thus to the working level. The seven departments of the Armed Forces Staff are composed mostly of military officers. Division III is responsible for all political-military affairs, including military strategy, NATO-related issues, armaments planning, and arms control. Division III is further broken down into nine desks, each headed by a full colonel, assisted by seven to ten officers.[17]

Desk 5 is the locus of responsibility for all arms control matters within the Ministry of Defense. Staffed by seven officers including the desk chief, the scope of the desk's activities is so broad that each staff member must routinely handle more than one issue area. As in the Foreign Office, working level officers focus mainly on operational issues. Moreover, a sharp division of labor between conventional and nuclear matters further limits the capacity of the desk to complete analytical studies that might be relevant to an independent German arms control position. Rather, MoD arms control positions, as described by one observer, reflect political desires but largely lack a sound analytical basis. Other tasks of desk 5 include advising division 2a of the Foreign Office. Additionally, an officer from desk 5 is usually sent with the German delegation to the MBFR and CSCE negotiations.[18]

A number of other MoD bodies may become involved at the working level in arms control decisionmaking. Desk 5 coordinates closely with desk 3, which is responsible for NATO and WEU and serves as a link to the United States and other Western allies. Other MoD actors include desk 1, responsible for general military policy, desk 2, for military strategy, and desk 4, which handles armament planning. All desks work together with the MoD's intelligence unit—division II.[19]

As in the Foreign Office, responsibility in MoD for arms control matters is divided among bureaucratic levels. The minister, aided by his secretaries and, sometimes, the planning staff, is ultimately responsible for ensuring MoD input into the decisionmaking process. At the intermediate level, the inspector general and the Armed Forces Staff may only be involved marginally. Policy implementation and coordination is accomplished at the working level.

The Federal Chancellor's Office

While limited constitutionally to establishing general policy guidelines, the chancellor may exercise an indirect influence on specific policy outcomes in three ways. He may create or abolish ministries and define their jurisdiction without parliamentary authorization. He alone recommends the appointment and dismissal of ministers. And, he may issue general policy guidelines that are binding upon ministers.[20] Additionally, the chancellor's government policy statements (*Regierungserklaerung*), periodic reports on the state of the nation, and other public statements are vehicles to address policy issues, including arms control.[21] The chancellor's leadership style within the Cabinet also affects the decisionmaking process. Helmut Schmidt, for example, was not adverse to taking an active hand in resolving conflict among ministers and, consequently, played an active role in the actual formulation of policy.

The role of the Chancellor's Office in arms control decisionmaking generally has been quite limited. The Chancellor's Office's task is to coordinate interdepartmental policy and oversee compliance of the various ministries with the government's general policy guidelines. Specific responsibility for security affairs lies with division 2, which is further subdivided. Three units deal in some capacity with arms control matters: Desk 212, which is responsible for East-West relations and bilateral relations with Eastern Europe, the Soviet Union, and North America; Group 23, responsible for defense, arms control, and disarmament, as well as the Federal Security Council. Group 23 is composed of four military officers who advise on the military implications of arms control and function as a secretariat to the Federal Security Council.[22]

In recent years, the Chancellor's Office (rather than the chancellor himself) has become a more visible player in security matters. The current head of division 2, Horst Teltschik, is a long-time associate of Chancellor Kohl and a key personal advisor on foreign and security policy. Teltschik seems to be attempting to carve out a greater role for the Chancellor's Office in security policy broadly defined, which could spill over into specific arms control policy. In September 1985, he led a twenty-eight-member delegation to the United States to gather information on the Strategic Defense Initiative. Foreign Minister Genscher was highly critical of Teltschik's mission; the resulting conflict between them was reported in the national press. Teltschik supports German participation in SDI, a position clearly at variance with that of the foreign minister. According to one well-informed observer, the influence of Teltschik's views on Kohl should not be underestimated.

The Cabinet's role is to approve position papers that have been prepared by the various governmental departments.[23] As a consequence of the principle of departmental autonomy, ministers tend to identify more closely with their respective ministries than with their cabinet function. This fact, taken with the lack of an independent bureaucratic infrastructure, prevents the Cabinet from acting as a collective decisionmaking body.[24] The Cabinet exercises influence on arms control decisions only to the extent that conflicts over policy cannot be resolved at working or ministerial levels and consequently must be hammered out at the highest political level under the chancellor's guidance.

Similarly, the Federal Security Council functions primarily as a forum to discuss political-military policy on the basis of decision papers already prepared by both the Foreign Office and Ministry of Defense. Its members include the chancellor, who heads the Council, the ministers of foreign affairs, defense, justice, finance, and economics, the inspector general of the Bundeswehr, and the commissioner of the federal government for disarmament and arms control. The relative infrequence of its meetings supports the view that the Council is primarily responsible for providing the stamp of approval to arms control positions that have already been taken. Between 1976 and 1980, for example, the Federal Security Council convened approximately twenty-five times.[25] Though the Council could provide a forum to resolve differences between ministerial policy positions, other mechanisms of conflict resolution usually ensure that a compromise has been hammered out before the issues reach either the Federal Security Council or the Cabinet.

Coordination and Conflict Resolution

The legal and actual division of responsibility for arms control policy makes the problems of interagency coordination and conflict resolution particularly acute. Conflicts between the Foreign Office and MoD or the Chancellor's Office can and do arise. Recent examples include differences between the Foreign and Chancellor's Offices over West German participation in the American Strategic Defense Initiative, or between the Foreign Office and MoD on the terms of an INF agreement. Though the predominance of the Foreign Office is firmly grounded, personalities may also make a difference to the resolution of these disputes, on occasion undermining the Foreign Office's power and enhancing the influence of contending agents. Mechanisms to resolve conflict start at the lowest level but, if necessary, proceed up through the bureaucratic hierarchy until compromise is achieved.

In civil-military disputes over arms control policy, the balance of power clearly favors the Foreign Office. As the center of foreign and security policy decisionmaking, its voice usually outweighs that of MoD. Most German representatives to bilateral or multilateral councils are Foreign Office staff members. The Ministry of Defense sends delegates as well, of course, but the instructions for negotiating terms are coordinated and transmitted through the Foreign Office, allowing it to monitor all incoming and outgoing information. An attempt in 1972 by the MoD to expand its role in arms control decisionmaking processes by establishing a specific department responsible for security affairs (similar to DOD/ISP in the United States) failed.[26] The Foreign Office enjoys the ironic, but nonetheless real advantage bestowed by Germany's tortured history of civil-military relations. This history provides a powerful constraint on too visible a role for the military in foreign policy matters.

When conflicts do occur, however, the Ministry of Defense has several ways to promote its views. Senior officers tend to be sophisticated politically, and the MoD may be more likely to make its views known through NATO than through domestic channels. Though the Bundeswehr may be a secondary actor at home, in the NATO context it is perceived as second only to the U.S., thus ensuring that its voice is heard.

Conflicts may also arise between the Foreign Office and the Chancellor's Office, again depending on the occupants of the leadership positions. During the early years of the Kohl government, for example, disputes between the Foreign Office and MoD were less evident. As previously noted, however, many disputes have surfaced between the Foreign Office and the Chancellor's Office.

Interagency coordination and conflict resolution is achieved through formal and informal mechanisms. Three instruments are usually available at the working level:

1. The telephone is usually most effective for routine matters.

2. The right of concurrence provides the legal basis for the involvement of agencies other than the Foreign Office. Based on the right of concurrence, for example, group 21 of the Chancellor's Office regularly communicates with the planning staff and desk 5 of MoD, and with the planning staff and divisions 2 and 2a of the Foreign Office.

3. Temporary interdepartmental working groups (IMAGs) are sometimes created for the more difficult issues which may affect several departments in the ministries.[27]

This third instrument was used, for instance, to prepare the German position on SALT I. The IMAG-SALT was directed by the commissioner for arms control and included the head of desk 220 in the Foreign Office and a member of desk 5 of MoD. [28] Its reports were sent to division 2 (division 2a's predecessor) in the Foreign Office, division II of MoD, and group 23 in the Chancellor's Office. Similar mechanisms evolved in the formulation of German positions on CSCE and during the course of the MBFR negotiations.[29] The actual influence of the IMAGs on policy outcomes, however, is limited by the *Ressortsprinzip*, which safeguards the Foreign Office's prerogatives in arms control matters. Moreover, when the issues are complex, the IMAG may be too large or unwieldy to have much impact on decisionmaking or longer term planning. This was the case with the CSCE interministerial group, which met only two or three times a year, and served more as an information channel than an autonomous decisionmaking body.[30]

The resolution of interagency conflict proceeds at all points in the hierarchy, but there is a great deal of pressure to work out disputes before they reach the highest levels of decisionmaking. Through extensive horizontal contacts, desk officers in all likelihood know which initiatives are liable to provoke objections from other quarters and take care to preempt conflict by avoiding the more controversial policies.[31] The realities of coalition politics constitute an additional source of pressure to reach compromise below the ministerial level, as disputes, for example, between the foreign and defense ministers automatically raise the politically sensitive issues of the relative power of the coalition parties. The result is often "anticipatory conflict resolution"—strong efforts are made to obtain a consensus before policy is submitted either to the Cabinet for approval or to the chancellor for his consideration.

THE BUNDESTAG AND POLITICAL PARTIES

The role of legislative actors has been shaped by the historical weakness of German representative institutions and by the nature of the parliamentary system itself. In 1949, there simply was no precedent in German history for a strong and active parliament. In the early postwar years, the Bundestag's role was limited by the supposedly provisional nature of the state and by Konrad Adenauer's iron hand over foreign affairs.[32] Moreover, the very structure of the parliamentary system prevents the Bundestag from exercising a true controlling function. The majority parties in the Bundestag usually will support the government's policies. The line of division is not between the executive and the Bundestag but between the government and the parliamentary minority.

The Bundestag and national political parties help to shape the arms control policy agenda, but have no direct power over decisions. Members of the Bundestag have two avenues by which they may attempt to influence decisionmaking: (1) The Bundestag can function as a forum for public debate on arms control issues; and (2) the Bundestag's committees serve to convey the views of parties' security experts to executive agencies. Plenary sessions, the committee structure of the Bundestag, and the parties' corresponding system of working groups all provide the theoretical capacity to perform these functions; in fact, however, legislative influence is marginal. Plenary debates on security questions are infrequent, and the committees more often resemble information-gathering and discussion bodies. Moreover, legislative deference to the executive and party loyalty in the Bundestag place strict bounds on potentially confrontational activities. The political parties may have a more significant, although still subtle influence on arms control policy. Party positions are indicators of trends in public attitudes on arms control, and may help to shape policy agendas in the government and ministries.

Bundestag

Parliamentary plenary sessions provide a forum for public discussion of the government's arms control policy. There are three primary methods of initiating debate in the Bundestag: the "major interpellation" (*Grosse Anfrage*), the question hour, and the hour for the discussion of current affairs (*Aktuelle Stunde*). All three tend to be used more frequently by the opposition than the majority parties.

If more than 5 percent of the Bundestag deputies submit written questions on a current topic to the government—a "major interpellation" (*Grosse Anfrage*)—a plenary debate may be held on the question and on the government's reply. Many debates, particularly heated ones, are televised. For the opposition, the *Grosse Anfrage* is an opportunity to level criticisms, to dispute conceptions, to challenge specific policy decisions of the government, and to mobilize support for an alternative policy view through an appeal to the attentive public. For the coalition in power, the *Grosse Anfrage* provides the chance to explain and rally support for its current policy. For all parties, it offers security experts an opportunity to prove their competence and to gain exposure and recognition in leadership circles and in the public eye.[33] In practice, the "major interpellation" has been employed during periods of intense political debate over security issues, such as the NATO dual-track decision, and otherwise has occurred only infrequently.

The question hour is an additional means of challenging the government's policy. The question hour takes place before each plenary session and offers a Bundestag deputy the chance to pose a concrete question and two follow-up questions. Other deputies may pose additional related questions, so that, with previous coordination within the party, a minister or his secretary can be forced to provide a sustained defense of the government's policy. In the past, the question hour has been the tool of the opposition, constituting one means by which opposition parties may force the government to debate publicly sensitive political topics, particularly when the timing is unfavorable to the government.[34]

The *Aktuelle Stunde*, instituted in 1965, is intended to supplement the question hour with an opportunity for discussion of current events. Debate is limited to one hour, with each deputy restricted to five minutes speaking time. Designed to encourage more spontaneous discussion, the *Aktuelle Stunde* is more suitable for deputies who are thoroughly versed in security issues—the parties' "experts." But such experts have the opportunity to debate in other parliamentary bodies, so that, once again, the *Aktuelle Stunde* has not been frequently employed.[35]

The Bundestag's committees also provide the potential to influence arms control decisionmaking. The system of Bundestag committees (*Ausschuesse*) mirrors the jurisdictional organization of the ministries: the Foreign Affairs Committee, whose members usually include prominent party figures; the Defense Committee; and the Subcommittee for Disarmament and Arms Control, which draws its membership from both the Defense and Foreign Affairs Committees. The selection of committee chairmen and members is proportional to party strength in the Bundestag.

In practice, however, the involvement of the committees in arms control decisionmaking is limited. As a rule, committee members lack the expertise essential for an active role in policy formulation and, unlike the case of the United States, have only small staffs. Committee members also are handicapped by the problem of access to pertinent information on security and foreign affairs. Information from the ministries and the government trickles down to the Bundestag only selectively. The sub-committee on disarmament and arms control is briefed weekly by the arms control commissioner or his staff, but the information cannot be disseminated beyond the members of the subcommittee; the meetings are closed and members are bound by a secrecy oath. Hearings involving outside experts are the exception rather than the rule.

For these reasons, the committees cannot function as independent actors in the decisionmaking process; their influence is indirect. Committee meetings provide forums for discussion among party experts, whose views and ideas can then be related directly to the commissioner for arms control and his staff, and to the MoD and the Foreign Office.

Political Parties

The parties' most direct contribution to arms control decisionmaking is achieved through the committee structure and the working groups that provide them with support functions. As a result of the limited resources available to individual committee members, parliamentary working groups have taken on the function of secretariat and staff. The parliamentary caucus (*Fraktion*), its functional working groups, and the research institutes associated with each of the three parties' political foundations provide background information and advice on specific issues to the Bundestag members. The working groups are the key link in the informational chain. Each parliamentary caucus has numerous "working groups" (*Arbeitskreise*), which are further subdivided into smaller groups (*Arbeitsgruppen*) that include those deputies who sit on the Bundestag committee corresponding to the working groups' area of competence. For each committee, the party designates a spokesperson who, as a rule, has developed special expertise in the field and can influence the decision-making process within the *Fraktion*. Working groups meet once a week to discuss particular topics and prepare resolutions for plenary sessions.[36]

The parties also possess less formal channels for input into ministerial decisionmaking, exerting a subtle and diffuse influence on arms control policy. Foreign Office staff members pay attention to ongoing security debates within the various parties, and in particular to party resolutions passed at the local and federal level. Discussions at meetings of the governing parties can have a direct impact on the perceptions and preferences of government officials, especially those on the political level. While opposition party policies are most unlikely to be adopted by government officials, they indicate public attitudes and can thus influence internal government policy debates. The heightened public awareness of arms control and security matters in recent years may put particular pressure on ministerial staffs to ensure their policies are acceptable; the parties' positions provide a guide to that acceptability.

In sum, direct legislative input into the arms control decisionmaking process is minimal, but the parties do influence internal government debates to a degree. The Bundestag provides opportunities for public debate on policy decisions and serves to convey the views of party activists and the public to executive agencies. But the contraints inherent in the parliamentary system, limited information, lack of expertise, and practically non-existent support staff prevent the parliamentary committees from expanding their participation in the process. All parties attempt to shape government or ministerial policy agendas, but without access to the expertise and power of the ministries, opposition parties can only rally support for alternative policy conceptions, and prepare for a return to power by training their security experts and exposing them to public view.

NONGOVERNMENTAL ACTORS

In addition to executive and legislative agencies, a number of nongovernmental actors provide limited inputs into the arms control decisionmaking process. The Research Institute of the Foundation for Science and Policy (*Stiftung Wissenschaft und Politik*) is the sole official outside source of information for the Foreign and Defense Ministries; as such, it may influence the range of policy choices considered by ministerial officers. The German Society for Foreign Policy (*Deutsche Gesellschaft fuer Auswaertige Politik*), roughly the West German equivalent of the U.S. Council on Foreign Relations, prepares research papers on arms control issues and provides opportunities for discussion on security topics. Similarly, the foundations of the four established political parties, the

Social Democratic Party (SPD), the Christian Democratic Union (CDU), the Christian Social Union (CSU), and the Free Democratic Party (FDP), also support research; in addition, they provide background information and security expertise for the parliamentary party groups, sponsor political education programs, and may facilitate contacts between party members and American and European security experts. Finally, a small number of journalists with an interest and experience in security affairs report regularly on arms control issues, both reflecting and shaping public and elite attitudes on arms control issues.

The Foundation for Science and Policy
(Stiftung Wissenschaft und Politik)

Designated in 1966 as the sole official research unit of the Federal Government, the Foundation for Science and Policy (SWP) may influence to a degree the flow of information on arms control to working levels of the Foreign Office and the Ministry of Defense. Located in Ebenhausen outside Munich, the SWP is financed primarily through funds allocated by the chancellor's office (in 1986, approximately 9 million DM). The foundation is nevertheless considered independent. The seventeen members of its advisory board include six scientists and economists, six members of federal ministries; the Minister of the Bavarian State Council; and a representative of each of the parties' parliamentary groups.[37] The research institute employs approximately forty analysts with seventy additional support staff, producing about sixty studies and working papers annually. The Foundation possesses an extensive collection of resource and research materials.[38]

At its headquarters in Ebenhausen, security issues are handled by two divisions. The first is headed by Uwe Nerlich, and focuses on American security policy and strategy. The second division is led by Karl-Peter Stratmann and handles NATO issues. The overall approach of both divisions is solidly pro-NATO and pro-American, with little or no criticism leveled against U.S. policies. Division chiefs are said to maintain close contacts with members of the Foreign Office and MoD planning staffs, with the state secretaries, and with those in the international research community who study security and arms control issues.

The foundation has two important channels to influence arms control decisions, one involving the dissemination of information, the other of political advice. The results of SWP studies are made available to a group of about 250 recipients in the Federal Republic. About twenty-five persons receive all reports and working papers. This select group includes prominent personalities in foreign and security policy, such as Theo Sommer (*Die Zeit*), Karl Kaiser (DGAP), and Hans Ruehle (MoD). The rest of the recipients are selected members of the ministries, parliamentary party groups, party research institutes, and journalists. Recently the Foundation has also begun to offer a "clipping service" to ministry officials, supplementing SWP reports with other relevant articles and documentation. It is not unusual for a foreign service officer, newly transferred to a post, to request foundation materials related to his new responsibilities.

Direct working level contacts with SWP researchers constitute a second, more direct channel of input into the decisionmaking process. Though such instances are not readily documented, MoD or Foreign Office desk officers maintain contacts with foundation researchers or are familiar enough with researchers' work to pick up the phone to request information or advice. Moreover, SWP analysts are sometimes invited to participate in inner-ministerial meetings or to testify before the Bundestag. In at least one case, the preparation of the German position on MBFR in 1968, SWP input was decisive. Uwe Nerlich and Dieter Kalix prepared numerous working papers and gave written and oral advisory opinion on general policy and specific negotiating positions. Moreover, there was said to have been an almost constant exchange of information and advice between the SWP analysts and designated members of the Foreign Office.[39]

In sum, though its isolated geographic location prevents it from taking a routine role in decisionmaking, the SWP can nevertheless influence long-term perspectives on arms control. As an important source of information for ministerial officials, the Foundation may help to set policy agendas and outline the alternative options. Political counseling rendered over the telephone or in hearings reinforces the written material funneled into the ministries. Both of these channels may be important, especially given the relative inattention to long-term strategic planning at the ministerial working level.

German Foreign Policy Association (Deutsche Gesellschaft fuer Auswaertige Politik [DGAP])

The German Foreign Policy Association (DGAP) plays a role analogous to the U.S. Council on Foreign Relations. The presidium of the DGAP includes many prominent practitioners and academics in the foreign policy field: Helmut Schmidt; Hans Merkle; Hans-Peter Schwarz; and Karl Kaiser. Moreover, members of the DGAP are drawn from all major political parties: Hans Apel (SPD), Martin Bangemann (FDP), Horst Ehmke (SPD), Volker Ruehe (CDU), and Gerhard Stoltenberg (CDU). The DGAP's declared tasks and goals are to explicate and promote research on the problems of international and European security and economics, to collect documentation on such issues, and to promote and enhance the understanding of international problems through lectures, study groups, and publications. To achieve these goals, the DGAP supports a research institute, headed by Karl Kaiser, staffs a documentation center on international politics, and publishes the widely respected international affairs periodical, *Europa-Archiv*.[40]

Within this broad framework, a number of DGAP activities deal specifically with security and arms control issues. Since January 1962, the DGAP has organized a study group on international security, disarmament, and arms control. (A similar group deals with the more general topic of East-West relations.) The arms control group has been chaired by prominent figures in the security field: Fritz Erler (1962–67), Helmut Schmidt (1967–70), Karl Mommer (1970–77), Alfons Pawelczyk (1977–81), and Egon Bahr.[41] Topics of discussion are varied, but the list of invited speakers usually includes well-known academics and executive level officers from the ministries or military. The study group thus provides an informal contact point for outside analysts and actual decisionmakers, and a vehicle for testing new ideas. In February 1964, for example, the inadequacies of the then-existing arms control decisionmaking apparatus in the Federal Republic were thoroughly discussed in the DGAP working group, which was then chaired by Fritz Erler, an SPD security affairs expert. The opinions articulated in the discussion group were later echoed in the Bundestag and contributed to the push for organizational reform.[42]

In addition to these study groups, the DGAP issues frequent publications and sponsors specific research projects, conferences, lectures, and small discussion circles. These activities may have a very minor impact on arms control policy decisions. The publications of the DGAP by and large represent the views of a West German foreign policy establishment and, as such, may help to shape elite attitudes on arms control. Specific DGAP research projects, conferences, or discussion groups—like the study groups—bring together German and international practitioners and analysts, and promote informal exchange among members of a well-defined group of foreign and security policy decisionmakers.

Political Party Foundations

The foundations of the political parties are best described as "auxiliary organizations."[43] All four—the Friedrich Ebert Foundation (SPD), the Friedrich Naumann Foundation (FDP), the Konrad Adenauer Foundation (CDU), and Hanns Seidel Foundation (CSU)—are financed almost entirely with federal funds.[44] Though nominally independent, each foundation is, in fact, linked inextricably to its parent party. The board of directors of each foundation includes the most prominent member of the relevant party; membership lists read much like party membership or Bundestag representative lists.

The party foundations are active in three main areas:

1. "Political education." Programs of courses, seminars, meetings, and colloquia are offered on a variety of topics. The political philosophy of the particular party and its analyses of security issues are presented at these meetings and may play a minor role in shaping public attitudes.

2. Study and research activities. The research institutes of the party foundations constitute a kind of "academic infrastructure" for the parties, and may train party experts or provide background information on security issues, especially when the party is in opposition.[45] In recent years, the research institute of the Friedrich Ebert Foundation particularly has dealt extensively with security policy issues. Conversely, the staff working on international security issues at the Konrad Adenauer Foundation has shrunk considerably since the CDU entered the government, no doubt reflecting a shift to reliance on ministerial sources of expertise.

3. Developing ties with Americans. All party foundations have offices in Washington, D.C. and organize conferences and smaller meetings, providing opportunities for Germans and Americans to meet in an unofficial and often informal setting. Party foundations also set up meetings between visiting party delegations and U.S. officials and private citizens involved in security affairs, though the Washington embassy retains primary responsibility in this area.

Journalists

The last major group of non-governmental actors includes a small number of prominent journalists who report on security and arms control issues.

Die Zeit, a respected weekly that covers topical political and economic themes, is a particularly important outlet. Its staff includes Theo Sommer and Kurt Becker; Christoph Bertram, former director of the International Institute for Strategic Studies (London), is also a periodic contributor to *Die Zeit* and, in January 1984, Helmut Schmidt became co-publisher of the weekly. Other commentaries on defense appear regularly in the daily *Frankfurter Allgemeine Zeitung (FAZ)*.

The impact of newspaper articles on arms control decisionmaking is, of course, difficult to ascertain. In one analyst's view, these occasional contributions may be more significant for the formation of opinion within the government than the more detailed research and working papers prepared by the SWP or the ministries.[46] This may be particularly true if the journalists' views are taken as a reflection of broader public or elite concerns and attitudes. Prominent journalists may be able to bring indirect pressure to bear on the government at least to consider specific arms control options before actual policy decisions are made.

BILATERAL CHANNELS

Because of West Germany's political/military position, arms control decisionmaking at the national level may also be affected by external actors, in particular by the United States and specific Americans. From the outset, Bonn's national defense policy, strategy, and doctrine have been embedded in the NATO and European framework; FRG security is grounded ultimately in the American nuclear guarantee. Bonn's alliance orientation and emphasis on close bilateral coordination apply just as much to arms control policy. Through the formal NATO infrastructure and more informal mechanisms, American perspectives are injected into the decisionmaking process. Bonn, in turn, also attempts to use bilateral channels to influence American policy, but in the final analysis, these two-way channels are more of a constraint on Bonn than an opportunity for influence.

NATO and Diplomatic Channels

Formal bilateral channels between Bonn and Washington can be divided into three groups. A primary instrument of influence is the NATO infrastructure itself and, within this framework, working contacts between the U.S. military and the Bundeswehr. Second, elaborate mechanisms have evolved within the context of various arms control negotiating forums. A third group is normal diplomatic channels at the working and executive level.

Over time, NATO has developed a complex network of consultative bodies and procedures to deal with arms control issues (see Figure 2–2). The hub of allied consultation in NATO is the North Atlantic Council. Multilateral consultations occur formally within the council, but they are supplemented by ongoing informal trilateral or bilateral discussions. In addition to inputs from national capitals, the North Atlantic Council receives guidance from other NATO bodies at the subcouncil level. The Political Committee, Senior Political Committee, and the Military Committee are all involved indirectly in the process of multilateral consultations. The Defense Planning Committee provides the infrastructure for consultations among defense officials. Within this broad framework, defense ministers consult on arms control issues in the Nuclear Planning Group, which is supported by contacts at the working level. Other NATO forums for arms control consultation include the High Level Group and the Special Consultative Group. Though not formal NATO institutions, they were created to coordinate NATO positions on theater nuclear arms control. The decisions and recommendations of these additional consultative bodies are fed into the North Atlantic Council, which, in turn, can advise on particular arms control negotiations.[47]

Further bilateral points of contact exist at the location of ongoing arms control negotiations. Elaborate multilateral procedures have been developed, for example, in the case of the MBFR negotiations in Vienna and for the CSCE process. In the first case, the MBFR working group and the ad hoc group in Vienna both include representatives from Bonn and Washington. The CSCE working groups provide a support function for the North Atlantic Council, helping to coordinate Allied positions.[48]

The German delegations to all of these bodies include representatives from the Foreign Office and the Ministry of Defense. The Foreign Office controls all communications and guidance to national delegations, but MoD representatives may outnumber Foreign Office delegations within specific negotiating forums, for example, in Brussels (NATO) and Vienna (MBFR).[49]

Direct contacts between West German and American military personnel may help to shape MoD attitudes on arms control. Regular conferences between American and West German staff officers, joint training exercises, or service together at the operational level may facilitate the

Figure 2–2.   NATO Structure for Arms Control
Consultations.

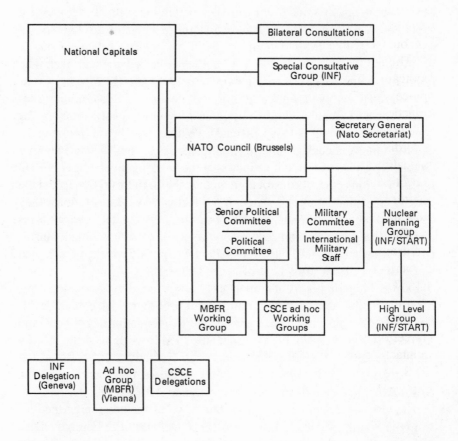

Source: Adapted from Stanley R. Sloan, "Arms Control Consultation in NATO," in *Decisionmaking for Arms Limitation: Assessment and Prospects,* ed Hans-Guenter Brauch and Duncan . Clarke (Cambridge, Mass.: Ballinger, 1983), p. 226.

establishment and cultivation of close contacts between the two military services. In addition to American military personnel stationed in Germany, a large contingent of German military personnel is stationed routinely in the United States for military training. Coodination and joint training are especially well-developed in the case of the two air forces. Moreover, in Washington, German military personnel are frequently in contact with officials of the Departments of State and Defense. It is difficult to determine the exact impact of these numerous ties, but at the very least they provide military personnel with separate sources of information and may encourage a certain unity of views between the two militaries.

Though the structures of consultation described above would seem to indicate a two-way flow of influence, in fact, the U.S. dominates this process. In the first place, NATO "consultative" bodies more often function as information clearinghouses than true collective decisionmaking bodies. (Though in MBFR and CSCE, the NATO bodies created to coordinate Allied positions probably played a more significant role in the actual decisionmaking.) In cases where West Germany has no seat at the negotiating table, such as START and INF, Allied consultative procedures more often are used to inform European allies of U.S. negotiating positions that have already been determined in Washington.

The overall predominance of the United States in questions of arms control gives added weight to the American input. The penetration of American views reflects not only its status as the major nuclear power in NATO, but its far greater research and analytical capabilities.[50] West Germany may simply lack the necessary analytical capabilities to prevail against the United States. In sum, rather than offering opportunities for forceful bargaining and lobbying for the West German position, bilateral contacts may constrain the development of independent, or at least U.S.-divergent FRG positions on arms control.

CHANGES IN THE DECISIONMAKING PROCESS

Personalities, arms control developments at the international level, and domestic political and social changes have shaped and will continue to shape arms control decisionmaking in the Federal Republic. A potentially powerful source of change is the coincidence of two recent developments: the "securitization" of West German politics, and the revival in new form of the German national question. Both could have a significant and long-term impact on the arms control decisionmaking process.

"Securitization" of Politics

The revival of the West German peace movement and active opposition to the deployment of INF have been interpreted by a number of analysts as evidence of the "democratization" of foreign policy in the Federal Republic. The implication is that foreign and security policy-making are no longer the privilege solely of a small body of security "experts"; instead, there will be new opportunities for popular participation and input into the decisionmaking process.

There is little evidence that the decisionmaking process, in fact, has been "democratized." As we have described, for the most part, foreign and security policy-making remains confined to the ministries, with a varying degree of input by other institutional actors. Moreover, the Bundestag and its committees have not visibly expanded their role in the process. New means of channeling public demands have not emerged from the turbulent period of protest in the early 1980s.

What has happened in recent years may more aptly be described as the "securitization" of West German politics. In the past, the saliency of security issues has been sporadic, being confined largely to the periods preceding German rearmament and the first deployment of nuclear weapons in the Federal Republic. In each case, interest waned soon after policy decisions were taken and implemented. In contrast, the current phase of "securitization," which was provoked by the controversy over the INF decision, may endure. Though broad concern over security issues is now less visible than in the early 1980s, the West German public may be so sensitized to security issues that any controversial policy decision might rekindle debate. Opposition parties, apparently, continue to see benefit in raising arms control concerns. The Social Democrats, for example, in early September 1987 called for a special session of the Bundestag to debate the government's policy on Pershing 1a modernization and an INF agreement; the debate took place only weeks before regional elections in Bremen and Schleswig-Holstein. Though elections still turn primarily on economic issues, security policy receives considerable attention in party forums, particularly within the SPD.

As a result of this "securitization" of politics, public acceptability will be an increasingly important criterion in arms control decisionmaking. Most importantly, "securitization" has a number of implications for executive agencies. For desk officers within the ministries, the function of the Bundestag and the parties as conduits of information and public opinion may gain in significance. Parliamentary and party resolutions, as well as committee discussions and hearings, are handy barometers of public opinion and attitudes. At higher decisionmaking levels, especially in the Chancellor's Office, greater efforts are made to predict public reaction to government decisions on arms control and to flush out potential problem areas, so that a public backlash does not erupt unexpectedly. The government also makes every attempt to appear an active advocate of the arms control process. In this view, strong popular support for an INF agreement may have been one factor in the Kohl government's acceptance in 1987 of a "double zero" solution on INF and its pledge not to modernize West German Pershing 1a missiles.

The "securitization" of politics is less likely to affect the parliament's direct role in decisionmaking. It has not, for example, provoked the Bundestag and its committees to develop their roles more fully, for example, by upgrading the Subcommittee on Arms Control, holding more frequent hearings, or expanding the Bundestag's support staff.[51] Whether from lack of will or resources, or simply because of the inherent constraints of the system, the legislative branch seems likely to remain a marginal player in arms control policy.

Revival of the "German Question"

The revival of interest in the German national question and national identity has reinforced the impact of "securitization" on decisionmaking processes. During the period of INF protest, the "German question" emerged as a topic of political discussion and reflection. Rather than a renewed demand for national reunification, the new German question manifests itself in a reexamination of national identity and an awareness of special German security needs and interests. Such popular recognition of special German vulnerabilities may reinforce the pressure on any Bonn administration to support the continuation of the arms control process and to champion German interests. Indeed, such pressure may be behind Foreign Minister Genscher's repeated exhortations to develop distinctly European positions on arms control. Greater cooperation with Bonn's European allies would be one means of protecting national interests, to the extent that European and German interests were perceived to be compatible.

The SPD has taken the step of linking explicitly an inter-German dialogue with security interests. Following more than a year of contacts between the SPD's parliamentary working group and the East German Socialist Unity Party (SED), the SPD on June 19, 1985 announced the successful completion of a draft treaty "outline" to create a chemical-weapons-free zone in Europe. The agreement is designed as a framework for negotiations at the governmental level.[52] In the words of SPD delegation head Karsten Voigt, "The agreement with the SED is one of the pilot projects, which the party will use to prepare a second phase of *Ostpolitik*."[53] Though the government has criticized the SPD for conducting an "ancillary" foreign policy, (*Nebenaussenpolitik*), the inter-German arms control dialogue continues. On December 6, 1985, working groups from the SPD and SED met in East Berlin for the first time to discuss the creation of a tactical-weapons-free corridor in central Europe; these talks continued during 1986 and 1987.

Institutional Changes

The SPD has proposed a different solution to advance West German arms control positions—reorganization of the entire arms control decisionmaking process. The party has declared its intention to revive earlier initiatives and create an arms control office, which would probably be located in the Chancellor's Office and which, according to several observers, would be headed by Egon Bahr. The arms control office would have its own financial resources and support staff to ensure a greater degree of autonomy. The success of the initiative would depend, however, on two preconditions:

1. The SPD would have to rule alone, so that the new chancellor would not have to consider coalition interests in reassigning duties now housed in the Foreign and Defense Ministries to the new agency.

2. The initiative would need the full support of the new defense and foreign ministers, who might otherwise thwart the attempt to coordinate and control arms control policy through the Chancellor's Office.

The creation of a West German arms control ministry could have numerous implications for arms control policy. First, the SPD would possess a potentially powerful instrument to pursue its own specific arms control agenda without confronting the entrenched opposition likely to exist in long-established bureaucratic channels. This would be true particularly for any continuation of an inter-German arms control dialogue on an official basis, which would require a locus of authority other than the Foreign Office. The latter is responsible for international affairs; as Bonn does not (and legally cannot) treat the GDR as a foreign country, responsibility for German-German arms control negotiations could only be assigned to the Foreign Office with a good deal of legal hairsplitting, if at all. Above all, an arms control ministry could provide the Federal Republic with the institutional resources and personnel to develop greater expertise in arms control. As a consequence, Bonn might then also be better able to articulate its own specific arms control agenda, which could cause greater friction in U.S.-German or German-Allied relations.

Conversely, a West German arms control ministry could prove politically insignificant if the real source of power remained in the established ministries. The Foreign and Defense Ministries, after all, would continue to exercise responsibility for NATO and U.S.-German relations. Coordination and conflict resolution would become still more complicated by the appearance of a new actor on the scene; the arms control process would be fragmented further.

A cynical view would suggest that the creation of an autonomous arms control ministry would serve primarily to deflect public pressures. Establishment of this visible office, and the apparent insertion of an actor at the highest decisionmaking levels, motivated solely to advance arms control, would indicate the new government's commitment to progress in this area. At the same time, it would not be difficult for the traditional ministries to retain real authority within the system.

Arms control decisionmaking processes have not been static over time, but have been affected by domestic political and social change. Electoral outcomes decide who will fill key positions in the decisionmaking structure, and thus indirectly, the nature of interagency conflict. In a broader sense, the "securitization" of politics sparked by the controversy over INF has brought debate on the fundamental principles of West German security into the public arena, while revitalized interest in the questions of German national identity may also have enhanced public awareness of German security interests. The coincidence of these last two domestic developments is likely to give each a lasting impact on the decisionmaking process. Whatever the nature of the coalition in Bonn or the personalities involved, public reaction to arms control policy may have to be taken increasingly into account before any decision is made. Further, whether through greater European cooperation or organizational reform, the Federal Republic may seek more effective means to protect what are perceived as special German security interests.

CONCLUSION

Reflecting a mixture of tradition and legal administrative principles, the West German arms control decisionmaking process is fragmented, decentralized, and bureaucratized. The formal structure gives weight to the executive agencies, above all the Foreign Office, but within each institution, responsibility for arms control policy is subdivided. The importance of working level operations—the desks of division 2a in the Foreign Office, and desk 5 of the Armed Forces Staff—should not be underestimated. This complex hierarchical and bureaucratic matrix system produces what one well-informed observer calls "administrative" (*Verwaltete*) foreign policy.[54]

Yet the formal decisionmaking structure represents a potential, rather than an iron, division of power among contending institutions. Legal principles may safeguard the Foreign Office's prerogative, but forceful personalities, personal capabilities and interests, special access, and useful contacts can bend the structure considerably. The current preponderance of the Foreign Office was preceded by periods when the Chancellor's Office or the MoD carried superior power.

The combination of fragmented arms control operations and individual power favors a system that guarantees periodic conflict. Moreover, the problems of coordination and conflict resolution at the national level are mirrored at the multi- and bilateral level, where American or Allied perspectives enter the process. Lacking a central organ with supreme authority but facing strong pressure to achieve compromise, West German officials may tend to settle for the least common denominator, or positions that broadly favor the continuation of the arms control process. This emphasis on progress in the process, on occasion, may lead to support for an initiative because it furthers the process, but opposition to the positions specified in the proposal. Such was reportedly the case when the West Germans welcomed an Allied initiative on MBFR, only to reject the specific suggestions for Soviet verification teams on German soil. What speeds along the process may be welcomed by all West German agencies; conflicts may arise over the specifics of proposals.

The arms control decisionmaking process continues to evolve. Developments at the international level, such as the creation of new arms control negotiations, have repercussions in Bonn. Over the past few decades, arms control policy has slowly but steadily been upgraded within the Foreign Office, as arms control has been institutionalized in NATO and more broadly supported at home. The final culmination of this trend would be the creation of a West German version of ACDA.

It remains to be seen whether the "securitization" of West German politics, coupled with a revival of interest in the German national question, will have a permanent impact on decisionmaking processes. If both prove long-lasting, then public acceptability of arms control policy will have to be taken as seriously as its technical feasibility. Though they will still lack a strong controlling hand, the Bundestag, parties, or non-governmental actors may be watched more closely by the "administrators"—the officials in executive agencies in Bonn— of arms control policy as gauges of public attitudes.

NOTES

1. "Basic Law of the Federal Republic of Germany" (Wiesbaden: Press and Information Office of the Federal Republic of Germany, 1974).
2. Hans Guenter Brauch, "Arms Control and Disarmament Decisionmaking in the Federal Republic of Germany: Past Experience and Options for Change," in *Decisionmaking for Arms Limitation: Assessment and Prospects*, eds. Hans Guenter Brauch and Duncan L. Clarke (Cambridge, Mass.: Ballinger, 1983), p. 139.
3. Renate Mayntz and Fritz W. Scharpf, *Policy Making in the German Federal Bureaucracy* (Amsterdam and New York: Elsevier, 1975), pp. 86–89.
4. Helga Haftendorn, "West Germany and the Management of Security Relations: Security Policy under the Conditions of International Interdependence," in *The Foreign Policy of West Germany: Formation and Contents*, eds. Ekkehart Krippendorff and Volker Rittberger, *German Political Studies*, vol. 4 (London and Beverly Hills: Sage, 1980), p. 12.
5. Guido Brunner, "Wozu einen aussenpolitischen Planungsstab?" *Aussenpolitik* 23 (September 1972): 546–51.
6. In 1977, two political scientists, Volker Rittberger and Hans Guenter Brauch, proposed the creation of a German Disarmament Agency within the Chancellor's Office. The SPD in November 1977 agreed at its party congress to evaluate the proposal. At its December 1979 congress, the SPD approved a number of resolutions for organizational reform, but Foreign Minister Genscher and Defense Minister Hans Apel both opposed the move.

Finally, in 1981, the Federal Committee of the FDP on Foreign Policy proposed a number of less drastic reforms, among them the upgrading of the arms control division in the Foreign Office. The latter was then approved. See Brauch, "Arms Control and Disarmament," p. 143.

7. Brauch, "Arms Control and Disarmament," pp. 144–49.

8. Helga Haftendorn, "Der Abruestungsbeauftragte. Zur Organisation der Abruestungspolitik in der Bundesrepublik Deutschland," *Politische Vierteljahresschrift* 13 (August 1972): 34–35.

9. In December 1986, Dr. Josef Holik succeeded Ruth as Bonn's arms control commissioner. Holik formerly headed desk 221 in the Foreign Office, responsible for European arms control issues, and had been chief of Bonn's delegation to the MBFR negotiations in 1985.

10. Brauch, "Arms Control and Disarmament," p. 149.

11. Jonathan Krause and Lothar Wilker, "Bureaucracy and Foreign Policy in the Federal Republic of Germany," in *The Foreign Policy of West Germany*, pp. 153–55.

12. Brauch, "Arms Control and Disarmament," p. 149.

13. Haftendorn, "West Germany," p. 16; Brauch, "Arms Control and Disarmament," pp. 153–55.

14. Catherine McArdle Kelleher, "Defense Organization in Germany: A Twice Told Tale," in *Reorganizing America's Defense: Leadership in War and Peace*, eds. Robert J. Art, Vincent Davis, and Samuel P. Huntington (New York: Pergamon-Brassey's, 1985), p. 91.

15. Ibid., pp. 96–8.

16. Haftendorn, "West Germany" p. 16.

17. Kelleher, "Defense Organization in Germany," p. 98.

18. Brauch, "Arms Control and Disarmament," p. 151.

19. Ibid., pp. 150–51.

20. Mayntz and Scharpf, *Policy Making*, p. 38.

21. The first of these—the chancellor's ministerial "organizing power"—is, of course, constrained by either intraparty or coalitional disputes over departmental jurisdiction, which may effectively block major reorganization initiatives. Coalition politics were doubtless a contributing factor in the failure in the late 1970s of a series of initiatives to create a German Disarmament Agency. The measure would have required both Foreign Minister Genscher and Defense Minister Apel to relinquish voluntarily certain powers and prerogatives. Because the distribution of cabinet positions is also an indication of the relative strength of coalition parties, the creation of a new agency was likely to upset this balance and reflect on the prestige and power of the coalition partners.

22. Brauch, "Arms Control and Disarmament," pp. 151–52; Haftendorn, "West Germany," p. 15.

23. Haftendorn, "West Germany," p. 13.

24. Mayntz and Scharpf, *Policy Making*, p. 43.
25. Brauch, "Arms Control and Disarmament," p. 152.
26. Haftendorn, "West Germany," p. 12.
27. Ibid., p. 18.
28. Heinrich Buch, "Die Rolle der Bundesrepublik bei SALT—Mitspieler oder Zuschauer?," in *Verwaltete Aussenpolitik: Sicherheits- und Entspannungspolitische Entscheidungsprozesse in Bonn*, eds. Helga Haftendorn et al. (Cologne: Verlag Wissenschaft und Politik, 1978), pp. 130–31.
29. Brauch, "Arms Control and Disarmament," pp. 152–53.
30. Ruediger Lentz, "Die Entwicklung der deutschen Position zur KSZE—multilaterale Problemstellung und innerorganisatorische Innovation," in *Verwaltete Aussenpolitik*, p. 159.
31. Mayntz and Scharpf, *Policy Making*, p. 74.
32. David P. Conradt, *The German Polity* (New York: Longman Inc., 1982), pp. 138–39.
33. Wolf-Dieter Karl and Joachim Krause, "Aussenpolitischer Strukturwandel und parlamentarischer Entscheidungsprozess," in *Verwaltete Aussenpolitik*, pp. 66–67.
34. Ibid., pp. 68–70.
35. Ibid., p. 70.
36. Ibid., pp. 71–75.
37. The Council is said to be politically neutral. At present, however, there is pressure from some quarters in Bonn to ensure a more partisan line at the SWP.
38. Stephan Hebel, "Eine Denkfabrik fuer Beamte und Parlamentarier," *Frankfurter Rundschau*, 21 April 1986, p. 21.
39. Martin Mueller, "Konzeption und Akteure. Die Entwicklung der MBFR-Politik der Bundesrepublik zwischen 1968 und 1971," in *Verwaltete Aussenpolitik*, p. 170.
40. Deutsche Gesellschaft fuer Auswaertige Politik, e.V, *Jahresbericht 1984* (Bonn: DGAP, 1985), p. 4.
41. Ibid., p. 8.
42. Helga Haftendorn, *Abruestungs- und Entspannungspolitik zwischen Sicherheitsbefriedigung und Friedenssicherung* (Duesseldorf: Bertelsmann Universitaetsverlag, 1974), pp. 79–80.
43. Reinhard Meier, "Political Party Foundations in Bonn," *Swiss Review of World Affairs*, February 1982, p. 25.
44. Following an unsuccessful attempt to block the dispension of federal funds to the political parties' foundations, the Greens in 1986 began to discuss the creation of their own foundation, the "Heinrich-Boell-Foundation." Like other issues, the project quickly became a contentious one within the party, as fundamentalist and realist factions argued over the foundation's function and organization.

45. Meier, "Political Party Foundations."

46. Haftendorn, "West Germany," p. 17.

47. Stanley R. Sloan, "Arms Control Consultations in NATO," in *Decision-making for Arms Limitation*, pp. 225–29.

48. Ibid., pp. 227–29.

49. Haftendorn, "West Germany," p. 12.

50. Simon Lunn, "Policy Preparation and Consultation within NATO Decisiomaking for SALT and LRTNF," in *Decisionmaking for Arms Limitation*, p. 262.

51. These are only a few of the suggested reforms to expand the role of the Bundestag in arms control policy-making. See Hans Guenter Brauch, *Abruestungsamt oder Ministerium?* (Frankfurt a. Main: Haag und Herchen, 1981), pp. 277–78.

52. Executive Committee of the SPD, "Chemische Abruestung: Modell fuer eine chemiewaffenfreie Zone in Europa," *Politik*, no. 6 (July 1985) pp. 5–7.

53. Karsten D. Voigt, "Wege zur chemischen Abruestung," *Deutschland Archiv* 18 (September 1985), p. 933.

54. The important role of officials in Bonn's executive agencies is depicted in Haftendorns comprehensive study of policymaking processes, *Verwaltete Aussenpolitik*.

3 THE CDU/CSU AND ARMS CONTROL

West German attitudes toward security policy, nuclear weapons, and arms control have been widely discussed on both sides of the Atlantic since the early 1980s. Yet relatively little attention has been paid to the perspectives of the Christian Democratic Union/Christian Social Union, the country's largest political party and, since 1982, its major governing party.

Part of the explanation lies in the Union's generally strict adherence to NATO orthodoxy as determined in Brussels and Washington during the past decade. This apparent conformity contrasts sharply with the Social Democratic Party's experiments in heterodoxy and the ecopeace movement's seemingly radical heresies. Similarly, there was little drama in the Union's comparatively harmonious deliberation over the question of deploying intermediate range nuclear forces, an issue that split the SPD and brought demonstrators onto the street throughout Western Europe. However in 1987 the party suddenly drew attention with its leadership's fierce effort to block the emergence of a superpower arms agreement and the resultant collapse of consensus within the Union.

The reasons for, as well as the exceptions to, the general rule of CDU/CSU conformity and harmony are critical to an understanding of West Germany's effort to deal with the changing nature of security and arms control policies. As this study suggests, a widespread and persistent conviction that nuclear deterrence is the key to West German security sets relatively strict limits on Union arms control policy. Above all, the party fears the perceived decoupling effect of many proposals for reducing nuclear weapons. Intraparty politics, especially the entrenched position of conservatives—led by the CSU—reinforce the commitment to traditional West German security policy, and thus reinforce suspicion of arms control.

The CDU/CSU has also been compelled to seek—and at times gently push the United States toward—more flexible arms control initiatives. The primary reason for this modification of CDU/CSU policy is the perceived need to reassure an uneasy public that nuclear deterrence need not mean an uncontrolled escalation of arms and tensions. Union leaders fear that such anxieties could in the long term undermine acceptance of the very security policies they deem vital. Reinforcing this factor are the exigencies of domestic politics, as the Union realistically can remain in control of the West German government only with the support of a coalition partner even more deeply committed to arms control.

This study first analyzes the extent to which CDU/CSU attitudes toward arms control are a product of the party's underlying assumptions about the Federal Republic's foreign and security policies. It next explores the impact of domestic political factors on the party's approach to weapon limitation issues. Finally, it assesses the likely future of Union arms control policy in light of the 1987 election and the emergence of a superpower accord eliminating intermediate-range nuclear arms. We begin with a brief word about the two parties which make up the CDU/CSU Union.

THE CDU AND THE CSU

The larger of the Union's two sister parties is the CDU, active everywhere in the FRG outside of Bavaria. More often than not, a CDU supporter is a Catholic *Buerger* from the FRG's western regions. Yet since its early days under Konrad Adenauer, first chancellor of the Federal Republic, the party has largely succeeded in making a broader appeal. Despite protest by some party activists, the "C" in its name has at most stood for a vague appeal to political action based on Christian values; it has avoided the image of either a religious or denominational Catholic party. Similarly, the CDU has appealed to voters across class lines, attracting workers as well as the middle class. It has campaigned nationwide (outside Bavaria), and has avoided overdependence on regional strongholds. Adenauer and his successors established the pattern of CDU's success: CDU strategy and policy first attracted diverse groups, then cemented their affiliations by identifying the CDU with a successful, internationally respectable, democratic, market-oriented state.

The result is a broad catch-all party, or *Volkspartei*, without an ideology. As a coalition of diverse interests, the CDU is held together primarily by its commitment to preserving the FRG's basic structures— and thus also by electoral victory over the SPD. Aside from the basic convictions already mentioned, the CDU is mainly concerned with effective management, stability, and prosperity.[1]

By contrast to its sister party, the Bavarian CSU is more homogeneous and ideological. Since the early 1950s, the CSU has nominally, and to some extent actually, been a catch-all party: its membership does span class and religious divisions. But not only has the CSU long been heavily Catholic and middle class, it offers an overriding appeal to Bavarian pride. The CSU considers itself Bavaria's party, representing the common, traditional values and interests of a region which, in spirit at any rate, is autonomous.

This translates into specific policies in many ways. Bavaria is a curiously successful blend of capitalism and social conservatism that reconciles economic modernization with traditional patterns of life in the countryside. In nationwide affairs, the CSU tries to uphold West German federalism in order to ensure the region's semi-autonomy, even while promoting Bavaria's version of conservatism as appropriate for the country as a whole. Stylistically, the CSU also reflects Bavarian combativeness and boisterousness.

Consequently, the CSU is more cohesive and ideological than its sister party. Bavaria and the FRG as a whole should, the CSU argues, constitute a "bulwark against Bolshevism."[2] The impact of this distinctive conservatism on Union defense and foreign policy will become apparent. The Union parties nonetheless are bound by a common commitment to established parliamentary-political structures, the social-market economy, and domestic order. More importantly, the strongest bond holding the Union together is an abiding commitment to Bonn's postwar foreign policy orientation—the *Westpolitik*, another Adenauer legacy.

After an initial debate within CDU ranks during the early postwar years, Konrad Adenauer steered the FRG into an enduring, institutionalized relationship with the Western states, and particularly with the United States. Today, the CDU/CSU believes that these ties to the Western democratic community have been the key factors in establishing West German respectability and in ensuring the survival of its basic sociopolitical structures. In the words of the late Alois Mertes, CDU spokesman on arms control, *Westpolitik* was a decision guided as much by political values as by national interests. It is with *Westpolitik* and its resulting security policies that any examination of CDU/CSU attitudes toward arms control must begin.

UNION FOREIGN/SECURITY POLICIES AND ARMS CONTROL

Two predominant strands in party thinking have determined Union positions on arms control issues. The first is party preferences concerning

West German security policy, the second its approach to relations with the East, or *Ostpolitik*.

West German Security

Instinctive anti-Communism, combined with a sober assessment of Moscow's postwar strategic aims, have sustained CDU/CSU convictions that the Soviet threat to West Germany is multifaceted. Party leaders have long believed that historical and ideological ambitions feed a Kremlin desire for political hegemony in Europe. Moreover, they believe an independent, democratic Germany inherently threatens the health of the Soviet Union's own sphere in Eastern Europe with the virus of freedom, represents a permanent democratic-irredentist appeal to Communist East Germany, and poses an obstacle to the westward expansion of Soviet influence. In CDU/CSU eyes, Soviet military might thus is engineered to destroy West German independence through psychological intimidation. The Kremlin's *Realpolitikers* hope to avoid war, according to CDU/CSU beliefs, yet create instability, uncertainty, and a sense of isolation in West Germany, such that neutralization or "Finlandization" results. To that end, Communist-controlled East Germany is a valuable tool that can be used to lure Bonn into accommodation. Soviet military, political and diplomatic tools are all part of the same strategy in CDU/CSU eyes. There may be phases of confrontation, peaceful coexistence, and détente, but the objective is constant: domination without war.[3]

The CDU/CSU sees close ties to the West as indispensable. Since the FRG alone cannot offset Soviet pressure, Bonn must be part of a larger whole that can prevent its isolation and ensure its protection. Thus, the Union has been willing to defer, perhaps indefinitely, national reunification for the sake of gaining the FRG's full sovereign status as a Western partner, and integrating it into the Western economic, political, and military sphere. All of Adenauer's legacies, from rearmament and entry into NATO, to membership in the European Community, serve these purposes.

Since late in Adenauer's era (1949–1963) however, there has been an underlying division between what could be labeled Union "Gaullists" and "Atlanticists." Though rarely used in recent years, these terms retain their validity if the Atlanticist-Gaullist split is understood, in Waldemar Besson's words, as a dispute over the implications of bipolarity.[4] Since the early 1960s, so-called Gaullists have feared that U.S.-Soviet preeminence makes Europe a marginal force in world politics, thus unable to shape its own destiny and helpless if—as they suspect—America's commitment to Europe should end. In their view only an assertive Europe, one that is a full and equal partner of the United States and shapes Western policy, can assure its own security. Atlanticists, on the other hand, have always regarded bipolarity as largely irreversible, and have argued that Europe must adapt to that fact or risk alienating its American partner while provoking its Soviet adversary. Both groups have feared that, in the long term, the wrong choice could isolate Bonn from those upon whom it must rely for protection; both thus have had security uppermost in mind.

This basic disagreement has led to a relatively permanent difference of emphasis, and periodic disputes, within the Union on foreign policy issues. Gaullist instincts have been most compatible with strong anti-Communism and, more importantly, an uncompromising political style; thus, the CSU and many notable CDU conservatives could still be considered Gaullists, while most CDU leaders, comfortable with compromise and pragmatism, fit the Atlanticist label.

Nuclear Deterrence.   Nuclear weapons have long played the key role in CDU/CSU security policy. The party has always contended that a conventional military balance must be achieved, but given the need to offset the peacetime effects of Soviet power, the West cannot merely equip itself for victory on a possible battlefield. Instead, it must strive to make war such an unthinkable risk that it is excluded as an option and renders Soviet military force irrelevant. In this view, conventional weapons are not suited to such far-reaching deterrence; they play an ancillary role. The effort to build up forces matching the Soviets' would, in any case, turn the FRG into a garrison state, tearing at its social fabric and opening the way for externally directed subversion.

From Adenauer's day until the present, the key variable in the CDU/CSU security equation has been America's nuclear guarantee. German nuclear weapons are an unthinkable option on historical grounds alone, and have been unilaterally renounced by the party. The Union's Atlanticist majority views a multilateral European nuclear deterrent built around Franco-British forces with skepticism, it has warned that any "concept of a self-contained and independent defense of Western Europe [is] illusory and dangerous."[5] It regards any potential European nuclear force as inherently incapable of equalling the deterrence value of U.S. central systems: from the Atlanticist perspective, Europe lacks the large land area and low population density that they believe necessary to make an entirely autonomous deterrent threat credible.[6]

To be sure, CSU chief Franz Josef Strauss and the CDU's Alfred Dregger still occasionally imply what Union Gaullists openly stated in the early 1960s: Paris, not Washington, is the FRG's most promising partner in the long run. Even in the late 1970s, the CSU's newspaper carried columns arguing that with ongoing modernization programs, "Paris understands its 'force de frappe' as an atomic shield for Europe."[7] Aside from providing a more reliable security partner, in Gaullist eyes, a European deterrent would end overdependence on the United States, revive Western Europe's will to defend its own interests, and restore Western Europe's status as an actor in, rather than merely an object of, world power politics.

Yet, in the short term, the Gaullist aim has been to find for Bonn the most realistic, credible nuclear "partner." In the early 1960s, and again late in the 1970s, when Gaullists assailed the Carter Administration, they often emphasized the European deterrent idea. In the 1980s, however, with a more assertive America and a more cautious Europe, they shifted ground and began to talk enthusiastically of a German "second key" for U.S. nuclear forces and less favorably of European options. Union Gaullists are not irrevocably committed to a European deterrent when the U.S. option appears more credible. For them the nuclear partner's credibility is more vital than its identity.

In any case, even Union Gaullists have been frank in their skepticism about the possibility of real progress toward creation of a European deterrent; national rivalries and political inertia are seen as nearly intractable obstacles. Strauss and Dregger have vented their frustration with the sluggish pace of European integration and Europe's skittishness about power politics quite bluntly. Moreover, both have openly criticized the discrepancies between talk by French politicians of an expanded deterrent and the French government's jealous treatment of the force de frappe as an exclusively national asset.[8] Atlanticists like Manfred Woerner and Helmut Kohl have been more diplomatic, yet even more certain in their view of inherent limits on European cooperation in the nuclear field.

Still, the Gaullist impulse underscores the central problem of traditional CDU/CSU security policy: the need, for lack of alternatives, to rely on a U.S. nuclear guarantee that can never be considered unquestionably viable. Despite commitments and verbal reassurances, the U.S. guarantee inherently lacks certainty; the vulnerability of U.S. cities beginning in the 1960s, the subsequent removal of U.S. missiles from Europe, the bilateral superpower *modus vivendi*, the acceptance of strategic parity all have nourished doubts. Despite public expressions of confidence that America's stake in Europe and a transatlantic "community of values" reinforce the U.S. nuclear guarantee, even CDU/CSU Atlanticists harbor concerns. Periodic American pressures to cut troop strengths in Europe or to remove nuclear weapons are taken as additional signs of waning U.S. interest in Europe. Atlanticists wonder whether it could ever be believed, above all in Moscow, that the U.S. would risk nuclear war on Europe's behalf.

NATO Strategy.   Given that Gaullist solutions have proven implausible, the Union has had to live with the inherent uncertainties of a U.S. guarantee and to prevent those uncertainties from growing. This has meant helping to fashion an Alliance strategy to guard against the possibility of transatlantic "decoupling," or even the emergence of perceptions that decoupling may be taking place.

Today the Union formally endorses the flexible response strategy as the key to secure coupling between Europe and the United States. The party proclaims that NATO must possess sufficient forces at each level of conflict to deny the Warsaw Pact a battlefield victory; it maintains that this permits a controlled but certain process of escalation, which alone can assure a credible threat of escalation to strategic warfare. With a "seamless web of deterrence" to assure rapid escalation, the party argues, war remains an unthinkable risk, and Soviet military power is thus neutralized.[9]

Yet, Union Atlanticists, and especially Gaullists, implicity distrust the strategy in many respects. The emphasis on intermediate stages of escalation at the conventional and tactical nuclear levels is problematic, they believe. It dilutes the dissuasive threat of strategic nuclear conflict which makes war unthinkable, and in Gaullist eyes, offers the United States options to pause rather than escalate. It implies the breakdown of initial deterrence and the conversion of Germany into a battlefield. It entails the financial and social burdens of continuing major defense expenditures, which tear at the country's social fabric by weakening the welfare state. It is an unattractive political package for any party to sell.

The Union, revealingly, thus puts little more than rhetorical emphasis on providing NATO with the necessary tools for flexibility. Manfred Woerner and party defense elites do outline specifically what must be done to provide NATO with the options necessary for controlled escalation. But even they, and certainly their colleagues with less expertise, seem comparatively unconcerned about meeting those operational requirements.

Despite its professed anxiety about a conventional imbalance, since its accession to power in 1982 the CDU/CSU-led government has failed consistently to meet NATO spending targets.

Similarly, the Union accords low priority to battlefield nuclear weapons. Woerner and party defense elites do state that only those weapons that defend can also deter, meaning that NATO must have the capacity to "deny" Moscow domination at each potential stage of escalation and not merely to "punish" it through retaliation. In practice, however, they show little enthusiasm for the tactical "warfighting options" implicit in this theory. Their nonspecialist colleagues are even less interested in the precise military applications of "usable nuclear weapons," especially at the battlefield level.

As for longer range weapons, defense experts believe systems able to strike Soviet targets best assure escalation dominance. But for most colleagues controlled escalation is still, in fact, an abstract and unrealistic notion.

For most party leaders, the true utility of flexible response lies in the doctrinal rationalization it provides for retaining: (1) U.S. nuclear forces in Europe; (2) a rough East-West equilibrium in European nuclear forces; and (3) a Bonn-Washington nuclear partnership. With U.S. forces present, Moscow simply cannot count upon resolving a potential conflict without risking a U.S.-Soviet nuclear exchange. By ensuring the stationing of U.S. systems in Europe, flexible response thus helps to preserve this reassuring ambiguity (or perhaps this ambiguous reassurance). Secondly, flexible response requires forces sufficient to ensure against Soviet achievement of a capacity for resolving conflict at the substrategic level. In CDU/CSU eyes, this ensures a rough equilibrium, preventing any perception that America's weapons are a token force, relics of a commitment made when the United States enjoyed a substantial strategic nuclear advantage. Union defense experts might worry about decoupling through "lack of options," but most party leaders emphasize the danger of decoupling through "lack of will." A perceived military equilibrium, offsetting Soviet forces with "a corresponding NATO potential" at each level of conflict, demonstrates such will—including the American readiness to share in the risks of extended deterrence.[10] Thirdly, Union Gaullists in particular have come to accept flexible response because it reifies the kind of U.S.-FRG nuclear partnership they consider a substitute for a European deterrent.

Admittedly, Union Gaullists and Atlanticists alike have also promoted Franco-German cooperation in the nuclear field. The Kohl government quickly moved to revive the defense clause of the 1963 Bonn-Paris Treaty, while pressing for—and achieving in 1986—formal consultative procedures for the use of French tactical nuclear weapons on German soil. This implied nothing, however, about French readiness to extend a strategic nuclear shield over the FRG. Indeed, the Union's aim in this area has been more modest than Gaullist, as it aims primarily to *reinforce* the U.S. guarantee. Only a "two-pillar" Alliance with credible Western European defense efforts will allay U.S. concerns about uneven burden-sharing and a lack of European will. For most Union leaders (including Kohl and Woerner), then, Franco-German nuclear cooperation provides a hedge against U.S. neo-isolationism but a *replacement* for U.S. protection only under the worst-case scenario of an American withdrawal.

Security and Arms Control.   In CDU/CSU eyes, arms control has long been the most uncertain variable in the security equation. No CDU/CSU party program since 1949 has been without an expression of commitment to the general proposition that negotiated arms reduction can reduce the risks and damage of potential conflict, minimize tension, enhance FRG security, and ideally make peace more secure.[11] Yet just as clearly, the basic premises and implications of CDU/CSU security policy have created a presumption against arms control. Party leaders have always feared that, if poorly conceived, arms control could weaken the credibility of America's nuclear guarantee, or even sever Bonn's Alliance ties altogether. In the Union's view, these would be the logical aims of Soviet arms control initiatives, and just as easily the unintended consequences of Western initiatives.

As a result, CDU/CSU arms control policy has been exclusively defensive, its primary aim lying not in arms reduction, but in risk reduction—reducing the risks arising from the arms control process itself. The party has considered arms control proposals only under certain circumstances: If they (1) reaffirmed the U.S. guarantee; (2) preempted an undesirable alternative; (3) did not isolate the FRG; and (4) did not weaken the credibility of transatlantic coupling. Union Gaullists applied still another condition: East-West arms control must not discriminate against the nonnuclear FRG. In addition, the Union has stipulated that arms control not prejudice its stance on the German question (as will be discussed in the following section).

1.   In certain cases, the party has seen arms limitation as a useful way of *reaffirming the U.S. security guarantee.* Foreswearing acquisition of independent German nuclear weapons, for example, served this

purpose during Adenauer's tenure. In 1954, he helped smooth the FRG's entry into the West European Union and NATO by incorporating into the Paris Accords a renunciation of German intent to acquire nuclear, chemical, or biological weapons. A similar, if more controversial move was the government's decision in 1963 to sign the Partial Test Ban Treaty. Union Gaullists opposed this accord for its alleged discrimination against nonnuclear West Germany and because it carried an East German signature. Yet ultimately Adenauer gave precedence to harmonious ties with Washington, and thus a more secure nuclear guarantee, by signing the Treaty.[12] The party still lists both the 1954 and 1963 decisions as two of its major contributions to arms control and as evidence of its willingness to pursue disarmament.[13] At the same time, however, both decisions also demonstrate the primacy of America's nuclear guarantee, and not arms control, in CDU/CSU thinking about security.

2.   CDU/CSU endorsement of comprehensive disarmament during the 1950s must be seen in the same light. While also cited by the party as evidence of a commitment to arms reduction, these appeals were defensive in nature, *designed to preempt an undesirable alternative.* More precisely, the Union sought to ensure U.S. nuclear protection by warding off initiatives to demilitarize Central Europe. Adenauer, and at times his successors, insisted on *global* disarmament as the necessary prerequisite for the Molotov, Rapacki, Kennan, and SPD proposals, among others, that envisioned placing limits on German rearmament, along with strictly regional denuclearization or disengagement. The CDU/CSU also feared the consequences of these plans for its *Ostpolitik*, as discussed below. Even when endorsing or initiating arms control proposals in the past, the CDU/CSU has done so defensively in order to avert proposals considered even more odious.

3.   The CDU/CSU has feared that Moscow would use arms control talks to *isolate Bonn from its allies.* Throughout recent decades, the party worried that the limited area covered by the Vienna troop reduction talks (MBFR) could create separate zones of security within Europe, splitting Bonn from Paris and London. The CDU/CSU saw this as a military risk and one likely to handicap West European integration as well.[14]

The Union has also resisted notions of an arms control dialogue with East Germany (even after it had tacitly recognized that state); it has feared that Moscow would use the lure of East German concessions on the national problem to win West German compromises on arms. This, the Union fears, would split Bonn from its Western partners, weaken the Alliance, undercut the credibility of America's nuclear guarantee, and hasten the process of "Finlandization."

4. Of even graver concern to the CDU/CSU for two decades, however, has been the *prospective decoupling impact of arms talks*. It worries that U.S.-conducted arms control talks, under certain circumstances, could erode the credibility of the U.S. nuclear guarantee. Specifically, in the 1960s, the CDU/CSU saw the Non-Proliferation Treaty as likely to cancel, perhaps by design, the Multilateral Force (MLF). Washington had just persuaded Bonn to accept the MLF as a vital step in offsetting Soviet medium-range missiles and restoring the credibility of NATO's nuclear deterrent. CDU/CSU Atlanticists in an oblique way voiced their concern about U.S. willingness to permit "an erosion of the Alliance"; Gaullists were characteristically more blunt. But both were concerned with the U.S. nuclear guarantee, and thus made German support for the NPT strictly conditional: it must leave the MLF untouched, or it must leave open the option of U.S. help in constructing a multilateral *European* nuclear deterrent force. Although the MLF was indeed scuttled, Union Atlanticists were eventually satisfied to a certain extent by creation of the NATO Nuclear Planning Group, which formally brought Bonn into Alliance nuclear decisionmaking.[15]

With some exceptions, party leaders also viewed the SALT process uneasily. The imperative of transatlantic political solidarity prohibited outright opposition, yet party politicians did express their wariness openly. Manfred Woerner observed in 1973 that the key question for Bonn was whether America, SALT notwithstanding, would still extend a nuclear guarantee to Europe; if not, the negotiation process made NATO's deterrence strategy of flexible response noncredible.[16] Gerhard Stoltenberg, like Woerner a cabinet minister in the Kohl government a decade later, observed that SALT "contains at least the danger that existing Alliance obligations will be superceded."[17] Hans Ruehle, then with the Konrad Adenauer Foundation, later chief of the planning staff in Woerner's Defense Ministry, was also worried by SALT. In his eyes, the

U.S.-Soviet pledge to work toward "eliminating the danger of the use of nuclear weapons" signaled U.S. desire to get out of the security business.[18]

SALT II aroused similar anxieties. Some Union leaders were concerned that in "ratifying parity" it underscored the same problem as its forerunner. Given formal recognition of its own vulnerability, would the U.S. remain committed to European security, and would that commitment be taken seriously in Moscow and in Europe itself? CSU leaders explicitly, and some CDU spokesmen indirectly, criticized America for permitting its edge in strategic nuclear weapons to be eroded by the Soviet arms buildup. Unrepentant Gaullists argued that with America fixed on SALT II it was time to seek French protection.[19]

What CDU/CSU spokesmen found most objectionable about SALT II were its implications for Europe. It ratified strategic parity, but omitted any limits on "grey area" weapons—nuclear forces between the strategic and the battlefield level. The treaty thus was perceived to "magnify" an imbalance in European medium-range nuclear forces, an imbalance worsening at the same time as the deployment of Soviet SS-20 missiles proceeded. In military terms, CDU/CSU spokesmen argued, this cast doubt on the viability of flexible response. More importantly, by underscoring the perception of a European disequilibrium, it created doubts about American protection. Soviet weapons aimed at Europe could be used to exploit these doubts about the U.S. guarantee. The result would be an atmosphere of appeasement, especially in nonnuclear West Germany, hastening the process of decoupling.

In Union eyes, this general problem posed by SALT II was exacerbated by some specific treaty terms. Limits on "grey area weapons" were left to future talks. There was a noncircumvention clause and a treaty protocol restricting cruise missile development, which raised the possibility that in the future Washington would not be able to deploy offsetting systems in Europe.[20] Then SPD leader and Chancellor Helmut Schmidt shared some of these reservations but endorsed the treaty; most Union leaders could not overcome their doubts. They called U.S. ratification of SALT II a purely domestic matter in which Europe, and above all West Germany, should not interfere. However, there were audible sighs of relief from the Union when Carter shelved SALT II following the Soviet invasion of Afghanistan.[21]

Theater Arms Issues.   CDU/CSU alarm about the militarily or psychologically decoupling effect of an imbalance in European-based nuclear arms dominated its approach to theater arms control. For example, it opposed NATO's 1975 "Option III" offer in the MBFR talks, which proposed reducing U.S. battlefield nuclear weapons in exchange for substantial reductions in Soviet conventional forces.

The CDU/CSU also had been unwilling to use U.S. enhanced radiation weapons (ERW) as a bargaining chip in multilateral arms talks. Regardless of its actual battlefield features, ERW was seen by most Union leaders as useful in restoring a perceived theater balance, especially given ongoing Soviet deployments and uncertainties about U.S. defense policy under Jimmy Carter. Woerner and party defense elites echoed U.S. arguments about ERW's usability: given the relatively low collateral damage associated with these weapons, they argued, NATO would not hesitate to use them against Soviet tanks. They were careful to stress, however, that this was an assurance of escalation and thus deterrence, rather than a tool of warfighting.[22]

In January 1978, the CDU/CSU parliamentary group unanimously urged Schmidt to request deployment of ERW on German soil. Schmidt tried to satisfy Washington and his own party—which virulently opposed ERW—by outlining conditions for West German acceptance. He stipulated that another NATO country must deploy them as well (nonsingularity), and that the Alliance initially try to use the weapon as a bargaining chip. Union leaders criticized Schmidt's "conditions" for making it appear that Washington was forcing Bonn to accept a weapon necessary for deterrence. More importantly, the party contended that using ERW as a bargaining chip to win cuts in Soviet conventional forces was an attractive but impractical idea.

Several years later, upon regaining power, the Union de-emphasized ERW, despite these arguments. By that time, it implied, the deployment of intermediate-range missiles had restored a perceived equilibrium, thus ensuring escalation and deterrence. Of course, this rationale also permitted the CDU/CSU government to avoid the political problems of accepting deployment of enhanced radiation weapons. This conflict between the party's views on security issues and the actions it takes in response to political realities will be seen again.

SALT II and ERW foreshadowed the more lasting and divisive debate over long-range intermediate-range nuclear forces (LRINF). As early as the mid-1970s, before the full magnitude of Soviet SS-20 deployment had become apparent, and before Helmut Schmidt's London speech, the CDU/CSU called for additional longer-range U.S. nuclear systems in Western Europe. Woerner, Mertes, Werner Marx and other defense spokesmen argued that NATO lacked the forces to make flexible response credible in the long run. Existing U.S. systems devoted to the Alliance either lacked the necessary range, accuracy, and mobility to deny Moscow the option of an unanswered theater strike, they argued, or were part of the U.S. strategic sea-based deterrent. In either case, a U.S. President would be confronted with the "excruciating choice" of surrendering in Europe or escalating immediately to a U.S./Soviet exchange; Moscow might act on the assumption that the former alternative was most likely. These CDU/CSU spokesmen saw in the SS-20 buildup proof that Moscow was aiming to obtain a clear military monopoly in LRINF, while Soviet soil itself remained "sanctuarized" from retaliation by comparable NATO weapons.[23]

Most other CDU/CSU leaders were less specific, dwelling on the psychologically decoupling implications of a perceived Soviet monopoly in this category of weapons. Party chairman Helmut Kohl put the issue in the context of SALT II and Soviet SS-20 deployment:

If the impression gained foothold among the German and West European public, that the global-strategic and the European continental strategic power ratio is shifting to the disadvantage of the United States and the Atlantic Alliance, this might release tendencies toward a political understanding with the Soviet world power.[24]

Consequently, all Union leaders welcomed the U.S. offer of modernized LRINF. To deny the Kremlin the psychological victory of a theater imbalance and, more specifically, its hope for "sanctuarization," the CDU/CSU supported new medium-range "Eurostrategic" weapons capable of striking Soviet soil. To ensure a credible threat that they would be used, if necessary, it supported deployment on land in West Germany. Gaullists saw the new LRINF as a guarantee of the U.S.-FRG nuclear partnership. Strauss, alone, even broached the idea of "second key" in Bonn, partly to make the perceived certainty of use stronger, partly to reinforce the image of a U.S.-West German nuclear partnership. Other Union leaders argued overwhelmingly for exclusive U.S. launch authority, stating that it would strengthen the links between use of LRINF and American central systems, underscoring U.S. willingness to share the risks involved in extended deterrence.[25]

Significantly, Union leaders contended that the deployment of intermediate-range missiles was more urgent than the alternative— U.S./Soviet LRINF reduction talks. Before NATO formally proposed its dual-track plan, Woerner suggested that "as a general necessity," to ensure the credibility of its strategy, NATO must deploy new LRINF. He implied that NATO required force modernization on military grounds even if Moscow could be induced to cut back on its new INF arsenal. Other Union voices were heard to say that linking arms and arms control was unwise. At the very least, Woerner contended, NATO must station its own systems before beginning arms talks, to ensure a more credible bargaining position. He also suggested that the Alliance needed more LRINF than its planners were considering.[26]

While this aroused SPD charges of CDU/CSU "missile addiction," the Union only modified its stance when it became clear that NATO would indeed select a double decision, linking deployment of 572 INF systems to arms talks. Even then it gave deployment high priority and assailed the SPD for making West German willingness to deploy contingent upon first exhausting every possible opportunity for a negotiated settlement. This attitude, they were convinced, would be exploited by Moscow. Opposition leaders also charged Chancellor Schmidt with giving in to his party's left wing by insisting on nonsingularity—the condition that West Germany not be the only NATO country to deploy INF. Alliance-wide deployment might be ideal, Union spokesmen said, but Bonn must be willing to station INF, even—if necessary—through bilateral agreement with the United States. They rebuffed SPD charges that the Union would willingly create a special nuclear role for the FRG: precisely because Bonn had long ago foresworn its own nuclear weapons, CDU/CSU leaders maintained, it must convey to Washington Germany's commitment to maintain a theater balance and secure coupling. Insistence upon nonsingularity was, in Union eyes, like other SPD conditions—such as prior U.S. ratification of SALT II—only a pretext for undermining LRINF deployments.[27]

For three years, the CDU/CSU "supported" Helmut Schmidt and Foreign Minister Hans Dietrich Genscher's efforts to overcome obstructions erected by the chancellor's party. In substance, the CDU/CSU leadership's position on the need for LRINF and its skeptical view of the arms control option never changed.

CDU/CSU leaders did endorse the Reagan "zero option" LRINF proposal, and continued to classify it as NATO's optimal solution. Throughout the LRINF debate, they urged the Soviets to accept this plan for eliminating all medium-range nuclear weapons and rebuffed the SPD's criticism of it. But the party considered this offer useful primarily in winning the propaganda war with Moscow by showing Western good will. In fact, the Union considered the "zero option" not merely implausible, but undesirable. Indeed, it endorsed it in 1981 only for reasons of reassurance (discussed below) and only because its implausibility ensured Soviet rejection.[28] The CDU/CSU believed complete renunciation of INF in exchange for Soviet removal of Soviet SS-20s (and SS-4s and -5s) would vitiate badly needed efforts to recouple the United States and Europe psychologically and lend credence to flexible response. The SS-20s alone had never been the source of the Union's decoupling fears: the overall imbalance, indeed what it considers the inherent asymmetry, between East and West in Europe was the danger. Even without the SS-20s this imbalance was considerable given existing systems and deployment of new, shorter-range Soviet missiles, as well as the Kremlin's almost inherent edge in the conventional area. Union defense specialists added that "escalation dominance," and thus flexible response, required new U.S. intermediate-range forces in any circumstances short of comprehensive Soviet force reductions.[29] Other party leaders saw the LRINF as confirmation of the U.S. commitment to Europe.

Union leaders also pushed for the 1983 Reagan interim solution to the LRINF problem, which proposed deployment of a limited number of intermediate-range missiles on both sides. At the time, they praised it in public as further indication of Western flexibility. In substance, it was considered more desirable than the zero option, as it entailed deployment of some U.S. LRINF in exchange for Soviet reductions, thus restoring coupling and assuring a theater nuclear balance. By contrast, the Union had been ambivalent about the so-called "walk-in-the-woods" working paper, drawn up by U.S. and Soviet negotiators on their own initiative in 1982. It envisioned limiting U.S. cruise missiles and Soviet SS-20s to about fifty to seventy-five, permitting no Pershing II missiles, and leaving Anglo-French systems out of the NATO weapons count. For reasons discussed below, the CDU/CSU welcomed this concept's greater negotiability. Because most Union politicians were not inclined to consider the particular operational characteristics of any system as critical, many were willing to dispense with the Pershing II missiles. Party defense experts, however, countered that the credible implementation of flexible response required options that only NATO's proposed weapon mix could provide.

CDU/CSU security policy militated against all Soviet offers and SPD proposals on INF during this period. Its criteria for an acceptable Geneva settlement matched those of NATO itself, thus explaining Union rejection of these various compromise formulae. An agreement must, the party argued:

- provide for equal limits on U.S. and Soviet forces;

- not count Anglo–French forces in NATO INF totals;

- not accept mere removal of Soviet weapons to Soviet Asia, as their mobility permitted rapid redeployment;

- not include air forces unless all Soviet dual-capable planes capable of striking NATO Europe were counted;

- not restrict NATO LRINF to sea-basing modes, as that would undercut the credibility of their use; and

- permit on-site inspection to verify compliance with any agreement.[30]

In practice, the party eventually modified its INF arms control position, but on grounds other than security policy, as discussed below.[31] In late 1983, the party's parliamentary group voted unanimously for deployment.

Strategic Defenses.   President Reagan's vision of a protective shield for U.S. and Soviet populations undercut a major premise of CDU/CSU security policy: America's nuclear arsenal made war an unthinkable risk, and thereby neutralized even the political utility of Soviet power. Union Gaullists initially saw the proposal to build missile defenses as confirmation of earlier doubts about U.S. commitment to Europe. Other Union leaders (and military officials) worried that it could inadvertently call flexible response into question and cause decoupling because (1) the sheer cost would drain U.S. resources from its NATO commitments; (2) the prospect of an SDI shield over the United States would engender a "Fortress America" mentality; and (3) SDI could create two zones of security, as Europe would still be exposed to shorter-range Soviet missiles. (There also were CDU/CSU reservations on grounds less directly related to the party's security policy; they are discussed below.)[32]

After a time, the Union did come to support SDI formally and to advocate German participation in its R&D stage. Yet only a small minority of defense experts had been persuaded by U.S. arguments that a more secure American mainland would reduce U.S. reluctance to take risks in guaranteeing European security.[33] For the large majority, support for SDI was vital to retain German influence in Washington. Apparent U.S. determination to proceed convinced them that obstruction or coolness toward missile defenses would alienate the Reagan Administration. Rather than run this risk of political decoupling, they argued, Bonn must cooperate and shape SDI's development so as to guard against its potentially decoupling *military* implications. As Kohl's chief foreign policy advisor, Horst Teltschik, observed, this desire to retain influence underlaid Bonn's SDI policy.[34]

That many Union leaders remained ambivalent about SDI's security implications even after endorsing a German role in it is clear. Kohl himself has continued to speak of the "risks" for West Germany of a race to space-based missile defenses; parliamentary president Phillip Jenninger and Teltschik still spoke of SDI as a "challenge" for the FRG. All make it clear that they endorsed SDI research, but not necessarily deployment.[35]

The exception is the Union (mostly CSU) minority with residual Gaullist instincts. They support the U.S. SDI research and development phase, German participation in the program, and even eventual deployment, along with a theater defense system connected to the American program. They have argued that the nonnuclear FRG has every reason to help render nuclear weapons obsolete. Some observers believe that this reflects a genuine enthusiasm for missile defense, arising from traditional Gaullist desires to end nuclear bipolarity and its discrimination against countries like the FRG.[36]

Yet even for Union Gaullists, the primary, immediate motive has been to *reaffirm*, not *replace*, the transatlantic nuclear guarantee. As Strauss has argued, Bonn must help promote the SDI to preempt further U.S.-German alienation, alienation which could effectively cause decoupling.[37] Dregger more explicitly contended that helping with SDI would ensure that America took its security obligations vis-à-vis Germany and Europe seriously.[38]

Whether formalistic *or* enthusiastic, Union backing for SDI (and a German role in it) has thus reflected the party's lingering ambivalence about missile defenses. This was clear in the Union's continuing *conditional* endorsement of German participation: two of Bonn's five formal stipulations were that SDI must not create zones of unequal security or undermine NATO's flexible response strategy. Given that these doubts on security grounds remain, there is little question that most CDU/CSU leaders would hardly object to U.S. use of SDI as a bargaining chip in arms control.

The Ostpolitik Factor

Like its security policy, the Union's *Ostpolitik* has long been a major determinant of the party's views on arms control. For two decades, this factor reinforced the conviction, arising primarily from CDU/CSU security policy, that the scope of negotiated agreements was circumscribed. Although the party's security policy has not changed fundamentally since Adenauer's time, its approach to *Ostpolitik* necessarily has undergone a transformation.

Arms Control and the Open German Question.   For over two decades, the CDU/CSU contended that German reunification was a priority. Under Adenauer, to be sure, it had in fact deferred national unity in order to integrate West Germany into the West European community. The party then argued that, by solidifying Western unity and military power, reunification was more likely. Moscow would be compelled to give up its control of half of the nation, and the two Germanys could then be integrated into the emergent West European federation.

This argument was, in large part, a useful rationalization for *Westpolitik* decisions made in the name of security interests. However, it also reflected the genuine determination of Adenauer and his successors to avoid ruling out German unity altogether. Although not traditional nationalists, they felt that accepting Germany's divisions was tantamount to accepting the first phase of Soviet hegemony over Central Europe. Consequently, the CDU/CSU maintained that, *Westpolitik* notwithstanding, Bonn had not and could not indefinitely accept the existence of East Germany or the overall division of Europe. The status quo was said to be entirely provisional.[39]

The implications of this traditional *Ostpolitik* for CDU/CSU arms control preferences were profound. The party remained wary of super-power, pan-European, and above all German arms initiatives that explicitly or implicitly accepted the territorial and political status quo in Europe. Union leaders instinctively resisted proposals in which Europe's division, including Germany's division, was the point of departure. Even the promise of actual arms reductions thus implied risks from the Union's perspective. Consequently, the party long sought to modify any such initiatives, or to rechannel them in a direction that would not "cement" the status quo.

These concerns generated some initial CDU/CSU hostility toward the Partial Test Ban Treaty and the Non-Proliferation Treaty, for example, because both accords were to be signed by the GDR as well, thus implying worldwide recognition of that state. CDU Atlanticists ultimately endorsed both accords to avoid having them appear with an East German, but no West German signature. However, Strauss and others still opposed them on the *Ostpolitik* issue.

CDU/CSU efforts to block or rechannel arms control initiatives to defend its *Ostpolitik* became highly problematic in the mid-1960s, as gradually the prospect of reunification waned and was replaced by an increased public willingness to ameliorate the harsh effects of national division through "regulated coexistence." The German question, moreover, stood athwart the path to U.S.-Soviet détente, including a superpower arms accord. Ludwig Erhard's government responded in 1965 by issuing a "peace note" to Moscow. It included several proposals for easing tensions and reducing arms, none of which, however, would tacitly accept the status quo. Most notable was the offer of mutual "renunciation of force" agreements between Bonn and Soviet bloc capitals (including eventually, if not initially, East Berlin), but even these contained no provisions even tacitly acknowledging postwar borders, much less the GDR's existence as a state.

The New Ostpolitik and Arms Control.   Over time the linkage between arms control and *Ostpolitik* necessarily changed in ways that both *strengthened* and, in part, *moderated* CDU/CSU suspicions of arms control. Willy Brandt's tacit recognition of the postwar settlement, including the GDR's existence as a state, combined with overall East-West détente, paved the way for greater inter-German cooperation in the early 1970s. The tangible benefits were increased trade and human contacts, as well as more secure access to Berlin and generally lowered tensions. When East-West confrontation again mounted in the mid- to late 1970s, the SPD government was concerned that these gains were at risk. It sought to help preserve détente in Europe (and Germany above all) by promoting reestablishment of the East-West dialogue. Arms control, having played a key role in the U.S.-Soviet and East-West détente initially, was seen as a necessary concomitant of revived cooperation.

Despite its vigorous and prolonged resistance to this policy, the CDU/CSU eventually adapted to it, while still in opposition, albeit grudgingly. By the mid-1970s, as its hopes of returning to office grew, the party was not merely pledging to honor binding treaty commitments, but promising to utilize these treaties to their fullest. This was an indirect way of acknowledging that cooperative arrangements with the East bloc, rather than reunification, were increasingly the sine qua non of successful *Ostpolitik*.[40]

As a consequence, the CDU/CSU tacitly acknowledged the irreversibility of Brandt's fait accompli; a Union government would have to treat the territorial and political status quo as its point of departure in relations with the East. This acknowledgment made it easier for the party to adjust psychologically to a position to which, in any case, Bonn was bound by treaty and by the desires of the great powers. That, in turn, removed one previous impediment to CDU/CSU acceptance of arms control.

Ostpolitik and the Atmosphere for Arms Control.   Does it follow that preserving and pursuing *Ostpolitik* have increased the CDU/CSU's stake in East-West arms control? Within limits, yes. As an opposition party, and especially since returning to office, the CDU/CSU has come to see East-West arms talks as a necessary element of smooth relations with the East bloc and the GDR. In practice, the *Ostpolitik* imperative has generated a preoccupation with the "proper atmosphere" for arms limitation that would not be warranted by strict adherence to CDU/CSU security policy. Especially after deployment of LRINF in late 1983, some Union leaders urged steps to improve the East-West, and thus the inter-German atmosphere.[41] Most CDU/CSU leaders share in the general consensus of West German elites that détente is intrinsically valuable for the FRG and should be preserved.[42] Moreover, Union leaders have begun to depict *Ostpolitik* as part of an overall policy to reduce tensions.[43]

Yet there are clear limits to the role that *Ostpolitik* plays in CDU/CSU thinking on arms control. The party still gives security policy clear precedence over détente considerations, and does not believe that the latter significantly enhances the former. This is reflected in surveys that reveal strong support for deterrence among Union elites, little faith that détente can complement security, and no confidence that détente could ever replace it.[44]

Unlike the SPD, the CDU/CSU thus has never espoused a concept of East-West "security partnership" or a "pan-European peace structure." In other words, it does not envision gradual demilitarization and extensive political cooperation across the East-West divide, as does the SPD. For the Union, these scenarios are unacceptable on security grounds, represent an unthinkable concession to Moscow's design for Europe, and would "Finlandize" West Germany—the very scenario its foreign policy since Adenauer has sought to avoid.

As even many party spokesmen agree, the CDU/CSU's adaptation to *Ostpolitik* has been in large part pragmatic, perhaps even expedient. Given their own long-standing convictions about security and unity, Union leaders do not share the SPD belief that *Ostpolitik* should be the first phase of a long-term solution for postwar Europe's division. The most that is consistent with Union beliefs is the notion that cooperation with the East can reduce certain tensions and provide humanitarian benefits. Thus, the party *desires* East-West cooperation, but is unwilling to cast doubt on Bonn's traditional security policy in any way by trying to promote *Ostpolitik* through a different, more ambitious arms control policy.

This was apparent during the opposition years, even after the Union had clearly adapted to the new *Ostpolitik*. In the ERW case, for example, party leaders pressed for German support of deployment despite SPD protests (and Soviet threats) that it would freeze inter-German relations. The Union blasted the SPD's conditions for German support of ERW and LRINF as preemptive concessions to preserve *Ostpolitik*. It also criticized the SPD's stipulation of nonsingularity and its insistence on exploring all avenues for a negotiated settlement. Union leaders then and since have remained wary of an inter-German arms control dialogue; they have contended that humanitarian concessions and harmony between the Germanys would become tools of blackmail to undermine Western unity on arms control. SPD leaders have responded that these arguments resulted from the CDU/CSU's continuing inability to accept *Ostpolitik* in all of its dimensions; it was "a fight against the Eastern treaties with other means."[45]

The Union Government, Ostpolitik, and Arms Limitation.   Since regaining power, the Union has rarely allowed *Ostpolitik* considerations to propel it very far toward a more active arms control policy, beyond the limits set by the need for Western unity. For reasons already discussed, it has not allowed relations with Moscow and East Berlin to determine its position on arms control policies; the party worries that any such influence could arouse fears of neutralism or in other ways could seriously complicate relations with Washington or Paris. Just as in opposition, the CDU/CSU in government resists all notions of a nuclear-free zone in Central Europe, a declarative no-first-use policy, an East-West nonagression declaration; each of these initiatives has been endorsed by the SPD as part of its effort to revive détente and *Ostpolitik*.

During the early 1980s, Union leaders did express hope that LRINF deployments would not create "a new ice age" in inter-German relations.

It was not this concern that led Kohl in 1983 to urge a revision of Washington's bargaining position in Geneva. Indeed, Helmut Kohl and Franz Josef Strauss took extraordinary measures to ensure that the threat of a stalemate in inter-German relations following the initial LRINF deployments could *not* be used as an argument to pressure Washington to modify its arms control position further. After deployment they enticed the GDR to help preserve Germany's form of détente with a one billion mark trade credit.[46]

Similarly, the CDU/CSU saw the reopening of U.S.-Soviet arms talks in 1985 as conducive to greater inter-German cooperation. *Ostpolitik* considerations, however, did not cause it to push the Reagan Administration toward Geneva. Nor have subsequent CDU/CSU concerns with *Ostpolitik* generated visible dissatisfaction with Washington's insistence on the Strategic Defense Initiative, even though Moscow has made abandonment of SDI its condition for a successful outcome of the talks.

SPD criticism of the Kohl government offers additional evidence that inheriting *Ostpolitik* has not significantly altered CDU/CSU arms control policies. From the 1983 campaign on, Social Democratic leaders have lambasted their rivals for failing to use Bonn's influence in Washington to bring about change in U.S. policy. Initially, these attacks took the form of SPD complaints that a submissive CDU/CSU-led coalition disregarded "German interests" in arms reduction for fear of offending Washington. Since then, SPD leaders have argued that an alleged stalemate in inner-German cooperation has resulted from lack of West German initiative in arms control and Bonn's support of SDI. Such SPD leaders as Willy Brandt and Egon Bahr have further underscored what they consider the Kohl government's lack of initiative by themselves arranging "pilot projects"—unofficial arms control agreements between the SPD and the Soviet bloc Communist parties, including the Socialist Unity Party of East Germany; a nuclear weapons-free corridor and chemical weapons-free zones have been discussed. Unequivocal Union condemnation of such accords indicates that *Ostpolitik* does not shape party arms control policy.

Reassuring Public Opinion

To the extent that CDU/CSU has in some circumstances actually supported arms control, it has not been because party security policy or *Ostpolitik* pointed in that direction. In general these two policies have set narrow parameters within which arms limitation is, at most, cautiously tolerated, and even then only under restrictions. The primary positive impetus for the CDU/CSU with respect to arms control is concern about public attitudes toward the FRG's foreign policy. Party leaders have come to see the promise of serious arms control as vital in sustaining a consensus for nuclear deterrence, as well as for co-opting sentiment for pursuing *Ostpolitik* without careful regard for Alliance commitments. The extent and nature of CDU/CSU support for arms limitation are largely functions of its implicit concern for the fragility of West Germany's foreign policy consensus. In short, the party sees arms control, or at least arms control talks, as vital means of reassuring a population that lives on what Helmut Kohl calls the geopolitical fault line between East and West.

In the 1950s Adenauer often talked of global disarmament to deflect public protest over his plans for rearming Germany and stationing U.S. nuclear arms in the FRG. But Adenauer's relative imperviousness to signs of public anxiety about both decisions was evident in his unreadiness to alter the substance of his policy. Years later Union leaders would paraphrase Adenauer's response to an aide who warned him that polls showed opposition to German rearmament: "Those are interesting statistics; how do you intend to change them?"[47]

Reassurance in the Early 1980s. It was in the 1980s that CDU/CSU leaders for the first time showed a willingness to give reassurance *precedence* in their approach to arms control. The debates over ERW and LRINF were a turning point.

As indicated above, the CDU/CSU initially described ERW in the late 1970s as a defensive weapon; it voiced support for deployment and skepticism of the Schmidt government's hopes to use it as a bargaining chip. The Union also declared LRINF deployment critical for the credibility of transatlantic coupling; it proposed deployment *before* negotiating reductions with Moscow, and at most seemed willing to tolerate the second track of the NATO plan.

This relatively unambiguous support for ERW and LRINF occurred in the late 1970s. While the party's position regarding LRINF deployments remained substantially the same thereafter, its view of ERW changed markedly. More importantly, while the Union never could shake its suspicion that arms control was unlikely to obviate the need for LRINF, its emphasis on seriously pursuing an accord in Geneva became unmistakable. Even before it regained power, the Union's concern with the "second track" indicated a significant change in its view of arms control.

To be sure, some polls showed a strong majority of CDU/CSU identifiers unequivocally opposed to ERW.[48] A not insignificant minority of party sympathizers consistently opposed LRINF deployments, and a majority expressed concern as well as hope that a breakthrough in Geneva would make the issue moot.[49] However, there was little reason for concern about erosion of the Union's own voting base, or even about the party's ability to attract new support; there certainly was not enough concern to account for a shift in the Union's traditional position on arms control. Indeed, from early 1981 on, the likelihood that Schmidt's government would collapse grew to near certainty; polls showed voter disapproval of the SPD, a lower job rating for Schmidt, and overwhelming conviction that the SPD/FDP team was falling apart.[50] Concomitantly, the Union was consistently rated more favorably than at any period during its decade in opposition. By late 1981 and early 1982, surveys showed the Union with an absolute majority of support among voters.[51] By early 1982, 71 percent of those polled in one survey considered a new Union government all but certain.[52]

Relentless criticism of the SPD/FDP and steadfast espousal of traditional CDU/CSU themes might well have sufficed to return the Union to power. Given the SPD/FDP coalition's collapse, even if the CDU/CSU had disregarded the arms issue altogether and emphasized its own competence in running the economy, it would have gained strength. Simply waiting for Schmidt's government to fall was another option. Concern with its own image and voting base alone provided inadequate reason for the Union to modify its stance on arms control. Indeed, the CDU/CSU modified its position most substantially *after* having regained office and having won a convincing election victory in 1983 on a platform of full support for LRINF deployment.

What then caused the shift? To the extent that it began showing greater interest in arms reduction after 1982, the Union was motivated largely by concern that antinuclear *Angst* was undermining foreign policy consensus in the FRG. It feared a public backlash against *Westpolitik*.

As early as 1981, surveys had begun to show that despite persistent pro-American sentiments, Germans wanted the FRG to distance itself from the Reagan Administration's "hard course."[53] Nearly one-half of the Union's identifiers voiced agreement with this course of action. By 1982, 70 percent of all West Germans (and 61 percent of Union identifiers) polled by a major television network agreed that Bonn must reorient its policies toward its own interests, even if it created friction with the U.S.

government.[54] One major reason for this perceptible public coolness toward Washington was a growing conviction that the United States was more intent on deploying than limiting intermediate-range missiles. One survey indicated that 70 percent of all West Germans, and again 60 percent of the Union's adherents, believed Washington and Moscow were equally responsible for the persistent failure of the Geneva talks.[55] Offhanded U.S. comments about nuclear war being limited to Europe exacerbated the situation.

Although they discussed the issue openly, Union leaders came to fear that an unconvincing arms control policy could compound resentment against the United States and Bonn's NATO commitments; they feared increased support for a more ambitious *Ostpolitik* with neutralist overtones might result. Arguments like these raised in public could be dismissed as polemics to malign the SPD. However, when the CDU/CSU began modifying and even compromising on its long-standing arms control policy, there could be little doubt that its concern was genuine. This was especially evident when first the Union opposition and later the Union-led government began prodding the U.S. administration to modify American arms control positions. As a Kohl advisor was to observe:

> We will have a year of intensive debate. And a key to winning the debate— and to de-emotionalizing it—is the extent to which we will be able to persuade the public that arms control is a serious undertaking. We have a basic interest in insuring that arms control will remain a coupling instrument within the alliance.[56]

Polls indicated that this general connection between Western arms control and transatlantic harmony did exist in the minds of citizens.[57]

ERW reflected the impact this preoccupation with reassurance was having on CDU/CSU attitudes. When the Reagan Administration surprised Bonn in early 1981 by announcing its decision to resume production of the weapon, Manfred Woerner labeled the move "unfortunate."[58] Party leaders gently warned Washington that the European and German public's mood toward nuclear weapons in Europe was changing. They plainly feared the ERW decision could cause a "sensory overload" and spark even more animosity toward LRINF. In part, the Union wanted to avoid the politically damaging label of a nuclear missile party, but its concern with the deterrence consensus was considerable.

The result was an unmistakable reluctance to press for deployment. While labeling ERW a "classical defense weapon," CDU foreign affairs spokesman Werner Marx hastily added that the question of stationing could not be answered with a "simple yes or no."[59] Most significantly, in contrast to its 1977–78 response, the CDU/CSU encouraged Foreign Minister Genscher's effort to incorporate ERW into multilateral arms talks, thereby deferring any question of deployment.[60] This was Alois Mertes's solution, while Richard von Weizsäcker proposed Western renunciation of ERW in exchange for a clear reduction in Soviet armored forces.[61] Eventually, the Union fully supported production of ER weapons, but by then it was clear that none were to be deployed soon in the FRG.

By 1981, ERW was but a sideshow, LRINF the main event. Here, too, the imperatives of reassurance often took precedence in CDU/CSU treatment of arms and arms control issues. Strauss, among others, hastily disavowed President Reagan's remarks suggesting that a nuclear war could be limited to Europe. Union leaders sought to identify their party with the burgeoning peace campaign, in large part to co-opt it. CDU General Secretary Heiner Geissler sponsored a nationwide campaign, using conferences, literature drives, and resolutions to present Union arguments for nuclear deterrence *and* arms control.[62] Geissler urged a dialogue with the peace movement. Even other party figures were increasingly careful not to dismiss antinuclear protesters as naive, let alone as leftwing, but instead described them as people of goodwill victimized by misleading propaganda.

This effort to restore public confidence culminated in the CDU's 1981 party conference in Hamburg. Kohl won his loudest applause by ad-libbing in his statement of greeting, "We are part of the German peace movement; we want détente and arms control." Geissler had invited several hundred young nonmembers for a dialogue on nuclear arms. As CDU leaders listened impassively, these guests spoke of their *Angst* and criticized the Union's own comfortable assumptions about deterrence. A resolution was added to the program, declaring that "the most important current foreign policy goal is the comprehensive limitation and reduction of arms and an equilibrium at the lowest possible level—contingent upon unreduced security."[63]

While there was little patience with open questioning of traditional NATO (and CDU/CSU) security policies, the Union campaign of reassurance did go beyond literature drives and somewhat contrived efforts at dialogue. Party leaders quietly stressed the importance of answering Soviet arms control offers with more than a "mere no." To demonstrate the willingness of pro-LRINF forces to keep negotiating, Woerner advanced counter-offers (consistent with NATO policy) on his own initiative.[64] He argued for improving conventional forces to reduce NATO's reliance on *early* use of nuclear weapons.[65]

Shortly after his convincing electoral victory in March 1983, Kohl applied mild pressure on Washington to modify its bargaining position. For months he had warned against dropping the zero-option "like a hot potato" simply because Moscow had rejected it. Now he told American journalists that Bonn hoped the United States would give arms control a "new impulse." While keeping the zero option as a long-term goal, the Chancellor added, "It certainly is time for new proposals," namely proposals for an "interim solution."[66]

Union leaders foreswore any desire to push Washington toward arms control, yet Kohl stressed that Bonn was "asking" Washington to explore Soviet proposals seriously, and to give arms talks new impulse.[67] His chief advisor, Horst Teltschik, more explicitly emphasized the vital need for such influence. Indeed, the party began selling Bonn's *Westpolitik* as the vital prerequisite for Western consideration of the German interest in arms control.[68]

Kohl left the details of what he had in mind to his associates—Volker Ruehe and, above all, Teltschik—who spoke of an initiative for reducing U.S. Pershing IIs and cruise missiles to between 75 and 150 (rather than the 572 envisioned).[69] Significantly, these were the figures discussed by U.S. and Soviet negotiators during their 1982 "walk-in-the-woods." That initiative had failed at least in part because it would have eliminated the Pershing IIs, which defense experts in the U.S. and the Union saw as a vital link in recoupling the Europe and the American deterrents. In 1983, however, Teltschik ambiguously conceded that the Pershings could be reduced "if not eliminated entirely."[70] Behind the scenes Kohl advisors spoke more plainly: "The 'walk-in-the-woods' was certainly something we could live with."[71]

When the Geneva talks failed to produce a settlement, Kohl's government went ahead with deployment of the Pershings; the CDU/CSU parliamentary group voted unanimously in favor. Yet after Moscow broke off the talks in protest, Kohl proposed a new negotiating format to entice the Kremlin: Britain and France should now be included in the negotiations, thus satisfying a long-standing Soviet demand.[72] In late 1983–84, the Kohl Chancellery was anxious to be seen urging Washington to revive the East-West dialogue. It feared the effect of an unanswered Soviet peace offensive on post deployment opinion. Union leaders proclaimed that Bonn's reliability on the deployment issue made Washington sympathetic to its concerns.[73]

In 1984, the CDU also delicately urged a resumption of strategic arms talks. Washington, it implied, could take the initiative to improve the atmosphere. As Horst Teltschik declared:

> The breakdown of negotiations should give each side the opportunity to rethink its position. Both world powers should jointly examine what the maximum thresholds for the various weapons systems should be. . . The examination should cover the seas as well as space. As long as there is no agreement on these points the danger will remain of partial disarmament or arms control agreements being undermined on different levels.[74]

SDI and Reassurance.   Its treatment of SDI, finally, further reflects the Union's recent preoccupation with reassurance, and thus its modified approach to arms control. As noted above, the CDU/CSU was an ambivalent backer of missile defenses on security grounds alone. Concern with preserving a public consensus for the CDU security policy's main component, nuclear deterrence, heightened its ambivalence.

Party spokesmen worried about Ronald Reagan's condemnation of deterrence and his vision of a nuclear-free world. They warned Washington that such rhetoric before SDI was in operation might continue what the LRINF debate had begun—an erosion of public understanding for the moral, political, and military foundations of current NATO policy. Union leaders also feared that Moscow could divide and weaken the West if SDI were seen to undercut arms control.[75] In this connection, they worried that Moscow could use the SDI as a pretext to block new talks; U.S. violation or renunciation of the 1972 ABM Treaty would further undermine arms limitation; and a full-scale, defensive arms competition, sparking new offensive countermeasures, might destabilize the rough strategic balance, causing a total collapse of arms limitations.

Consequently, most Union leaders accepted (some with enthusiasm) Foreign Minister Genscher's plan for a "cooperative U.S. Soviet solution"—a policy that integrated SDI into the ongoing arms limitation process.[76] CDU spokesman Volker Ruehe specified a "desirable" three point U.S.-Soviet agreement: a "mutual, coordinated construction of defense weapons," along with dismantling of offensive systems; continued respect for the ABM Treaty, which he did not clearly reconcile with the previous point; and agreement to honor the Treaty's clause on exchanging information about future developments.[77] In May 1985, the party backed a list of government conditions for German support of, and participation in, SDI. It stipulated, among other things, that missile defenses must be implemented in conformity with the ABM Treaty, must not destabilize the strategic equilibrium, and must remain consistent with the general aim of arms control.[78] Teltschik and Ruehe also encouraged respect for the ABM Treaty during SDI's research period and changes in that accord only in cooperation with the Soviets.[79]

Teltschik went furthest, describing SDI in 1985 as a bargaining chip to win Soviet reductions in offensive missiles.[80] Few colleagues openly agreed, but all did underscore indirectly its usefulness as a bargaining chip. They stressed SDI's positive effect in bringing Moscow back to the Geneva talks. Even an arms control skeptic like Juergen Todenhoefer called SDI the West's "trump card" at the bargaining table; he lambasted the SPD not for its willingness to negotiate on SDI, but for its overeagerness to bargain it away quickly.[81] Kohl's government deferred formalizing its role in SDI until after the 1985 Geneva summit, indicating that it hoped for, and did not want to complicate, SDI's incorporation into arms control.[82]

Reassurance and Other Arms Issue. The Union has been most willing to push Washington toward arms control for purposes of reassurance regarding chemical weapons. Underlying uneasiness about the large arsenal of NATO chemical weapons on German soil was exacerbated by the crises of the early 1980s and U.S. plans for introducing binary systems into Alliance stocks. CDU/CSU leaders thus began urging the Schmidt government before 1982 to press for completion of a worldwide ban on chemical weapons (if not a chemical weapons-free corridor in Central Europe), and openly spoke of dissuading Allies from developing new systems. They also took an active interest in the Geneva talks on chemical arms. In April 1986, CDU conservative Alfred Dregger announced that he had secured U.S. Defense Secretary Weinberger's assurance that old chemical weapons would be removed from the FRG and that new binary systems would be deployed there only when necessitated by rising tensions. Weinberger quickly denied that claim, embarrassing Dregger, but President Reagan gave such assurance to Chancellor Kohl at their June 1986 summit.[83]

Other signs of Union preoccupation with reassurance came in Kohl's 1986 call for a gradual, phased-in reduction, followed ultimately by complete suspension, of nuclear testing. As the *FAZ* observed, "Kohl wants to counter the impression that the West always only says no to Eastern initiatives which have an effect on the public."[84]

It should be noted that a significant Union minority—the latter-day Gaullists led by Strauss, Alfred Dregger, and other prominent conservatives—often downplay the importance of arms control as a means of reassurance. Before the 1979 Brussels decision, they echoed Manfred

Woerner's skepticism of, and resistance to, the link between LRINF modernization and arms control. Even after Woerner's concern about reassurance and the defense consensus led him to underscore the importance of pursuing a settlement in Geneva, Strauss, *et al.* remained critical. As late as 1982, they held that the Brussels decision was flawed. Strauss startled his own party by describing the Reagan zero-option as impractical, a salve to European antinuclear anxiety; he urged deployment without further efforts at compromise settlements in Geneva. Strauss, Dregger, *et al.* have also downplayed the negotiability of SDI. In short these conservative Gaullists give military security policy precedence over *Ostpolitik* and argue that preoccupation with reassurance weakens Bonn's credibility; the Union must resist uncompromisingly, rather than co-opt forces undermining the consensus favoring *Westpolitik* and nuclear deterrence.

The absolute primacy of security considerations was well expressed by the CDU's Juergen Todenhoefer, former arms control spokesman for the Union parliamentary group. In a 1985 article, he assailed the "false premises and false expectations" of even his own government's approach. It was routinely assumed, he wrote, that fewer arms meant greater security, when in fact the critical criterion is stability rather than quantity. This "fatal" premise reflected a willingness to give "domestic political" and "tactical" considerations priority over the actual military requirements of the stable deterrent. Arms control had become the policy of diplomats and politicians rather than strategists. He blamed all parties for trying to outdo each other by offering ever more generous arms control proposals. NATO's position at Geneva was continuously diluted by a "scurrilous" process whereby the Western partners negotiated among themselves and disregarded their own security. In some cases "the worst thing that could happen" would be Soviet acceptance of the West's own positions.[85]

To be sure, even conservative Gaullists have acted on the imperative of reassurance at times. It is simply less often—and less easily made compatible with their emphasis on the primacy of credible military security. But for most party leaders, reassurance requires a more positive approach to arms control, even if this means changing the emphasis of Union security policy.

THE DOMESTIC POLITICAL DIMENSION OF UNION ARMS CONTROL POLICY

Not surprisingly, CDU/CSU attitudes toward a critical issue like arms control are by no means strictly a function of security and *Ostpolitik*, or even concern with public consensus on these critical issues; arms issues are also often influenced by political competition in the FRG. Domestic political factors determine many questions of priority and rhetorical tone, if not fundamental assumptions, and thus shape the way the party and its leaders handle arms control issues.

Intra-Union Factors

Both intraparty and intracoalition factors play a critical role in shaping the CDU/CSU approach to arms control issues. This section deals with the first set of considerations—the constellation of forces within the Union itself, and how the Union sells itself to the public. (The following section will address the effects of the Union's coalition with the FDP.)

The CDU/CSU's Rank and File and Arms Control.   As noted at the outset, the CDU is guided by several basic convictions but lacks an overarching ideology, largely because it consciously appeals to a heterogeneous voting base. It has always been a party of diverse interests, held together by a commitment to preserve the status quo it claims credit for shaping, and by the goal of electoral success over the left. In consequence, as an organization the CDU typically is not consumed by discussions of policy, let alone doctrine, as is the SPD. The rank and file tend to focus on organizational matters and political strategy. Where the basic interests of party subgroups or the electoral fortunes of the party as a whole are not directly affected, policy debate beneath the CDU's top level is rare. This is especially true in those areas in which prevailing CDU policy has become sacrosanct because of its proven success, including its electoral rewards. Where a special level of expertise is seemingly required, rank and file involvement shrinks even further.

With rare exceptions, then, CDU positions on arms and arms control since 1949 have not been shaped by rank and file political pressure. Debate has not been suppressed; it has rarely ever broken out, given the party's character and the prevailing consensus on *Westpolitik*. In contrast to SPD activists' bitter debates over official party policy, CDU conferences are "theaters of conformity." One irreverent British journalist compared them to gatherings of an East European party, with demonstrations of unity, prolonged applause, pro forma debate, and near reverence for the *Spitzenpolitiker*, the CDU elite.[86]

An illustration of the CDU's style was provided during the height of controversy over LRINF deployments. While the SPD leadership in Bonn struggled to hold its regional and local party groups in line behind their chancellor's policy, there was comparatively little restiveness in the CDU. Admittedly, this reflected consensus support for NATO policy and general acceptance of the U.S. bargaining position at Geneva. But it also illustrated the readiness of CDU activists to let their leaders determine party policy on arms and arms control. A faction of top officials, supported almost solely by the youth auxiliary, did suggest that Union serenity in the midst of the raging public debate might seem like disregard for the widespread nuclear *Angst*. At that point, a cautious CDU campaign of dialogue with the peace movement was launched, culminating in the previously mentioned, somewhat contrived debate at the 1981 party conference in Hamburg. But even that minor event did not result from rank and file pressure. As one disgruntled dissenter complained, "With us, the party is not debating over [INF]; with us, the leadership is debating over whether the party may discuss it."[87]

Factionalism and Arms Issues.   Although there is little rank and file influence on major policy decisions such as arms control, the CDU is far from centralized. On the contrary, its heterogeneity, its diverse interests, and its pragmatism make for very loose organization. Above the level of party activists (those who attend party conferences and work at the local level), there is considerable factionalization. Party executive committee members, parliamentarians, and regional government leaders often fall into different factions.

As a rule, genuine factions do not crystallize around issues, let alone conflicts between ideological purity and political pragmatism (as is often the case with the SPD). There is no basic CDU/CSU ideology to interpret and apply, and rhetoric notwithstanding, there are few insoluble differences over the substance of policy within the CDU/CSU leadership; this is particularly true of foreign policy. Rather, the CDU/CSU is most often rent by factions grouped around rival leaders or rival strategies. This form of factionalization has often had clear implications for party decisions on policy.[88]

Arms and arms control issues have been fodder in leadership battles in the Union. Debate over the Test Ban Treaty and the NPT between Gaullists and Atlanticists was in the larger sense a struggle for the succession to Konrad Adenauer. The CDU/CSU's divisions over détente, including its response to SALT I, CSCE, and MBFR, were also part of a leadership battle. Even after Helmut Kohl's accession in the mid-1970s the problem persisted. Despite having waged an effective campaign in 1976, Kohl was compelled not to run for Chancellor in 1980, undercutting his hopes of gradually encouraging the party to adapt its security policy, even modestly, to the *Ostpolitik*. And shortly before the party returned to office, many of its maverick and liberal leaders sought to replace Kohl; they considered him unsuited for the Chancellory. Consequently, they assailed him for overcaution in shaping an arms control policy suited to the imperatives of reassurance during the LRINF debate.

Arms control issues have also been caught up in intraparty strategy disputes. CDU moderates, long a minority, have long contended that the party must further broaden its appeal. Since the early 1980s, this has implied the need for a more forthcoming position in arms control. It was not merely the need for reassurance that generated pressure for a shift in CDU policy during 1981–82; it was also the need for votes. As Matthias Wissman complained, "Till now we have not been able to convey publicly to citizens the feeling that for us both parts of the NATO agreement matter: arms modernization and negotiations."[89] CDU moderates felt that a bit more aloofness from the Reagan administration and greater understanding for the peace movement were also necessary. Union moderates in 1981, led by Heiner Geissler and Kurt Biedenkopf, pushed for an effort to co-opt the peace movement by opening a dialogue with it—partly against Kohl's wishes.[90]

Yet, the offsetting force of CDU conservatives has generally slowed any momentum toward a new emphasis on arms control. Parliamentary chief Alfred Dregger has led at least a sizable minority in stressing the absolute primacy of security policy considerations. Dregger is most resistant to softening traditional hostility to arms control at the expense of deterrence. In this he has the support of CDU nationalists and expellees from the East bloc, who are generally suspicious of any emphasis on détente (as well as the CSU, of course).

The CDU Chairmanship.   Because of this factionalism, CDU party chairmen have always had to struggle to hammer out a tenuous consensus on strategy. Even Kohl, who at times has enjoyed greater authority than anyone since Adenauer, cannot unilaterally set CDU political strategy or policy. Even as chancellor, he at most has been first among equals in a factionalized leadership. The CDU party structure itself was for decades merely a campaign committee for chancellor candidates, and even though its importance has waxed in the past decade, a CDU chairman has little direct control over the party's elites. At most, the chairman can broker decisions on strategy and, above all, policy. To accomplish this, he must arbitrate among different subgroups, factions, interests, *Laender* (states) leaders, personal rivals, and strategists, with the goal of preserving unity through consensus. Party "barons" have largely determined the shape of CDU policy in an ad hoc bargaining process, sometimes in public view, often in closed sessions. One figure can dominate CDU decisionmaking only by satisfying the barons; it is easiest, but by no means always possible, to do so from the chancellory.

The party strategy and policy that results is, at best, capable of vague concessions to numerical minorities and incremental changes. Even at the height of the LRINF debate, Kohl—contrary to his personal predisposition—dug in his heels when pressed by some for a more flexible arms control position. He permitted cosmetic changes in party programs, but was too concerned about the CDU's delicate internal equilibrium to do much more.

The CSU.   The leverage of CDU conservatives would not be nearly so strong without the unique relationship between the CDU and CSU. Indeed, while it is a separate party, the CSU in a sense is the CDU's strongest faction. As noted previously, the Bavarian sister party's compositional and philosophical cohesiveness greatly exceeds that of the CDU; its homogeneity and unique ideology have forged a bond between leaders and activists so integral as to subsume, override, or preclude factional and doctrinal disputes—except in rare but notable cases.

This has meant not only that CSU party activists fall in line behind the party leadership, but that the CSU leadership under Strauss acts as a unit, with resulting disproportionate leverage over the CDU in intra-Union policy-making. The sister parties nominate one Chancellor candidate; since Bavarian votes will provide the parliamentary majority, the Union candidate must run on a platform that satisfies the CSU. He also must appoint CSU members to cabinet and subcabinet posts. More importantly, before the CDU/CSU parliamentary group votes on bills, the Bavarian members caucus informally, determine their position, and confront their CDU partners with a bloc vote.

CSU leaders frankly concede their assertiveness within the Union, justifying it as an effort to provide Bavarians with a voice in federal politics. "Critical loyalty" to the CDU and a confrontational political tone are accepted readily in Bavaria. Strauss has also proclaimed that in its uncompromising defense of traditional Adenauerean policy, the CSU is "the hope of millions outside Bavaria."[91]

In government as in opposition, then, Strauss and his CSU colleagues have hectored the CDU, ridiculing its strategy and tactics, deploring its (above all Kohl's) indecisiveness. The CSU insists that a harder, candid, conservative CDU/CSU approach would win more votes. It routinely cites the CSU's 60 percent appeal in Bavaria as proof of the success that such a strategy offers.

CDU leaders in party, parliament, and government alike often have little choice but to shape party policy in a way that satisfies the CSU. Kohl has always been particularly sensitive to intra-Union harmony, however tenuous. As CDU/CSU parliamentary leader, Union Chancellor candidate, and later Chancellor, he has been careful not to challenge or confront the CSU openly. Concerned for its own credibility with the German public at large, the CDU leadership at the same time often attacks the CSU's bellicosity, intransigence, and obstructionism. Kohl wins applause by reminding party faithful that the CDU makes its own decisions, and that "today government policy is made in Bonn—not Munich."[92]

The CSU has used its influence to redirect overall Union policy regarding foreign and defense affairs, an area where its own unity is almost seamless. In its Gaullist days, it formed a bloc against CDU Atlanticists who adapted to U.S.-Soviet bilateralism. It has continued this effort in more recent years, urging support for U.S. defense initiatives to ensure that Bonn is taken seriously as an American partner. This has meant resisting efforts by some in the CDU to raise the priority of *Ostpolitik* and reassurance in framing arms control policy. As noted previously, it treated the LRINF decision's second track as largely irrelevant for years, and after 1983, resisted exploration of any proposal that might eliminate LRINF systems already deployed. Despite initial reservations about its decoupling effect, SDI was warmly embraced by the CSU. It scorned talk in the CDU of missile defenses as a bargaining chip, and urged rapid, unequivocal West German participation. It condemned Kohl for equivocation, and pushed for an early decision favoring a full U.S.-German, state-to-state treaty on missile defense cooperation.

Kohl's solicitousness toward the CSU has reinforced his own caution about giving German nuclear *Angst* greater weight in Union arms control policy. In his view, the image of CDU/CSU cohesion would be tested too severely by accepting a greater emphasis on arms control. Kohl and the CDU leadership do not, however, force more reassurance-minded colleagues to soft-pedal their own preferences; as noted above, that would be difficult. The result is often discord within the Union, as least in deciding how seriously Bonn should be seen to be pursuing arms limitation.

The Union and the FDP

All politics in the FRG are coalition politics. Although West Germany's party system is not nearly so fragmented as in the past (or in neighboring states), only once has a single party achieved an absolute majority and tried to govern by itself (Adenauer's CDU/CSU in 1957.) Proportional representation and, perhaps more importantly, public unease at the thought of one-party government, have made it difficult for either of the larger parties to govern without a partner. In almost all cases that partner has been the centrist FDP. Despite its claim to represent a distinct liberal philosophy and voting bloc, the FDP has, in fact, survived and often prospered as a balancer. It is the repository of floating voters, undecideds, or even Union and SPD identifiers who want to check the strength of their own party for fear it will be dominated by an ideologically extreme wing. West Germany's electoral system facilitates "tactical" voting for the FDP.

As a balancer the FDP possesses unique leverage. It has been a necessary component of the governing coalition during the FRG's entire history, with the exception of two brief periods: 1957–61 and 1966–69. In return for providing its partner with a majority, the FDP has extracted important concessions, namely a disproportionate share of government posts and considerable influence over policy. Above all, the FDP has dominated the Foreign Ministry since 1969; its former chairman and influential leader, Hans Dietrich Genscher, has been foreign minister since 1974, outlasting all postwar counterparts in Europe.

Another effect of its balancing role, however, is that the FDP's original, distinctly "liberal" philosophy has been diluted. While "liberalism" still influences party attitudes in many respects, FDP policy—like the FDP itself—has, in effect, become the middle ground between its larger rivals. By underscoring its moderation, and painting both the opposition and its governing partner as extremists, the FDP can secure a constituency for itself.

FDP Foreign Policy Perspectives.   Nowhere is the blend of liberalism and centrism more apparent than in FDP foreign and defense policies. The party was in the coalition that brought Bonn into NATO and the one that launched the *Ostpolitik*, and considers itself the defender of both established policies. It resists exaggerated versions of both the CDU/CSU emphasis on military security and the SPD's inclination toward cooperation with the East. With regard specifically to arms control, the FDP generally has not gone as far as the SPD in treating it as the necessary prelude to an extensive security partnership with the Soviet bloc. Nor has it given precedence to the requirements of deterrence strategy, as has the Union. For while the FDP is concerned with retaining U.S. backing and protection, and thus avoids any hint of neutralism, it argues that long-term security requires an institutionalized East-West dialogue with an active European component. It espouses the importance of political security, resting above all on an active arms control policy. Such policies, it maintains, would lower tension, undercut Soviet efforts to separate America and Europe, and permit the West to go on the public opinion offensive.

In practice, this means that since 1982 the FDP has encouraged the CDU/CSU to respect "continuity" in foreign policy by putting arms control atop its agenda. Despite the U.S.-Soviet tension of the early 1980, the party contended that it lay in Bonn's interest to encourage "a new phase in détente." To this end, the FDP has argued that Bonn must use its influence continually to promote and revitalize U.S.-Soviet arms control talks. There must be pressure for new proposals that stress negotiability, rather than the precise requirements of deterrence strategy. The FDP urged a last-minute revival of the "walk-in-the-woods" proposal shortly before LRINF was deployed in 1983, signalling its willingness to do without Pershing II missiles; thereafter, it argued for new initiatives of a similar nature. FDP officials contend that the West must seriously examine Soviet counteroffers and make an effort to meet Moscow halfway. It did not insist that an LRINF solution be unconditionally global (encompassing Soviet Asian-based SS-20s), though it has rejected Kremlin efforts to count Franco-British systems in NATO INF totals.

FDP spokesmen have been uniformly hostile to SDI and European participation in it. Publicly, they contend that it could decouple the Alliance, but their central concern is that it could destabilize the U.S.-Soviet strategic arms balance. In this way alone, in their view, SDI would undercut a superpower arms dialogue and thus the new phase of détente. Moreover, the FDP contends that SDI testing violates the ABM treaty, further damaging the basis for U.S.-Soviet—and thus East-West—arms talks and overall cooperation. Lastly, the party warns that Moscow could use SDI as a pretext for arguing that the West's arms control policy lacks seriousness, thus hurting NATO's credibility in multilateral forums and in the battle for public opinion. Almost without exception, the FDP has criticized SDI and argued that its only logical utility is as a bargaining chip at Geneva. Concern about the effects on *Ostpolitik* partly account for this opposition.

The FDP has argued that this new phase of détente must have a European component. The Europeans should not try to bind the superpowers, but they can contribute by giving new impulse to East-West cooperation. In practice, this means an active inter-German dialogue, the agenda for which should include arms control—provided neither state is obliged to cast doubt on its own Alliance commitments. To make sure, the FDP argues that Bonn and East Berlin should discuss issues connected with multilateral forums in which they are represented: Vienna and Stockholm, as well as CSCE. These multilateral talks are in themselves a vital element in the FDP's new détente: after LRINF deployments resulted in the collapse of U.S.-Soviet talks, the party argued that the new Stockholm talks on confidence-building measures must fill the gap. Before the 1985 summit, Genscher warned against "bilateralizing" arms control and urged all European states to help shape the U.S. position.[93]

In outlining FDP arms control policy above, it would have been possible, perhaps logical, to substitute the name Genscher for the party's title in each sentence. As Foreign Minister since 1974, he has been the framer of FDP foreign policy, the very embodiment of the continuity it preaches in conducting external affairs. There is such broad support within the FDP for his conduct of foreign policy (though not party strategy during his tenure as chairman) that Genscherism will surely outlast its namesake. The Liberals are closely identified with his conduct of diplomacy and feel it gives their party a distinctly popular profile between the "neutralist SPD" and "hardline Union." They thus not only embrace it, but have a political stake in sustaining it. Indeed, party rank and file and regional groups have urged the foreign minister along in their common hostility toward SDI.[94]

The Union-FDP Relationship.   Union conservatives, and above all the CSU, would like to see the FDP vanish beneath the 5 percent threshold level which all parties must attain to hold seats in parliament. The sources of this animosity are personal and institutional as well as political. Since 1962, when FDP pressure forced Adenauer to drop then Defense Minister Strauss from the cabinet over the *Spiegel* affair, the Bavarian chief has despised the Liberals.

Most persistent, however, has been the institutional source of tension. Within the CDU/CSU, the Bavarian wing enjoys disproportionate leverage. But within a CDU/CSU-FDP partnership, the Liberals offset this influence; the CDU must placate both partners. Liberals enjoy exploiting this position, and many CDU moderates make no secret of the fact that it pleases them as well. At the very least, the CSU thus worries about its identity in a three-way coalition; at the most, it fears total lack of influence. Yet, because its credibility depends on being Bavaria's voice in Bonn, it cannot realistically threaten to leave a government.[95]

Consequently, the CSU and its conservative CDU allies have long waged open political war on the FDP. Strauss has more than once proposed ways to absorb his despised rival. None has succeeded and, since 1982, the CSU has had to share cabinet seats with the FDP. To make matters worse, the portfolio Strauss has most coveted—Foreign Affairs—was reserved for Genscher. Admittedly, Genscher stepped down as FDP party chief, and his successor, Economics Minister Martin Bangemann, has made some effort to accommodate the Bavarians. But Genscher's leading role in coalition foreign policy still irritates the CSU leadership. The CSU's *Bayernkurier* has charged the FDP with treating foreign policy as "Genscher's private affair." It argues that the Liberals use their foreign policy leverage to create a moderate FDP profile at the Union's expense.[96] Some observers agree that the FDP finds Strauss's CSU useful: it allows the Liberals to present themselves as a stabilizing force, as a bulwark against reaction. FDP supporters consider such a profile critical to their party's survival.[97]

Many CDU leaders are lifelong proponents of a Christian-Liberal alliance. Like Kohl himself, they believe it can embody the FRG's antisocialist majority. More concretely, a CDU/CSU-FDP partnership is seen as all but indispensable. Most CDU politicians do not believe the Union could easily duplicate Adenauer's feat of an absolute majority and, if it did, would quickly arouse fears of a one-party government. Moreover, in a Union-only government, the CSU would be more heavily represented. Many CDU leaders prefer a three-way coalition in which the FDP's presence offsets the Bavarians' leverage.

To be sure, personal and institutional friction besets the CDU-FDP relationship as well. As a general rule, the CDU resents having to give a tiny coalition partner greater representation. It is outraged when FDP spokesmen charge Chancellory officials, like Kohl's main foreign policy advisor, Horst Teltschik, with "meddling in foreign affairs." Genscher has apparently been irritated by Teltschik's independent access to Kohl, and argues that he should be replaced by a professional diplomat.[98]

Nonetheless, Kohl has tried to preserve the three-way coalition, even at the expense of irritating some of his own colleagues and alienating the CSU altogether. As noted previously, he considers the three-way partnership defensible in principle, as well as desirable politically. The result is that "coalition" foreign policy is subject to an expanded version of the bargaining process that shapes Union policy positions.

Despite its small size, Genscher's FDP has thus enjoyed disproportionate influence. Much to the frustration of CDU and CSU conservatives, Kohl has allowed his Foreign Minister great latitude. Genscher has been able to refute his Union critics by pointing to Kohl's use of the term "continuity" and a "new phase of détente," and urging them to support their own Chancellor.

The FDP has gone too far in occasionally trying to act as a link between government and opposition by working for bipartisan cooperation. Genscher has tried this tact in certain areas, including arms control. His apparent aim has been to improve the FDP's own profile as the centrist party that preserves consensus, stability, and continuity in foreign policy. However, the result has often been to alienate both CDU and CSU, drive the Union sister parties into each other's arms, and make the FDP their object of mutual animosity. Most FDP leaders are thus wary of antagonizing the Union to this extent. They realize that, however much the CDU/CSU needs their party, too much contention could lead to collapse of the Christian-Liberal coalition. Were that to occur, the FDP would suffer considerable desertions by trying to reform its old partnership with an SPD that it considers too far left. The Liberals could fall into the, for them, fatal role of a minor opposition party, soon to be squeezed out of existence.

Coalition Arms Control Policy.   FDP influence has reinforced the Kohl government's emphasis on reassurance, such as during Bonn's last minute effort in 1983 to bring about modification of the Western negotiating proposals at Geneva. For reasons already discussed, Kohl and some CDU leaders wanted to press cautiously for revival of the "walk-in-the-woods" framework. The FDP pushed for it *openly*, and effectively created the image that this was coalition policy. Genscher's policy of a European contribution to détente also was largely adopted by the coalition after 1984. Due to Genscher, Bonn also avoided an unequivocal rejection of Soviet leader Gorbachev's 1985 LRINF arms proposal, and welcomed the U.S. response—a revival of the zero option—despite CDU/CSU reservations.[99]

On SDI, Genscher has also had success in shaping coalition policy. Despite its reservations, the Union was relatively unified in endorsing the U.S. project in early 1985. Given strong FDP opposition, however, the coalition's initial, formal statement was more cautious and conditional, especially in its insistence that SDI be conducted in strict conformity with the ABM Treaty and arms control.

Intracoalition wrangling intensified over whether and how Germany should participate in SDI research and development. Genscher's party feared the effects on arms control, détente, and *Ostpolitik* if Bonn spurred on SDI. He tried to delay a decision on Germany's role. Even after Kohl's party spoke in favor, the FDP argued that the question was still "if," not "whether" Bonn would participate. It criticized CDU politicians like Teltschik for "committing" Bonn to SDI before Bonn's final decision in late 1985.[100]

As for specific issues, Genscher's party insisted on, at most, a "minimal" German role, with no formal government-to-government accord and no financial contribution. Bonn, it argued, wanted no influence over SDI. Genscher insisted on "nonsingularity," openly pressed the United States not to reinterpret its obligations under the ABM Treaty, and tried to push Bonn into the European Eureka program—to undercut the argument that only SDI offered access to new technologies. His support of Kohl's position became so opaque that SPD leaders cited the foreign minister when justifying their *opposition* to SDI.[101]

Ultimately, SDI became the coalition's most divisive issue in 1985–86. The CSU sharply attacked FDP pressure. CDU leaders, including those around Kohl—Teltschik, Ruehe, Secretary General Geissler, Research Minister Heinz Riesenhuber, Chancellery Minister Schaeuble—also agreed that the Union's position must prevail on the issue. The FDP attacked their (especially Teltschik's) interference in a Foreign Ministry affair, but this only increased CDU/CSU unity.[102] By late 1985, non-singularity had become a moot issue because Great Britain had readied an agreement with the United States. The Union also agreed that Bonn should not contribute financially to the research program, and Kohl accepted a U.S.-German SDI accord of less than treaty status. However, he still insisted on more than an informal letter exchange regulating Germany's role, and succeeded in deferring any FRG commitment to Eureka.

This led to a compromise formula generally more favorable to the Union's position: FDP Economics Minister Bangemann would negotiate conditions of involvement for German firms within the context of a broader Bonn-Washington accord on technological cooperation. Genscher capitalized on the anti-SDI mood in his party to distance it from even this accord: he said it embodied economic but not political support for SDI, and was not in any way a military agreement. FDP spokesmen argued that the Bonn-Washington accord eventually reached permitted the new phase in détente and arms control to continue.[103]

Genscher has at times also made it appear that Bonn is trying to guide U.S. policy. The government attributed the result of the Geneva summit in 1985 in part to German input: that LRINF talks were delinked from SDI, the ABM Treaty upheld, and a proposal made for the worldwide ban of chemical weapons all "reflected the German impulse."[104] Genscher also prodded Kohl toward his 1986 appeal for a suspension of nuclear testing. The foreign minister actually submitted the government's statement on this issue to the chancellor, which—as one newspaper observed—showed the United States who determines policy in Bonn.[105]

Genscher in part also achieved his aim of a German-German arms control dialogue. Initially, he envisioned Bonn-East Berlin discussions and joint statements on all areas of weapons limitation, making Germany the driving force of East-West détente. Fearing that Moscow would link humanitarian gains vis-à-vis East Germany with a quiescent West German arms control policy, the Union long insisted that arms control be left at the superpower and interbloc levels. In the event, East and West German negotiators began meeting to discuss arms control issues, while "taking into account their duties" within their countries' respective alliances. This has meant focusing largely on topics already on the agenda at multilateral forums, like MBFR and the confidence-building measures conference in Stockholm, where the scope for bilateral initiatives is limited by the need for intra-alliance consensus. Nonetheless, even this level of dialogue makes many Union leaders uneasy.[106]

FDP Impact on CDU/CSU Policy.   Genscher's hand has been evident in the Kohl government's arms control policy since 1982. As noted, it has aroused protest from Union conservatives who feel that Genscher's positions compromise the primacy of military security considerations (and weakens their own influence); Strauss, for example, has deplored Genscher's policy of "unreason and irresponsibility."[107] Within the Union, a parliamentary group has formed around Alfred Dregger, aiming to resist the new phase of détente and continuity "as an end in itself." Dregger and other conservatives contend that Genscher's policies have been shaped by the FDP's desire to keep open the possibility of a future coalition with the SPD. They are especially irritated when Social Democrats praise the Foreign Minister's stand on issues like arms control, *Ostpolitik,* and South Africa, as they did frequently in 1986.[108]

At the same time, FDP influence has strengthened the hand of those in the CDU who, since 1981, have urged the Union to give *Ostpolitik* and, above all, reassurance greater weight when balancing Bonn's arms control options. These elements are generally if not uniformly comfortable with FDP policy. They are described as "Genscherists" by their conservative critics. Included in this group are—among others—deputy parliamentary chairman Volker Ruehe, Kohl national security advisor Horst Teltschik, Chancellery Minister Wolfgang Schaeuble, and representatives Lamers, Hornhues, Repnik, Stavenhagen, and Pfeifer.[109] More generally, the special political equilibrium in a three-way coalition has often required the Union as a whole to back positions closer to the Ruehe–Teltschik perspective than the Strauss–Dregger perspective.

Yet in threatening intra-Union unity, Genscher's personal diplomacy (especially with regard to arms control) has at times backfired and partially offset his influence over policy. Strauss, Dregger and their conservative colleagues have implicitly warned Kohl that, as chancellor, he must use his formal responsibility for shaping government policy or risk an intra-Union rebellion.[110] In the SDI case, this pressure led Kohl, ever concerned by threats to party unity, to consult more closely with the CSU. He showed more sympathy for conservative arguments that the Union must clearly distinguish itself from the FDP.[111] Consequently, the Union has subsequently prevailed on most issues in the debate over Bonn's role in missile defense; arms control considerations accordingly have been ranked lower in priority.

Other Domestic Factors

Union policy on arms and arms control is also subject to domestic influences from outside the coalition parties themselves. These factors include: (1) the force of bureaucratic continuity; (2) West German military-industrial interests; and (3) assorted private groups with input, including academics and churches.

The Foreign Ministry and Bureaucratic Inertia. Foreign Ministry officials, above all professional diplomats, could be said to have a special interest in arms control. The FDP for fifteen years (and Genscher alone for ten) has dominated the ministry. Liberals have been able to influence appointment of mid- and upper level diplomats and other public administrators during this time. The FRG's civil servants have not been so isolated from politics that their selection is merit-based alone; quite the contrary, there has always been an effort to politicize the civil service.[112] The diplomatic corps and civil servants affiliated with the FDP's Foreign Ministry have thus been chosen, promoted, and assigned in part with an eye to their attitudes toward arms limitation. Frustrated Union politicians see the foreign ministry as a bastion of "Genscherism."

Secondly, the Ministry has an institutional stake in arms control. With regard particularly to Bonn's positions at the multilateral MBFR talks in Vienna and CBM negotiations in Stockholm, the broad parameters are set by NATO policy and coalition leaders, but considerable latitude is left to the delegation to work out detailed bargaining positions. Foreign Ministry officials could thus be said to have developed a strong stake in the continuity of Bonn's arms control policy, and would prefer that "their" policies be preserved from political pressures. As in the CSCE process, the Foreign Ministry has also come to value the process itself and the intrinsic desirability of consensus at multilateral talks.[113] This prepackaging of FRG arms control policy frustrates Union leaders, although on larger issues like LRINF and SDI, their political input overrides bureaucratic inertia.

Private Industry and German Economic Interests.   Union leaders have close connections to German big business. The largest share of parliamentarians with business backgrounds are in the CDU/CSU; private lobbyists most often receive a sympathetic hearing from the Union; the Union's Economic Council institutionalizes these ties within the party structure; business leaders who join a party tend to join the Union; and most contributions from private industry flow into the Union coffers.[114]

How much influence industrial concerns gain over CCU/CSU policy as a result of these ties is difficult to assess. There is no satisfactory way to isolate and measure their input into specific party decisions or general party attitudes when it comes to arms control. Nonetheless, certain Union positions on arms and arms control issues have been affected by economic considerations, suggesting at the very least a coincidence of views between party leaders and certain industrial sectors.

1.   CDU/CSU reservations about the NPT throughout the late 1960s and early 1970s were reinforced by concerns about the possible effect on Germany's civilian nuclear industry. Politicians with business back-

grounds, like Kurt Birrenbach, or with economic expertise, like Gerhard Stoltenberg (Finance Minister under Kohl after 1982, and a chancellor-in-waiting), argued that NPT's restrictions on the transfer of technology and nuclear fuel would undercut the effort to construct a nuclear power industry and diversify Germany's sources of energy. This was by no means, however, the most serious obstacle to CDU/CSU support for the treaty, and even Stoltenberg and Birrenbach eventually voted to ratify, having been satisfied by U.S. assurances.

2. The party's initial, major reservations about an FRG role in SDI stemmed from its security policy, but as the depth of Reagan Administration enthusiasm for missile defense became apparent, the Union resigned itself to this project. It simultaneously developed considerable interest in the possible commercial applications of SDI spin-off technologies, coming to see the economic benefits as comparable to those of the Apollo program. Consequently, Union leaders became more and more attracted to the U.S. appeal for Allied cooperation in the research and development phase of SDI. As long as the program was underway, party leaders argued, West Germany should participate in the R&D so that German industry would be on the cutting edge of the next generation of high technologies. They referred to statistics showing lack of European and especially German competitiveness vis-à-vis the United States and Japan, arguing that SDI spin-offs could at least ensure that national industry did not slip further behind its rivals in the high tech era.

Consequently, in his May 1985 speech announcing West German support for SDI, Kohl declared, ''We shall and must be interested in putting at the service of our industry research findings that will have a revolutionary impact in their civilian applications.''[115] On other occasions the Chancellor was heard to say that West Germany risked becoming a second-rate economy if it passed up the opportunities presented by SDI.[116]

Some CDU leaders have even been led beyond SDI at least partly by technological considerations. CDU parliamentary chief Alfred Dregger has become Bonn's most enthusiastic proponent of a European defense initiative as part of SDI—a European theater missile defense within NATO and linked to SDI (as distinguished from a separate, civilian space-technology program like Eureka). After a meeting with U.S. Defense Secretary Weinberger, he expressed confidence that Washington would consider far more favorable terms for technological cooperation on such a project than on SDI. It would be a real "two-way street," giving Bonn and German firms an equal say in all decisions. Because such a project would come at a later stage, Dregger continued, it would also benefit from SDI research and thus be less expensive.[117]

Enthusiasm for SDI on technological-commercial grounds has been most marked within the CSU and the Baden-Wuerttemberg CDU. Despite initial reservations, Strauss became a missile defense advocate, routinely speaking of the commercial applications. Baden-Wuerttemberg Minister-President Lothar Spaeth, who presides over the FRG's "silicon valley," has echoed this approval.

Yet, there are many reasons for doubting that the CDU/CSU's position on SDI and SDI's role in arms control reflects in any substantial way the interests of German industry. For one, German industry appears uncertain that the economic cost-benefit ratio of SDI *is* so favorable. Not all industrialists, even in the sectors that are seen as benefiting the most, have demonstrated great enthusiasm for SDI. This applies all the more to a theater defense system, which would rely less on developing exotic new technologies than on perfecting existing ground-based ABM systems. Some CDU/CSU politicians closest to industry, such as Finance Minister Stoltenberg and Research Minister Riesenhuber, have often been perceptibly lukewarm about SDI.[118]

Moreover, while perceived commercial-technological spin-offs have made SDI attractive to many party leaders, this factor was not decisive in their support for the program. As Kohl noted, not disingenuously, in his May 1985 speech, economic considerations were certainly not uppermost in his mind. CDU/CSU approval of SDI has largely been a function of U.S. resolve to proceed with the program, and fear of what the transatlantic political and security implications of perceived West German obstructionism might be. Even those like Strauss and Dregger, whose enthusiasm has waxed, have been motivated primarily by political-military considerations. For other party leaders, the prevailing attitude remains a determination to make the best of an unchangeable situation.

Partly as a consequence of this resignation, there would be little CDU/CSU resistance to U.S. use of SDI as a bargaining chip at

Geneva. Teltschik and others have suggested as much, though under a Kohl government Bonn would never push the United States to negotiate SDI away. Nonetheless, except perhaps for Strauss and Dregger, the party would accept—with relief—a comprehensive U.S.-Soviet accord encompassing limitations on or cancellation of missile defense. Commercial interests could thus hardly be seen as a decisive factor in the Union's attitude toward arms control in this case.

3. In other cases, aside from NPT and SDI, it is still more difficult to establish a strong causality between the interests of German private industry and CDU/CSU arms control policy. Certainly in specific decisions, the interrelationship, if present, has been so minor as to be outweighed easily by other considerations. Still a case could be made that, in a more general sense, the attitudes and assumptions of West Germany's military/industrial complex do influence those of party leaders, as they emerge from and interact with a certain milieu. Strauss's close connection with leading Bavarian-based defense firms, for example, suggests a compatibility of outlook that reinforces the latter's generally strong resistance to arms control.

Retired Military, Academics, Church Groups.   The role of three other private groups in CDU/CSU arms control policy warrants brief mention.

1. Retired *Bundeswehr* officers have access to CDU/CSU decisionmaking circles as individuals because of their expertise and ties forged with the political establishment during their years of service. Moreover, organizations like the German Strategy Forum, organized by retired General Juergen Domroese, were established to provide an institutional setting for discussion among ex-military officers and CDU/CSU politicians.

   This relationship exposes the party to expertise on strategy, and in general reinforces their predisposition to give security concerns precedence in formulating arms control policy. It would be difficult to measure with any precision the overall input of ex-military officials, as in many cases they disagree; disagreements, however, arise as much from the legacy of intraservice rivalries as from conflicting strategic perspectives. SDI provided a case in point, with many retired officers fearful that it would drain funding from conventional forces.

2. Academics also have considerable access to CDU/CSU decisionmaking. In part this results from the share of party leaders with advanced

university degrees, which is much higher than in the United States. More important is the general aura of the academic and intellectual in Germany, which compels parties to maintain close affiliations with this milieu. "Dialogue" with intellectuals was one of Kohl's major aims in his early days as CDU chairman. Not surprisingly, however, the CDU/CSU has sought reinforcement from intellectuals known to support party positions, rather than objective input from the academic community at large. Thus, while the CDU/CSU has held numerous conferences with leading academics and consults them informally as well, the net result in party policy is negligible.

It should be added that the CDU's Konrad Adenauer Foundation and the CSU's Hanns Seidel Foundation play a major role in facilitating party contacts with industry officials, retired military officers, and academics. The directors of these foundations themselves also enjoy considerable independent input. As director of the Adenauer Foundation's Social Science Research Institute, for example, Hans Ruehle acted as advisor to Manfred Woerner on security policy. Ruehle moved with Woerner to the Defense Ministry in 1982.

3.   Lastly, West German church groups are also of some significance in CDU/CSU arms control planning. As noted above, the "C" in the party's title has long since ceased to be decisive in its policy. Yet a sizable minority of CDU Protestants and Catholic "Christian-Social" activists remain sensitive to the state of opinion on arms issues within the two churches. During the LRINF debate, this relationship reinforced the conviction of these CDU leaders that reassurance must take greater precedence in party thinking on arms control.

CDU/CSU ARMS CONTROL POLICY IN 1987 AND BEYOND

The Crisis of 1987

For the CDU/CSU's arms control policy 1987 proved fateful. Events on the international and domestic fronts that began late in the previous year combined to create a serious challenge for the party's consensus on foreign and security affairs. These events were, first, an inept election campaign with predictably discouraging results and, second, emergence of a major superpower arms accord. The result was a full-fledged crisis for the Union. As one newpaper put it, by May there was "Panic in Bonn."

The Election Campaign. In a sense, the CDU/CSU's greatest asset during the 1987 campaign was the fact that it was not the SPD. But, paradoxically, the Union, along with its junior coalition partner, was also its own greatest liability.

Many West Germans still doubted the SPD's capacity for pragmatism, given its barely concealed sectarian strife and flirtations with the Greens as a potential coalition partner. The SPD platform contained many vague positions—especially on nuclear energy and security—designed to placate leftists and moderates.[119] For example, while SPD Chancellor candidate Johannes Rau and fellow centrists stressed their support for NATO, left-wing SPD security policy spokesmen aroused controversy by signing an accord with the East German Communist party endorsing a nuclear-free corridor, and others spoke of unilateral disarmament gestures.[120]

By contrast, the Union had proven itself largely immune to the temptation of ideological fervor and major experiments in policy. Its leaders instead stressed Bonn's improved relations with Washington and the successful implementation of LRINF modernization in particular, steps they said not only assured recoupling but prevented Moscow from undermining NATO cohesion and pressuring the West into concessions. The party claimed credit for enhancing the West's ability to bargain confidently and on an equal footing with Moscow, and suggested that the SPD's neutralist drift—which Rau was powerless to resist—would weaken and divide the Alliance.

The Union also argued that its firmness gave the FRG solid Alliance credentials, thus enhancing its influence in Washington and Europe, winning Allied understanding for the country's special concerns, and compelling the Soviet bloc to take Bonn seriously. The party hoped to convince voters that it could thus promote arms talks and convince Moscow to accept continued intra-German cooperation, thereby capturing or at least neutralizing the arms control/détente/*Ostpolitik* issue.

Perhaps more decisively, Kohl's government had presided over a fairly solid economic recovery that created public confidence, if—given the persistently high rates of unemployment—not enthusiasm. Along with the FDP, the party thus hoped to capture the vital political center.[121]

Yet the coalition's very pragmatism and populism had been accompanied by largely nonideological, personal, and factional quarrels. Each partner jostled for power, position, and profile in an unseemly manner.

Kohl's preference for arbitration rather than the exercise of authority had done little to offset the resultant image of pettiness and, at times, even chaos. Public opinion had wearied of the bickering and drawn-out bargaining process on issues like a national identity card, labor rights, internal security, immigration, and South Africa. Gaffes and scandal made the picture even less attractive, as did the spate of questions about Kohl's ability to keep his position atop the Union.

All of these problems surfaced time and again during the campaign itself. Strauss lambasted Genscher over foreign policy, precipitating more internecine political warfare. Consequently, the FDP stressed its role as a vital counterbalance to the CSU. Far from exercising some discipline, Kohl added to the confusion—and annoyed the FDP—by drawing controversial parallels between Gorbachev and Goebbels, and labeling East German prisons "concentration camps."[122] The SPD played up differences within the coalition, arguing that Kohl gave in to Union hardliners, whom they called the "*Stahlhelm*" (after a Weimar era paramilitary group), and ignored the FDP and CDU "Genscherists" who endorsed a new era of détente.

In January 1987, Germans went to the polls and delivered Kohl's party a clear setback. Support for the CDU/CSU dropped by nearly five points, down to just over 44 percent of the popular vote. Genscher's FDP reaped the benefits, picking up some of the Union's lost support and climbing to 9 percent. The SPD under Rau lost ground while the Greens made clear gains.

Analysts drew several conclusions from this outcome. One was the clearly negative impression many voters had of the Union, its internal bickering, CSU bombast, Kohl's apparent submissiveness to CSU pressure, and the chancellor's tendency for awkward overstatement. Equally clear was voter approval of the FDP and of Genscher's foreign policy. CSU attacks on the Foreign Minister had only permitted the Liberals to stress that they must remain in the coalition as guarantors of continuity—above all in relations with the East—and as a counterbalance to the CSU's clumsy meddling. Voters seemed to agree.

Its own setback and the FDP's gains weakened the Union by intensifying strife between party factions in 1987. CDU liberals like Heiner Geissler and Labor Minister Norbert Bluem urged the Union to regain lost ground by accentuating its broadly centrist appeal, taking stands designed to woo younger voters, women and workers; no gains were to be had on the right, they argued. Not surprisingly this annoyed the CSU, which insisted that the Union must remain true to its traditional principles and voters. Because the election outcome and this strife within the Union had been predictable, many observers agreed that "things would only really get exciting after the election," when deliberation over policy would begin.[123]

The Double-Zero Option.

West Germany's campaign took place against the dramatic backdrop of the Reykjavik summit. Union leaders had welcomed the event and, for the sake of reassurance, pushed for a U.S.-Soviet pact on LRINF. When the superpowers very nearly reached agreement on the old zero option, it startled Union leaders, who criticized the idea and began voicing concern about the drift of U.S. policy.

Their unease grew when in early 1987 Mikhail Gorbachev dropped all major preconditions for an agreement eliminating medium-range nuclear arms and preempted objections by pledging to expand the accord to ban shorter range INF, where Moscow enjoyed another clear numerical edge. Washington this time welcomed the opening for a so-called "double-zero option."

Almost all Union leaders feared that losing U.S. LRINF would hurt their conception of nuclear coupling: U.S. Pershing II and cruise missiles, able to strike Soviet targets, served the requirements of flexible response, gave Bonn status as a nuclear partner of America—which pleased the Gaullists—and, in general, reified the U.S. willingness to share the risks of extended deterrence. Shorter range INF or SRINF (of which NATO had none) played a less vital role in party thinking, but—in the absence of LRINF—could still serve a modest coupling function given that they could strike Warsaw Pact staging areas.

Banning these coupling mechanisms alone would have mobilized CDU/CSU opposition to the emerging accord, but party leaders sensed a longer term danger in the developments since Reykjavik. They worried that the United States and other NATO countries were willing either to denuclearize NATO altogether—meaning, in their view, the end of extended deterrence—or at least to eliminate all but the shortest range German-based systems. The latter scenario "singularized" the FRG, leaving it burdened with systems unsuitable as deterrents and bound to arouse public anxiety.

However, the party could not openly oppose an accord it had long endorsed. Not only was its credibility on the line, but Union leaders had to take into account the factor of reassurance: the progress of arms control could not be derailed without causing alarm among West Germans, and suspicion that deterrence as conceived by the Union meant only an endless buildup of missiles. This could lead to a backlash against the party's policy—and the party's political standing. Moreover, the Union knew that outright opposition to the accord could jeopardize improved relations with East Germany, including the planned visit by Erich Honecker to the FRG.

Union leaders from Strauss, Dregger and Woerner to moderate spokesmen like Ruehe, Teltschik and Schaeuble sought a way to divert the zero option without blatantly backing out on their long-standing commitment to it. In March they proposed modifying the original plan to retain a small number of LRINF systems. When that failed, they pressed for an expanded agreement to limit shorter range INF (SRINF). When Gorbachev pledged in April to do away with SRINF, the party pointed to the Soviet edge in shorter range battlefield weapons *and* conventional weapons, contending that until this advantage—and the threat it posed—were reduced, the West needed nuclear arms as an assurance of transatlantic coupling.

In May Union leaders pushed an alternative: low but equal ceilings on SRINF, permitting the United States to build up to eighty new SRINF systems. This would assure coupling, they argued, or at least give the West bargaining leverage for future negotiations: NATO could foreswear its right to deploy new missiles if Moscow accepted major cuts in battlefield and conventional arms.[124] But U.S. Secretary of State Shultz derided the idea of equal ceilings as "an empty right" unless Bonn was ready to deploy those new missiles immediately; neither NATO defense ministers nor the British and French governments backed the Union strategy.[125]

Genscher's FDP exploited the Union's isolation by making known its enthusiasm for the double-zero option and its full support of U.S. policy: "We have no fear of arms control." Polls showed far greater support for Genscher's position than for the Union's and unambiguous approval of double-zero. Some observers believed this led to CDU losses and FDP gains at two state elections in May, including one in Kohl's home region.[126]

Ultimately many CDU moderates could no longer support a stance that isolated Bonn abroad and the Union at home. Led by CDU General Secretary Geissler, they stressed that this obstructionism would create broad disenchantment with the party's overall foreign policy, allowing the SPD with its neutralist susceptibilities to capture an issue as crucial in the public mind as arms control. They also emphasized the purely political costs: the furor threatened to undo all their efforts to attract new, especially younger voters, and revitalize the CDU.

By mid-May of 1987 the Union was tearing itself apart, with Geissler's moderates attacking the leadership and the CSU responding with charges of "populism" and "opportunism." In characteristic fashion, Kohl tried unsuccessfully to mediate among the factions and between his party and the FDP. But ultimately he gave in, authorizing a compromise in June that in effect lifted all major preconditions for CDU/CSU acceptance of double-zero—provided that the superpowers continued discussions aimed at reducing both battlefield nuclear and conventional weapons.

Only the FRG's own seventy-two aging Pershing 1a missiles with U.S.-controlled warheads were to be exempted. While party leaders had downplayed the significance of these missiles when it had still appeared possible to keep LRINF or deploy SRINF, the old Pershings took on sudden significance after June. Strauss, Dregger, and Woerner insisted upon exclusion of these "third-state systems" from the superpower talks and spoke of the need to proceed with their modernization, scheduled for the 1990s. Geissler warned against this stance, while Genscher and the FDP urged that the Pershing 1a's not be permitted to block a superpower accord.

When in July the Kremlin offered complete global elimination of INF—which the United States desired—in exchange for a package eliminating the Pershing 1a's, the coalition seemed set for more internecine warfare. Dregger insisted that Moscow must at least also give up its *shorter* range missiles as part of the bargain. But Kohl faced varying degrees of pressure from Washington, Genscher, his party, and the calendar: two state elections and the historic visit by Honecker were set for September. Consequently he pledged to scrap the Pershing 1a's once the superpowers reached an INF accord, thus paving the way for a U.S.-Soviet agreement.

Union leaders had opposed each element of a superpower INF treaty as incompatible with their understanding of nuclear coupling and thus deterrence. Each time they had been forced to back down, in part due to the stance of Allies and the FDP. Ultimately the party's position also collapsed because it lacked credibility and CDU moderates—most never known as security policy experts—proved unwilling to risk the political and policy consequences of obstructing an historic arms agreement.

The CDU/CSU and Arms Control in the 1990s

U.S. readiness to reach agreement on INF caused some bitterly anti-American grumbling, and revived both a long dead strain of national-neutralism on the party's fringes and, more importantly, the Gaullist inclination to seek some form of European deterrent force.[127] Most Union leaders and party parliamentarians rejected such radical experiments with traditional party policy, yet sensed that events since Reykjavik signalled a new U.S. desire to do away with NATO missiles that assured automatic escalation. In mid-1987 party leaders were beginning the effort to find a policy which could take account of this new American position while satisfying Union concerns with coupling and reassurance.

On one hand, many Union spokesmen voiced hopes that NATO would carry out its plan to *modernize sea- and air-based INF forces*, perhaps by adding sea- and air-launched cruise missiles to the Alliance arsenal as coupling mechanisms that reduced the automaticity of escalation. As for shorter range battlefield systems, only Woerner spoke favorably of Alliance plans to modernize these arms, and even he downplayed the idea. Most party leaders instead wanted the next stage of superpower talks to reduce these systems—to avoid ''singularization.'' But rather than another zero option, which might lead to denuclearization, they proposed a package *reducing short-range nuclear arms to lower levels* with an agreed-upon ceiling *and* making *deep, asymmetrical cuts in Soviet conventional forces*.

Domestic and international events will determine whether Union leaders turn these points into a policy acceptable to the party, the coalition, and the alliance. Several scenarios seem plausible: at home, continuation of the CDU/CSU-FDP coalition or a retreat by the Union into opposition, and on the world scene, a broad superpower rapprochement, a partial superpower rapprochement, or collapse of U.S.-Soviet relations.

CDU/CSU–FDP Coalition.   After the 1987 election it appeared almost certain that the Union could remain in power only with the help of the FDP.[128] Even the bitterly disaffected CSU saw no alternative to this coalition short of giving up its place in government. For their part, the Liberals had the best of reasons for continuing the querulous partnership: they had profited at the polls. And while the FDP and SPD had again found some common ground, it was still too fragile to sustain a coalition.

Yet Genscher's party is certain to resist the Union leadership's emphasis on modernizing NATO sea- and air-based INF, especially if there is also resistance elsewhere in the Alliance. While Genscher did seem to accept the Union position on arms control (i.e., rejection of a zero option in battlefield systems and linkage between reduction of these arms and conventional cuts), both positions would clearly become negotiable for him in the effort to produce further superpower agreements.

This built-in discrepancy between the aims of the coalition partners could also exacerbate the Union's internal debate. Moderate politicians like Geissler would certainly worry lest the FDP capture the reassurance issue; to them, too rigid a CDU/CSU stance on INF modernization or linkage of nuclear and conventional cuts could appear as obstructionism, thus damaging the credibility of the Union commitment to arms control.

Assuming a *broad superpower rapprochement* encompassing more cuts in European-based weapons, the Union leadership would be all the more alarmed about denuclearization. Gaullists would call for a European deterrent, while most party leaders would push for modernizing NATO sea- and air-based INF and merely limiting—rather than eliminating—battlefield systems, while insisting on linking this accord to asymmetrical conventional cuts.

Yet, if this stance were seen as an obstacle to an emerging superpower accord, the result would almost certainly be a confrontation within the coalition. Genscher would press the government not to undermine an accord with demands to obtain new or retain old arms, and many moderates in the CDU would feel compelled to echo this argument, splitting the Union again.

If the superpowers were to achieve *partial rapprochement*—agreement on strategic issues but not on the European front—the Union leadership would be ambivalent. In this scenario the atmosphere for modernizing INF in some form presumably would be better, and fears of a zero option in battlefield systems would be reduced—both satisfying to the CDU/CSU. Yet Union leaders like Dregger and Ruehe have been emphatic that these latter systems at least be reduced, and might move for unilateral reductions, assuming that NATO was taking steps to upgrade its LRINF.

Genscher would again resist any modernization as an obstacle to arms control, and would press the Union to put Bonn on the record in favor of an accord involving a zero option for the battlefield weapons. CDU moderates like Geissler, fearful of neglecting reassurance considerations, would agree, precipitating confrontation with party conservatives.

Total *collapse of superpower relations*, including the 1987 INF accord, would provide Union leaders justification for pushing modernization of NATO's air- and sea-based INF, which would, in turn, increase their readiness to consider unilateral cuts in the unpopular battlefield systems to avoid "singularization." Yet even they—and above all CDU moderates—would still worry if blame were to fall on Washington (perhaps because of SDI) for undermining détente and arms control. Some common ground would reemerge within the coalition over the effort to revive dialogue for purposes of reassurance and thus consensus on NATO policy.

CDU/CSU Opposition. It is not inconceivable that the coalition's centrifugal tendencies could finally prevail: CSU intransigence or FDP opportunism could lead to revival of a Social-Liberal coalition, thus relegating the Union once again to the opposition benches.

In this case CDU/CSU arms control policies would still be fiercely disputed. Freed from the constraints imposed by formal responsibility for policy-making and coalition politics, the Union's conservatives could again assert themselves and urge that security considerations be given unquestioned precedence. In practice, this could mean vocal support for air- and sea-based INF modernization and sharp criticism of any emerging superpower accord that drifted in the direction of denuclearizing Europe.

Yet, at the same time, CDU moderates have taken a stance on arms control that they are unlikely to back away from, even if—in opposition—they could no longer use as supporting arguments the need for cooperating with the United States or preventing the FDP from stealing the reassurance issue. If anything, Geissler's group is likely to force a showdown with the CSU and party conservatives in the effort to finally put the Union on the right side of the arms control issue. Indeed, without the relatively centripetal force created by the need to maintain power, internal debates in the Union could even lead to a rupture between the sister parties.

The CDU/CSU Leadership

The shape of CDU/CSU arms control policy going into the 1990s will not depend only on the exigencies of party politics and international trends: personalities will also matter. Most significant is the identity of the CDU chairman, the chancellor or (if the Union loses power) the chancellor designate, and the possible successor to Strauss atop the CSU.

Ultimately Helmut Kohl has retained the CDU chairmanship and chancellery for several reasons. More than his rivals, he is an organization man, and most party activists are comfortable with him. Kohl remains, moreover, the CDU's "lowest common denominator," an unflattering reference to the fact that he does not polarize opinion; conservatives and liberals feel frustrated but not threatened by his consensus-oriented pragmatism. Lastly, even his critics have been reluctant to move against a sitting head of government. Consequently, the CDU/CSU lacks the customary "chancellor bonus"—the advantage of a popular statesman atop the ticket—but Kohl remains relatively secure in his two top posts.

Nonetheless Union members have often said obliquely what press commentators say openly: the party's internal bickering and its ceaseless drifting from crisis to crisis could best be halted by a stronger hand on the tiller; its drooping public image also makes a more respected helmsman necessary. Despite his endurance, Kohl could fall if the party's standing continues to plummet. Speculation about successors, both as CDU chairman and chancellor/chancellor designate, centers on several names.

Gerhard Stoltenberg.   The Finance Minister has long been considered the strongest candidate to replace Kohl. As director of the coalition's budget austerity drive, the competent, coolly decisive and pragmatic northerner has enjoyed widespread respect, if not overwhelming popularity. Many CSU and FDP leaders consider him better suited to help the coalition regain public confidence than the jocular, provincial Kohl, who for that very reason may be a more formidable counterpart in intragovernment disputes. Yet in 1987 his chances seemed to dim with the controversy over his tax cut plans and CDU setbacks in his home state. Lesser-known rivals have improved their positions so that if Stoltenberg is to replace Kohl, the succession must happen relatively early.

Stoltenberg stands squarely at the Union's center on foreign policy issues, yet his leadership style would cause certain changes. The northerner's firm, confident assertion of German interests (in his refusal to reflate the German economy and have the FRG act as a locomotive for the West, for example) contrasts sharply with Kohl's more acquiescent, consensus-oriented attitude toward Bonn's allies. This could carry over into more overt pressure on the United States to respect traditional NATO policy and to pursue arms control if as chancellor he considered it vital for Bonn's businesslike relationship with the East (which he supports), or especially if revived nuclear *Angst* made him fear for the FRG foreign policy consensus.

Ernst Albrecht.   Another northerner, Lower Saxony's Minister-President has been mentioned often as a possible successor to Kohl as chancellor and party chief. Long popular among young CDU members and liberals for his centrist policies, he would be a natural choice to head a Union-FDP team: he is comfortable philosophically and personally with the FDP. But he is not trusted by the CSU and would thus be a less likely opposition leader.

Albrecht made a name for himself in the mid-1970s by urging the Union to pursue a more adaptive *Ostpolitik*, and is in this sense a leader among

CDU liberals with regard to foreign policy. But he also stands squarely behind traditional Union security policy, and his consensus-oriented style—while more sophisticated than Kohl's—would ensure continuity in Union policy.

Lothar Spaeth. Baden-Wuerttemberg's Minister-President would be a logical CDU chairman if the party decided that his energy was needed to keep it in power or bring it back out of opposition. Spaeth has won praise for actively using government power to promote high-tech sectors of the local economy, industrial cooperation with trade unions, and ecological legislation. This distinguishes him from Kohl and the classical liberal Stoltenberg, and would also make him an uncomfortable choice as chancellor for the FDP. For these and other reasons, some observers began to suspect by 1987 that this "coming man" might never arrive.

Despite his somewhat unorthodox domestic policies, Spaeth would be expected to produce few changes in Union foreign policy. While he has enthusiastically advocated an active FRG *Ostpolitik* and has traveled East on several occasion, Spaeth shares Kohl's instinctive, consensus-oriented Atlanticism—exemplified by strong support for SDI (which also reflects his enthusiasm for high tech). As chancellor, Spaeth would not intensify Bonn's assertiveness vis-à-vis Washington with regard either to arms or arms control policy.

Walter Wallmann. Another rising star in the CDU is this former Frankfurt mayor who can claim the distinction of having brought the CDU to power in Hessen for the first time. Wallmann's persuasive skills are such that he was Kohl's choice to head the newly formed Environment Ministry after the anxiety created in the FRG by the Chernobyl disaster. As a Kohl protege, he is solidly within the CDU mainstream, an advocate of traditional party security policy tempered by concern with reassurance. In policy terms Wallmann could hardly resemble Kohl more closely, and stylistically he follows the same path of mediation—albeit with greater skill and sophistication.

Strauss and the CSU. Strauss and his party have long considered him the man best equipped to be chancellor as well as Foreign Minister. Yet the CSU suffered losses in the 1986 *Land* election and the 1987 federal election. In subsequent months it became painfully apparent just how skillfully the Bavarian chief had been outmaneuvered by Helmut Kohl, who offered him only cabinet posts Strauss was sure to reject, overruled him on several major issues (including the Pershing 1a question where Strauss was not consulted), and permitted CDU liberals to modify the party's image. Experts concluded that despite his anger the CSU chairman had no alternative but to accept such rebuffs: pulling out of the coalition, let alone the partnership with the CDU, could cost the CSU its cherished influence over federal policy and could weaken it in Bavaria.

A bitter Strauss is nonetheless certain to remain a factor in Union and Bonn politics. Even without a cabinet post for himself or more portfolios for the party, he can make the CSU presence known simply by continuing to spearhead the Union's conservative wing and preserving its Gaullist tradition. Yet Strauss celebrated his seventieth birthday in 1985, stirring speculation about his eventual successor. The leading candidates are CSU General Secretary and party leader in the Bavarian parliament, Gerold Tandler; the party's top federal parliamentarian, Theo Waigel; FRG Interior Minister Fritz Zimmermann; and Bavarian Chancellery Minister Edmund Stoiber. Any successor is certain to represent the same views on security and arms control as Strauss, but with less force and vigor. Moreover, a successor probably will be forced to devote time and energy to consolidating control of the CSU itself (Strauss had few real rivals; his successors will not be so lucky) and rallying the party in its Bavarian bastion against both the right and the center.

CONCLUSION

The events of 1987 revealed flaws in the CDU/CSU approach to arms control that had been papered over for nearly a decade, and it is unlikely the party will soon be able to find a credible, consensus policy in this area.

Certain long-standing imperatives of CDU/CSU security policy—above all, preservation of transatlantic nuclear coupling—remain the major determinant of the party leadership's views on arms control. But since the events of 1987 indicate that coupling in the future can no longer be based on intermediate-range missiles, the Union leadership will have to promote alternatives, such as upgraded NATO air- and sea-based INF. And since Union leaders also fear an uncontrollable process of denuclearization, they will want to keep a modicum of what they otherwise view as less than optimal coupling mechanisms—battlefield nuclear arms. Clearly this will have implications for arms control, especially if the superpowers continue making progress. The Union would provide:

- No support for a zero option in battlefield arms without some steps to upgrade NATO's longer range air- and sea-based deterrent capabilities;

- No support for an accord that might restrict NATO's access to cruise missiles or other modernization measures;

- Full support only for a concept that links any further nuclear arms reductions with deep asymmetrical cuts in Soviet conventional arms;

- No support for a policy urging the United States to bargain away SDI and even some support for an FRG role in SDI to prevent further "political" decoupling;

- No support for any plans that single out the FRG or Central Europe as an arms control zone, such as nuclear arms- or chemical arms-free corridor;

- No support for a substantive Bonn-East Berlin arms control dialogue.

Yet since the early 1980s security considerations alone have not driven Union arms control policy. As the events of 1987 indicated, even party leaders suspicious of arms control—those who tried to modify the double-zero option or even opposed it altogether—fear that outright obstructionism could undermine public tolerance of any policy based on nuclear deterrence. In the near future, party leaders—especially under one of Kohl's successors—may temper their firm position on the above mentioned issues with gestures such as:

- Pressure on NATO to reach an accord cutting battlefield nuclear arms to lower levels (if not necessarily zero), thus precluding "singularization";

- Full support for deep if asymmetrical cuts in conventional forces;

- Subtle pressure for a "cooperative solution" on SDI to preserve the ABM Treaty and to find a formula deferring real movement toward SDI deployment;

- Further resistance to deployment of chemical arms and continued support for their withdrawal from Europe and a global ban on such systems;

- Strong rhetorical support for strategic arms reductions (if not as sweeping as envisioned at Reykjavik) and for the overall East-West dialogue.

As the events of 1987 also demonstrated, many CDU moderates may find such steps to reassure the public less than credible and opt for far-reaching efforts. Just as these moderates—generally younger and less well versed in the intricacies of security policy—endorsed the double-zero option, they may press the Union leadership not to attach any further conditions to FRG arms control policy that might hamper the pace of East-West arms talks. Their position will be strongest if the Union remains in government with the FDP and if superpower talks continue to produce results at any level.

The Union consensus on arms and arms control policy all but collapsed in 1987; how completely it can be restored remains uncertain. The party's basic assumptions about security, tempered by more recent concern with preserving the public consensus on nuclear deterrence, are the constants in its approach to arms control—generating some predictability if not complete harmony and coherence. However, 1987 exposed contradictions within that policy, as well as a rift between intransigent conservatives and impatient moderates, and showed how vulnerable the Union is to changes in the international and domestic political environments. On the threshold of a new decade, the party may have to rethink its policy or else concede that consensus is part of the past.

NOTES

1. On the CDU's history and character, see Geoffrey Pridham, *Christian Democracy in Western Germany* (New York: St. Martin's Press, 1977).
2. On the CSU, see Alf Mintzel, "Die CSU in Bayern," *Parteiensystem in der Legitimationskrise* (Opladen: Westedeutscher Verlag, 1973); "Conservatism and Christian Democracy in the Federal Republic of Germany," in *Conservative Politics in Western Europe*, ed. Zig Layton-Henry (London: Macmillan, 1982).
3. *Die Ueberruestung der Sowjetunion: Ziele kommunistischer Machtpolitik* (Bonn: CDU Bundesgeschaeftsstelle, 1983).
4. Waldemar Besson, *Die Aussenpolitik der Bundesrepublik: Erfahrungen und Massstaebe* (Frankfurt; Ullstein, 1973), pp. 300–6.
5. Manfred Woerner, "West Germany and the New Dimensions of Security," in *West German Foreign Policy, 1949–1979*, ed. Wolfram Hanieder (Boulder, Colorado: Westview Press, 1980), p. 41.

6. See, for example, Helmut Kohl's speech cited in *CDU Pressemitteilung*, November, 1974, pp. 8–11.

7. *Bayernkurier*, March 3, 1979.

8. *Frankfurter Allgemeine Zeitung* (hereafter *FAZ*), April 9, 1984; Alfred Dregger, "Paris muss Farbe bekennen," *Die Zeit*, March 30, 1984.

9. *Gemeinsam den Frieden sichern: Das Atlantische Buendnis—Garant unserer Freiheit* (Bonn: CDU Bundesgeschaeftsstelle, 1983), pp. 6–7.

10. Ibid.

11. *Zum Thema: Frieden: Politik der aktiven Friedenssicherung! Dokumentation ueber Abruestungsinitiativen der CDU/CSU* (Bonn: CDU Bundesgeschaeftsstelle, 1982).

12. Besson, *Die Aussenpolitik*, p. 292.

13. *Zum Thema: Frieden*, p. 4.

14. *FAZ*, August 27, 1973.

15. Catherine McArdle Kelleher, *Germany and the Politics of Nuclear Weapons* (New York: Columbia University Press, 1975).

16. *FAZ*, July 4, 1973.

17. *Welt am Sonntag*, July 15, 1973.

18. Hans Ruehle, "Entwaffnung Westeuropas?" *Die Politische Meinung*, July/August 1973, pp. 84–85.

19. *Bayernkurier*, March 3, 1979.

20. Manfred Woerner, "Die Bedenken Europas," *Deutsche Zeitung/Christ und Welt*, August 17, 1979, p. 8.

21. See remarks by Strauss, for example, cited in *Deutscher Bundestag, Stenographischer Bericht*, 8. Wahlperiode, 203. Sitzung, February 28, 1980, p. 16193.

22. See comments by Defense Committee member Willi Weiskirch, cited in *Deutschland-Union-Dienst*, January 6, 1978.

23. *FAZ*, February 1, 1979.

24. Cited in David S. Yost and Thomas S. Glad, "West German Party Politics and Theater Nuclear Modernization Since 1977," *Armed Forces and Society*, November 16, 1982, p. 548.

25. Ibid.; *FAZ*, September 9, 1977.

26. Rolf Seeligen, ed., *Koalition auf Entspannungskurs: Beitraege Zur Abruestungspolitik mit einer Dokumentation: CDU/CSU stoert Friedenspolitik in Europa* (Munich: Verlag Rolf Seeligen, 1979), pp. 62–65; 70–74.

27. *Deutscher Bundestag, Stenographischer Bericht*, 8. Wahlperiode, 141. Sitzung, March 8, 1979, p. 11165.

28. *FAZ*, February 25, 1986.

29. *FAZ*, February 26, 1986.

30. *Gemeinsam den Frieden sichern*, pp. 14–16.

31. *Frieden schaffen mit weniger Waffen: Referate des Friedenskongresses der CDU* (Bonn: CDU Bundesgeschaeftsstelle, February 3, 1983), p. 8.

32. *FAZ*, December 19, 1985; *Seventh German-American Roundtable on NATO*, sponsored by the Konrad Adenauer Foundation and the Institute for Foreign Policy Analysis (Washington: The Institute for Foreign Policy Analysis), pp. 3–7.

33. Ibid.

34. *FAZ*, December 7, 1985.

35. *FAZ*, May 21, 1985; October 19, 1985; December 19, 1985.

36. *FAZ*, April 25, 1985.

37. *FAZ*, November 21, 1985.

38. *FAZ*, September 27, 1985.

39. Hans-Peter Schwarz, "Das Aussenpolitische Konzept Konrad Adenauers," in *Adenauer-Studien I*, eds. Rudolf Morsey and Konrad Repgen (Mainz: Matthias Gruenewald, 1971), pp. 99–102.

40. This issue is the main theme of the author's recently completed doctoral dissertation at the Fletcher School of Law and Diplomacy, entitled "The CDU/CSU and West German *Ostpolitik*, 1969–82."

41. *Neue Zuercher Zeitung*, December 23, 1983.

42. Erich Weede, Dietmar Schoessler, and Matthia Jung, "West Elite Views on National Security Issues: Evidence from a 1980/81 Survey of Experts," *Journal of Strategic Studies* 6 (1983): 82–95.

43. See, for example, Kurt Becker in *Die Zeit*, November 3, 1983.

44. Weede, et al., "West Elite Views."

45. Seeligen, *Koalition auf Entspannungskurs* pp. 14–19.

46. Cited in Ronald D. Asmus, "East and West Germany; Continuity and Change," *The World Today*, April 1984, p. 145.

47. Schwarz, "Das aussenpolitische Konzept Konrad Adenauers," pp. 97–102; Gordon Drummond, *The German Social Democrats in Opposition: The Case Against Rearmament* (Norman, Oklahoma: University of Oklahoma Press, 1982), pp. 212–41.

48. See, for example, the results of an Emnid poll, cited in *Frankfurter Neue Presse*, September 26, 1981.

49. See the results of an Emnid survey, discussed in *Spiegel*, April 12, 1982.

50. See the results of an Emnid poll, cited in *Welt am Sonntag*, July 19, 1981; and an Allensbach survey, cited in *Die Welt*, August 28, 1981.

51. See the results of an Emnid poll, cited in *Welt am Sonntag*, September 13, 1981; and an Allensbach survey, *Die Welt*, October 26, 1981.

52. An Allensbach survey, discussed in the *Stuttgarter Nachrichten*, May 2, 1982.

53. See the results of a *Spiegel* poll, cited in that magazine, March 2, 1981.

54. See the results of a poll conducted by the ZDF Barometer, discussed in the *Bundespresseamt*/news division's newsletter, May 31, 1982.

55. See a Stern poll, cited in Peter Schmidt, "Public Opinion and Security Policy in the Federal Republic of Germany," *Orbis* 28 (Winter 1985) p. 740.
56. *New York Times*, March 18, 1983, p. A10.
57. Schmidt, "Public Opinion and Security Policy," p. 741.
58. *Sueddeutsche Zeitung*, February 16, 1981.
59. *Der Spiegel*, August 17, 1981, p. 22.
60. *FAZ*, August 12, 1981.
61. *Der Tagesspiegel*, September 22, 1981.
62. See the variety of pamphlets offered by the CDU Information Service, catalogued in the *Union in Deutschland 26/83 Aktion 10,000 Friedenstage*.
63. *30. Bundesparteitag der Christlich Demokratischen Union Deutschlands, Niederschrift*, Hamburg, November 2–5, 1981 (Bonn: CDU Budnesgeschaeftsstelle, 1981).
64. *FAZ*, February 26, 1981; March 2, 1981.
65. *Sueddeutsche Zeitung*, March 31, 1981.
66. *Washington Post*, March 13, 1983.
67. *Friedenskongress der CDU*, p. 11.
68. *FAZ*, October 1, 1985.
69. *Rissener Rundbrief*, Haus Rissen, April 1983.
70. Joseph Kraft, "The Euromissile Problem Isn't Over," *Washington Post*, March 10, 1983, p. A19.
71. Ibid.
72. *Washington Post*, December 19, 1983.
73. *Neue Zuercher Zeitung*, December 23, 1983.
74. Address given by Horst Teltschik in Moscow, June 1984.
75. *FAZ*, February 15, 1986.
76. *FAZ*, May 21, 1985.
77. *FAZ*, February 25, 1985.
78. *FAZ*, April 19, 1985.
79. *FAZ*, December 7, 1985.
80. Horst Teltschik, statement to the 13th German–American Conference, Dallas, March 29, 1985, cited in *Statements and Speeches*, 7, German Information Center, April 1, 1985.
81. *FAZ*, October 12, 1985.
82. *FAZ*, October 1, 1985.
83. *FAZ*, April 9, 1986; April 10, 1986; April 25, 1986.
84. *FAZ*, April 12, 1986.
85. *FAZ*, July 7, 1985.
86. *Financial Times*, March 11, 1981.
87. *Spiegel*, June 22, 1981.

88. Gordon Smith, *Politics in Western Germany* (New York: Holmes and Meier, 1982), p. 91.

89. *Spiegel*, June 22, 1981.

90. Kurt Biedenkopf, "Rueckzug aus der Grenzsituation," *Die Zeit*, October 30, 1981, p. 4.

91. *FAZ*, April 25, 1985; Paul Pucher, "Der Pfaelzer und der Bayer," *Der Spiegel*, August 26, 1985, pp. 64–70.

92. "Die Zukunft gestalten, den Frieden sichern," address by Helmut Kohl to the 31st CDU Federal Parteitag, Cologne (Bonn: CDU Bundesgeschaeftsstelle), p. 10.

93. *FAZ*, October 8, 1985.

94. *FAZ*, June 25, 1985; September 23, 1985.

95. *FAZ*, July 8, 1985.

96. *FAZ*, September 26, 1985.

97. *FAZ*, September 23, 1985.

98. *FAZ*, November 8, 1985; November 9, 1985.

99. *FAZ*, October 8, 1985.

100. *FAZ*, October 5, 1985.

101. *FAZ*, October 17, 1985; December 16, 1985.

102. *FAZ*, October 10, 1985.

103. *FAZ*, March 1, 1980.

104. *FAZ*, November 27, 1981.

105. *FAZ*, April 12, 1986.

106. *FAZ*, June 26, 1985.

107. *FAZ*, September 19, 1985.

108. *FAZ*, June 26, 1986.

109. *FAZ*, December 5, 1985.

110. *FAZ*, November 25, 1985; December 9, 1985.

111. *FAZ*, November 16, 1985.

112. Smith, *Politics in Western Germany*, pp. 68–69.

113. *FAZ*, November 30, 1985.

114. Lewis J. Edinger, *Politics in West Germany* (Boston, Mass.: Little, Brown, 1977), pp. 195–200.

115. Helmut Kohl, address to the Bundestag, April 18, 1985, cited in *Statements and Speeches* 7 (April 19, 1985); *FAZ*, July 2, 1985.

116. *Der Spiegel*, September 9, 1985, p. 27.

117. *FAZ*, July 2, 1985.

118. *Der Spiegel*, July 8, 1985, pp. 76–77; September 9, 1985, pp. 27–30.

119. *Die Zeit*, August 29, 1986.

120. Karsten Voigt, "Erneuerung und Neubestimmung einer sozialdemokratischen Sicherheits- und Abruestungspolitik," paper of the SPD's Frankfurter Kreis, discussed in *FAZ*, February 17, 1986.

121. Robert Leicht, "Das traege Pendel der Demokratie," *Die Zeit*, July 11, 1986.

122. *Der Spiegel*, January 12, 1987; *Washington Post*, January 22, 1987.

123. Robert Leicht, "Spannend wird's erst nach der Wahl," *Die Zeit*, January 23, 1987.

124. See the speech by Volker Ruehe, *Das Parlament*, May 23, 1987, p. 6.

125. *Washington Post*, May 15, 1987.

126. Rolf Zundel, "Vom Zug aus die Weichen stellen?" *Die Zeit*, May 15, 1987.

127. See Dregger's comments in *FAZ*, June 5, 1987.

128. Other scenarios—a Union-only government or a Union-SPD coalition— seemed highly unlikely after the 1987 election.

4 THE POLITICS AND IDEOLOGY OF SPD SECURITY POLICIES

Jeffrey Boutwell

The history of the German Social Democratic Party (SPD) is one of long-standing internal tensions between the party's doctrinaire socialist, and reformist social democratic, factions. Since the Gotha Conference in 1875, when the followers of Ferdinand Lassalle and Karl Marx debated the advantages of reformist versus revolutionary strategies, the SPD has been beset by internal schisms that have manifested themselves openly every generation or so.[1] These shifts in party policy were especially evident at the Erfurt party conference in 1891, at the Heidelberg conference of 1925, and, after the hiatus of the Third Reich, at the Bad Godesberg conference in 1959. It was at this latter conference that the SPD shed many of its more doctrinaire Marxist tenets and essentially accepted West Germany's role in NATO and the Atlantic Alliance, thus broadening its appeal to the "high middle ground" of West German politics.

Beginning in the late 1970s, however, the SPD began drifting back to the left. In the midst of the "Euromissile" debate of the early 1980s, a party conference at Cologne in 1983 essentially repudiated the security policies of former SPD Chancellor Helmut Schmidt. Despite suffering a severe setback in the 1983 national election, the party adopted a security platform, at its special party conference in Nuremberg in August 1986, that was increasingly at odds with established NATO policy. A second poor showing in the West German national election of January 1987 did little to temper the party's search for a more independent security policy. The SPD today seems to be in the midst of yet another generational change in its outlook and character.

The Roots of SPD Security Policy

In one sense, current attempts by the SPD to fashion new security policies that are less dependent on the superpowers and the opposing blocs of

NATO and the Warsaw Pact are but symptomatic of widespread unease throughout the West about the stability of military deterrence on the continent. At the same time, however, current SPD security policies are very much rooted in the party's antimilitarist and internationalist traditions, which trace their lineage to the SPD's formative experience during the Bismarckian Reich. The revolutionary nature of the party's Marxist ideology in the late 1800s, combined with the reality of a Germany dominated by a Junker elite and a Prussian military "state within a state,"[2] gave the SPD a less overtly nationalistic outlook than other left-wing parties in Europe (e.g., the French Communist party). When the SPD Reichstag faction voted in favor of war credits in 1914, it catalyzed the greatest schism in SPD history as first the Independent Socialists (USPD) and then the Communists (KPD) split off from the SPD in 1917. During the 1920s, the horrendous legacy of the First World War strengthened the party's commitment to disarmament and concepts of collective security, especially after the reintegration of the Independent Socialists in 1922. The travails of Weimar democracy ultimately led to the SPD being driven underground during the Third Reich; the party emerged in 1945 with an even stronger belief in the sentiments expressed by Friedrich Engels in 1892: "I believe that disarmament and the securing of peace are possible . . . and Germany more than any other civilized state has both the power and the responsibility to see it come about."[3]

In domestic politics, the SPD initially sought following World War II to maintain its working-class, Marxist identity in a society that was undergoing a fundamental transformation. Steady economic growth helped soften the class divisions and party allegiances of domestic politics. The SPD was further handicapped by having lost its natural base of political support in the industrial sections of what became East Germany. Moreover, the reality of a divided Germany and Cold War politics allowed Chancellor Konrad Adenauer to equate the policies of the SPD with those of the Communist regimes to the east, even though the SPD itself was staunchly anti-Stalinist. The existence of this "double security complex,"[4] where the citizens of the Federal Repulic looked to the Adenauer government for continued domestic economic growth and external security from the Soviet threat, prevented the SPD from breaking out of the "one-third barrier" and winning more than 32 percent of the vote in the 1953 and 1957 national elections.

During the 1950s, the SPD opposed both Adenauer's rearmament program and the decision to join NATO, largely on the grounds that these measures would jeopardize any possibility of German reunification. The

SPD also campaigned strongly against the delivery of nuclear-capable weapon systems to the Bundeswehr, and in January 1958 helped initiate the widespread public protest movement known as the *Kampf dem Atomtod* (Struggle against Atomic Death). Drawing parallels with the vote on war credits in 1914 and the party's less-than-effective opposition to Hitler in the 1930s, the more doctrinaire elements of the SPD advocated full use of both general strikes and mass protests to block what they saw as a militarization of West German society and possible German responsibility for the outbreak of a new conflict in central Europe. Yet, even though public opinion ran as high as 80 percent against deployments of additional theater nuclear forces in the FRG, the SPD was unable to capitalize politically on these sentiments. Having suffered a crushing defeat in the 1957 national elections (the CDU/CSU won an absolute majority for the first and only time in the FRG's history), the SPD was in no position to block Bundestag passage of Adenauer's armaments program in the spring of 1958. Even at the height of the mass demonstrations in mid-1958, the low electoral salience of nuclear weapons issues, compared with those of economic security and political stability, was demonstrated in July 1958 when the CDU swept the state elections in North Rhine– Westphalia, a traditional SPD stronghold. Finally, a combination of trade union unwillingness to engage in mass strikes in support of the SPD and Adenauer's success in equating SPD policy goals with those of East Germany and the Soviet Union convinced SPD party leaders to back away from a grass roots movement then out of its control.[5]

Unbeknownst to the broader public during the *Kampf dem Atomtod* demonstrations, a growing segment of the SPD was arguing the party's need to broaden its appeal and to shift from being a class party to a mass-based party (*Volkspartei*). A younger elite led by Fritz Erler, Carlo Schmid, Herbert Wehner, and Willy Brandt argued particularly that the SPD should accept the Federal Republic's role in the NATO alliance and demonstrate its unswerving support for the Bundeswehr.[6] As was the case earlier in the party's history, this centrist social democratic element (centered mainly in the party's Bundestag delegation), was opposed by the more doctrinaire socialist wing (in the party organization), which stressed the importance of adhering to the pacifist and antimilitarist roots of the SPD. With the electoral defeats of 1957–58 to bolster their argument, however, the reformist wing of the SPD (known as the *Gegenelite*, or counterelite) began to gain adherents to its view that the SPD must move toward the political center if it were to have any chance of gaining political power.

It was in 1959, at the special Bad Godesberg party congress, that the SPD finally shed its more doctrinaire Marxist tenets and began a process of bridge-building with moderate nonsocialist, democratic elements. Shaped largely by Erler and his colleagues, the Godesberg program enunciated the party's support for defending the democratic ideals of the West German state as a member of the Western Alliance. Equally, however, the party stressed that arms control and international law must complement national defense in providing a long-term solution to East-West tensions and the division of Germany.[7] The following year, in 1960, the Godesberg conversion was cemented with Herbert Wehner's landmark speech to the Bundestag that signalled SPD acceptance of a foreign policy firmly grounded in West Germany's membership in NATO and the EEC. This shift by the SPD to a more moderate and broad-based *Volkspartei* paid off first in 1966, when the SPD joined the CDU/CSU in the "Grand Coalition" government, and then in 1969, when Willy Brandt was elected Chancellor and the SPD formed a coalition government with the Free Democratic Party (FDP).

Detente and the West German Security Consensus

For the next ten years, through the late 1970s, there existed in the FRG a consensus, albeit fragile at times, on security issues among the dominant moderate wing of the SPD, the FDP, and the majority centrist elements of the CDU. The only exception to the consensus had been the bitter ratification debates over Willy Brandt's eastern treaties ("Renunciation of force" agreements with Moscow and Warsaw that implicitly accepted the postwar boundaries of Germany). The security consensus was based on the twin goals of deterrence (i.e., military parity with the East) and détente, as enunciated in the 1967 Harmel Report of NATO. However, this domestic political consensus in West Germany depended greatly on the confluence of détente policies of the FRG and the United States.[8] As long as Willy Brandt's *Ostpolitik* was in step with U.S. efforts to negotiate arms reductions with the Soviets and lessen political tensions in central Europe, the more leftist elements in the SPD, as well as conservative figures in the CDU/CSU, found themselves isolated. Once superpower détente began to sour in the mid-1970s, however, internal fissures within the SPD became more pronounced as the party found itself increasingly divided over pursuing *Ostpolitik*, on the one hand, and supporting U.S. and NATO policies that at times conflicted with West Germany's deepening relations with the GDR and the Eastern bloc.

By the late 1970s, this split within the party had been exacerbated by the neutron bomb affair, as well as by the growing political challenge posed by the Green Party. Long before the rise of the West German peace movement in the early 1980s, a growing segment of the SPD left wing voiced its concern with the centrist policies of the Schmidt "government wing" of the party. At the Hamburg party conference in 1977, for example, Schmidt was confronted with widespread SPD opposition to any deployment of enhanced radiation weapons (ERW). Egon Bahr led the opposition to the neutron bomb, calling it a product of "perverted thinking"; one SPD motion from the floor of the conference referred to ERW as a "grotesque sadism of military planning."[9]

By 1978, Bahr, Brandt, and others on the SPD left were formulating a new security and arms control policy that they hoped would be adopted at the 1979 party conference in Berlin as the party's platform for the 1980 election.[10] In writing that arms control is "no more and no less a political partnership for the protection of peace," Brandt presaged the "security partnership" concept that came to the fore in the early 1980s and that has aroused intense debate, both within the FRG and among its allies. In seeking to formulate a new strategy that would provide momentum to the stalled talks on strategic forces in Geneva, and on conventional forces in Vienna, Brandt and Bahr hoped as well to win back those younger voters who had been attracted by the environmentalist and antinuclear policies of the Green Party. Thus, both men stressed the North-South aspect of the East-West military competition (i.e., the need to divert defense funds to Third World development projects), as well as the possibility that a new European security system might be created within which the two German states could further develop their relationship.

By the time of the 1979 Berlin conference, then, held just one week before NATO made its important INF "dual-track" decision, the party itself was more divided on security issues than the SPD government of Helmut Schmidt and the CDU/CSU opposition.[11] Indeed Schmidt was able to get his party's approval of the NATO "dual-track" decision on deploying intermediate-range nuclear forces (INF) only by exerting considerable pressure on party delegates, including the threat of refusing to run for reelection in the 1980 elections.[12]

This growing split between the Schmidt-led "government" wing of the party (which included Defense Minister Hans Apel and Schmidt aide Hans-Juergen Wischnewski) and the "party" faction of Willy Brandt,

Egon Bahr, and others was then exacerbated by the debate in early 1980 over an appropriate Western response to the Soviet invasion of Afghanistan.[13] The need for party unity prior to the national elections in September 1980, given that Schmidt's popularity with the German electorate was much greater than that of the SPD, maintained a semblance of order within the party only until the election.

Following the election, in which the SPD-FDP government actually increased its plurality in the Bundestag, the SPD found itself increasingly divided over three main issues: Alliance security policy (especially the INF issue); economic policy differences within the SPD-FDP government; and the electoral challenge posed by the Greens. A combination of the first two issues led FDP leader (and Foreign Minister) Hans Dietrich Genscher to bring down the Schmidt government in September 1982. The growing strength of the Greens manifested itself in the March 1983 national election in which the SPD suffered a devastating defeat, winning less than 40 percent of the vote for the first time in twenty years.

The final breakup of the West German security consensus occurred during the campaign for the 1983 election, when the SPD advanced the concept of an East-West "security partnership" (*Sicherheitspartnerschaft*) that, by seeming to give equal weight to its neighbors to the east, for many questioned the party's allegiance to NATO and the West. As set forth by Egon Bahr, Horst Ehmke, and others, the "security partnership" concept, to the extent that it went beyond generalities regarding the primacy of politics over conflict in the nuclear age, implied a greater role for the FRG in stabilizing East-West relations, largely because of West Germany's special relationship with the GDR and other Warsaw Pact countries.[14] While Bahr and Ehmke asserted that the "security partnership" concept was predicated on continued West German membership in NATO and the Western Alliance, rising SPD criticism of INF deployment plans and U.S. arms control policies suggested to many that the SPD was seeking a quasi-neutralist, third way for West Germany between the superpowers. Such fears in the United States and France especially, were fueled during the electoral campaign by statements from the SPD chancellor-candidate, Hans-Jochen Vogel, and other party figures including Brandt, Eppler, and Oskar Lafontaine.

The importance of the "security partnership" concept for SPD policy will be discussed at greater length below. Suffice to say here that the SPD emphasis on security issues during the campaign was clearly ill-advised. Polls taken shortly before the March 1983 election showed that, although the SPD was considered the more competent party on such issues as *Ostpolitik* and the environment, these issues were of relatively low importance to most voters. Conversely, the CDU/CSU was deemed the more competent party to handle precisely those issues (unemployment, pension security, government deficits) that were of greatest importance to the German electorate.[15]

Following the election, the first won by the CDU since 1965, the SPD continued its leftward drift on security issues. At a special party congress held in Cologne in November 1983, SPD delegates voted overwhelmingly for a moratorium on the soon-to-be-deployed Pershing intermediate-range ballistic missiles, thus repudiating the earlier policies of the Schmidt government.[16] In addition, many members of the SPD participated in, and helped to coordinate, the mass demonstrations against the NATO INF systems that took place in Bonn and other West German cities during this period. Perceptions that the party was embarking on an increasingly unilateral security policy were further fueled when, in the spring of 1984, the SPD announced that it was beginning a series of talks with the East German Socialist Unity Party (SED) regarding the creation of a chemical weapons-free zone in Europe.

The failure of the West German Peace Movement and its supporters in the SPD, the Green Party, and other political groups to block the initial deployments of the Pershing IIs in November 1983 signalled the cresting of public concern with the INF issue. The stated willingness of the Reagan Administration to negotiate a global ban on intermediate-range ballistic missiles, set forth in the President's "zero option" speech that same month, dampened some of the West German opposition to the Pershing and cruise missiles, even though the Soviets made good on their threat to walk out of the Geneva INF negotiations. By the time the United States and Soviet Union resumed arms control negotiations in March 1985 on a wider range of both offensive and defensive weapon systems, antinuclear movements in the FRG and elsewhere in Western Europe could not mobilize hundreds of thousands of citizens for public demonstrations as they had during the 1981–83 period. Yet the activist core of the West German peace movement remained strong and, in conjunction with its allies in the SPD, the Green Party, the Evangelical Church, the media, and several research and peace institutes, continued to seek strategies with which to rekindle public concern with nuclear weapons, as well as to formulate alternative security strategies for the FRG.

The SPD in Transition

Before examining the current status of the internal SPD debate on security policies, it is important to note that the leftward drift of the party in the late 1970s and early 1980s was not simply the product of rising public concern with the INF issue and deteriorating U.S.-Soviet relations. Certainly, the reemergence of a powerful West German peace movement contributed to this internal party debate; by the same token, many in the SPD hoped the party could take electoral advantage of increased public opposition to INF deployments. Yet, as was the case in the relationship between the SPD and the antinuclear *Kampf dem Atomtod* movement in 1957–58, ferment within the party developed well before there was widespread public protest. Moreover, again in a fashion similar to the situation in the 1950s, internal debate within the SPD was shaped above all by the exigencies of domestic politics, and only secondarily by foreign and defense issues. There is yet a third parallel with the late 1950s, that of an emerging counterelite (*Gegenelite*) within the party that challenged the party leadership on the SPD's security platform. Of course, the major difference in the two periods is that, in the late 1950s, the SPD was moving toward the political center; in the early 1980s, the SPD was veering back to the left.

A major factor contributing to the SPD's leftward drift was a growing dissatisfaction among many, especially younger, Germans with the centrist policies of all three major West German political parties. To a great extent, many West German citizens sought to maximize their political influence, particularly at the state and local level, on clearly defined issues such as civilian nuclear power, environmental concerns, housing, and restrictions on public sector employment. By the late 1970s, total membership in environmentalist organizations and citizen-initiative groups (*Bürgerinitiativen*) rivalled formal party membership in the SPD, FDP, and CDU/CSU.[17] It was out of these "antiparty" organizations that the Green Party coalesced in the late 1970s, and quite quickly posed a serious challenge to the SPD in several state *Länder* elections. This appearance of a political competitor to the left of the SPD, for the first time since the German Communist party was outlawed in the 1950s, sparked a debate at the 1977 Hamburg party conference that continues to this day on whether the SPD should move to the left and seek to coopt those voters being won by the Greens. Main protagonists in this debate were then party Chairman Willy Brandt, who stressed the need for the SPD to broaden its appeal to stem the flow of voter defections to the Greens, and Richard Löwenthal, a deputy chairman of the SPD Commission on Basic Values, who countered that the SPD "must opt for the majority of the working population and against peripheral groups."[18]

With the fall of the Schmidt government in 1982, however, the Brandt/Bahr wing of the party gained the upper hand. The influence of the older party moderates (Former Defense Ministers Hans Apel and Georg Leber, Wischnewski, Löwenthal) was waning, and Schmidt himself became more influential in international circles than in SPD party politics.

By the mid-1980s, then, the SPD was in full swing back to more fundamental socialist values, which many in the party felt had been compromised by the exigencies of being the party in power under Schmidt. The adoption of a party platform in Nuremberg in August 1986 put the SPD at odds with much established NATO and U.S. policy and signalled the final breakup of the security consensus that had existed between the Schmidt government and the opposition CDU/CSU. More generally, the SPD Commission on Basic Values was working on a new Basic Program for the party, to be debated at a special party conference in 1988, that continued the tradition of generational reevaluations of the party's ideology and political strategy. As with the Brandt-Löwenthal debate over political tactics vis-à-vis the Greens, the battle over future SPD security policies and the new Basic Program split along the lines of those in favor of modifying the Bad Godesberg program and those who favored a return to fundamental socialist principles that would clearly distinguish the SPD from the FDP and CDU/CSU.

The Security Debate in the SPD

No security issue more aptly characterized the leftward drift of SPD policy in the 1980s than its position on intermediate-range nuclear weapons. From the late 1970s, when the SPD-led government of Helmut Schmidt was a prime architect of the NATO dual-track decision, to 1983, when SPD delegates at the Cologne party conference voted overwhelmingly to postpone deployment of Pershing and cruise missiles in order to allow more time for arms control negotiations, party debate on security issues became increasingly dominated by the Brandt/Bahr search for ways to construct an East-West security partnership that often was at odds with NATO policy.

Nowhere was this more evident than in a draft report on security prepared for the 1986 Nuremberg party conference, authored by Andreas von Bülow, a former cabinet minister in the Schmidt government.[19] Entitled "Strategy for a Confidence-building Security System in Europe: The Way to a Security Partnership," the von Bülow paper outlined a method for implementing the "security partnership" concept of Bahr, Ehmke, and Brandt through a combination of bilateral arms control efforts and unilateral security measures on the part of the FRG and NATO.

In doing so, von Bülow and the party commission he chaired drew on diverse sources for their recommendations. For instance, from those advocating a nonprovocative defense posture for NATO, the report advocated an antitank belt of 7 to 25 kilometers along the inter-German border and a corresponding decrease in tanks and combat aircraft to minimize the potential for offensive operations. From the Palme Commission, named after the former Swedish Prime Minister, von Bülow adopted the concept of a 300 kilometer nuclear-free zone in Central Europe and a drastic reduction in short-range nuclear weapons. From a series of bilateral talks between the SPD and the East Germans on chemical weapons, the report urged the withdrawal of chemical weapons from the two Germanys, even in the absence of a U.S.-Soviet chemical weapons treaty. Finally, the report favored a number of major changes to the West German Bundeswehr, such as reducing the conscription period from fifteen months to seven to eight months in the 1990s, and either dissolving active Bundeswehr units or reducing them to cadres in order to allocate a greater share of defense tasks to reserve units.

Along with these concrete recommendations, the von Bülow report was controversial to many for what was seen as its sense of "moral equivalency" in portraying NATO and the Warsaw Pact as being equally responsible for the military confrontation in Europe. Taking its cue from the "security partnership" concept, the report stressed the need to eliminate the nuclear threat that is a central component of the NATO deterrent, greatly reduce the presence of U.S. and Soviet troops in Europe, and eventually dismantle the opposing military blocs.

Predictably enough, the report was not only castigated by the CDU/CSU, but became the subject of a full-scale Bundestag debate.[20] In addition, there was some criticism of the report from within the SPD. Party experts on security issues, such as Erwin Horn, as well as members of the SPD Executive Board, sought to disassociate themselves from the report and downplay the unilateral aspects of von Bülow's recommendations.[21] In particular, the SPD Executive Board issued a statement saying that the party was not contemplating advocating unilateral withdrawal of U.S. troops, that a militia structure like that of Switzerland for the FRG was "out of the question," and that, while some restructuring of the Bundeswehr in the 1990s might be necessary for demographic reasons, there was no intent to reduce the conscription period drastically. More broadly, the statement reaffirmed West Germany's role in NATO as a necessary precondition for the FRG's *Ostpolitik* and drew an explicit link between any future withdrawal of U.S. and Soviet troops and the creation of a European security system that could accommodate eventual German reunification.[22]

In seeking to downplay the more radical elements of von Bülow's report for SPD policy, the party leadership instructed the SPD commission on security to submit a new draft in advance of the Nuremberg party conference. However, it was by no means certain that the majority of the SPD was dissatisfied with von Bülow's report. In January 1986, for example, a paper was published by the Friedrich Ebert Foundation, a research institute affiliated with the SPD, that spelled out in detail the concept of an enlarged security partnership between West and East Germany. Written by Wilhelm Bruns, a specialist in inter-German relations, the paper listed a number of steps for institutionalizing a security dialogue between Bonn and East Berlin.[23] Among other items, Bruns proposed that the two Germanys:

1. Formulate joint proposals at the Stockholm conference on Confidence-Building and Security Measures in Europe;

2. Seek to establish tradeoffs between those elements of NATO and Warsaw Pact force structures that are most threatening to the other side, such as NATO adopting no first-use policy on nuclear weapons in exchange for the Warsaw Pact giving up its superiority in tanks;

3. Enter governmental negotiations on establishing a chemical weapons-free zone covering the FRG and GDR, along the lines proposed by the SPD and SED, without waiting for a U.S.-Soviet agreement;

4. Reduce their military budgets and make available some of the savings for Third World development aid;

5. Take joint steps to speed up progress at the MBFR talks and the U.S.-Soviet negotiations in Geneva.

In proposing such steps, Bruns drew on those elements of a new security policy for the SPD that Brandt and Bahr formulated as early as 1977, and also reiterated some of the recommendations of the von Bülow report. In essence, what was proposed was a widening of the inter-German relationship beyond its traditional socioeconomic focus to include formal ties between the two Germanys, including negotiations on security issues, that West German governments previously had handled within the context of NATO and the Western Alliance. Taken together, the von Bülow report and the Bruns article provided a good indication in early 1986 of the likely direction of SPD security policies. In April 1986, the SPD Executive released the revised draft of the security platform that would be debated in Nuremberg, and it indeed contained many of the unilateral initiatives advocated by von Bülow and Bruns for breaking the East-West arms control stalemate.[24] It is true that the document forcefully acknowledged West Germany's role in the Western Alliance, saying that its concept of an East-West security partnership could only be carried out with an FRG firmly anchored in NATO.[25] In doing so, the document sought to answer the criticisms of many in the SPD that the original von Bülow draft had gone too far in espousing a unilateral role for West Germany in mediating East-West tensions. Nonetheless, the platform contained numerous items that were greatly at odds with official NATO policy, the more important being:

1. A reaffirmation of an earlier SPD call for an immediate halt to INF deployments and the withdrawal of those Pershing and cruise missiles already deployed;

2. A freeze on all deployments of nuclear weapons, on nuclear testing, and on development and testing of antisatellite weapons and other space-based weapons, for the duration of the arms control negotiations in Geneva;

3. The withdrawal of battlefield nuclear weapons and the creation of a nuclear-free corridor in central Europe, as proposed by the Palme Commission;

4. The withdrawal of all chemical weapons from central Europe and the establishment of a chemical weapons-free zone in Europe; and

5. The rejection of NATO deep-strike strategies, such as "AirLand Battle 2000" and "Follow-on Forces Attack".

In addition, the security platform criticized the American SDI program and made clear that an SPD-led government would reject West German participation in both SDI and any European effort to develop antitactical ballistic missile (ATBM) defenses, as had been proposed by the CDU Defense Minister, Manfred Wörner.[26] Also, the SPD pledged to cut the West German defense budget; to oppose extending the period of conscription from fifteen to eighteen months; and gradually to assign a greater role for reservists as a means of dealing with the manpower problems facing the Bundeswehr.

The report did criticize the Soviet Union for its steady military buildup, noting in particular that the deployment of the short-range ballistic missiles in Eastern Europe contradicted Soviet statements regarding a "no first-use" policy. Well before it was evident that the United States and the Soviet Union would successfully negotiate an INF treaty, the SPD called upon the Soviets to reduce deployments of its SS-20 missiles to 1979 levels and withdraw those tactical ballistic missiles (the SS-12/22 especially) that were deployed in eastern Europe following the NATO INF deployments. Also, Moscow was urged to abandon the Warsaw Pact's offensive-oriented strategies in Central Europe, and show greater flexibility in reaching accords on nuclear weapons, troop levels in Europe, chemical weapons, and confidence-building measures.

Finally, the platform went to great lengths to assert that, although the FRG and GDR were considered to have a special role in bringing about an East-West security partnership, "the two German states are not following a separate course but seeking support in their respective alliances for aims which they cannot achieve alone." By working within their respective alliances, the report noted, a "second phase of détente" could be initiated with the aim of making Europe a "zone of peace," at which time "the alliances will have lost their significance and served their purpose."[27]

In sum, the revised draft of the party's security platform distributed prior to the Nuremberg conference contained most of the policy initiatives raised earlier in the von Bülow draft, even though it was more moderate in tone and paid more attention to the FRG's role in the Western Alliance. On the other hand, little was said about how and whether the GDR and other members of the Warsaw Pact could exert the kind of pressure on the Soviets that an SPD-led West Germany could be expected to wield within NATO. The one-sided criticism of U.S. nuclear weapons policies that earlier had characterized the West German Peace Movement led many, both within the FRG and elsewhere, to feel that the SPD was indeed searching for a third way between the superpowers that was in fundamental conflict with NATO policy.

The Nuremberg Party Conference and the 1987 Election

The SPD conference held in Nuremberg in August 1986 signalled the beginning of the party's national election campaign, and provided the first substantive indication of the policies on which the SPD would seek to regain the Chancellorship in January 1987. The revised security report was adopted by the 400-plus party delegates with virtually no dissent. If anything, many delegates felt that the party's security policies did not go far enough; most of approximately 100 amendments and motions offered from the floor called for more radical security initiatives. One amendment that was defeated stipulated that a newly elected SPD government must ensure that the U.S. Pershing and cruise missiles be removed from West Germany within six months, whether or not an arms control agreement had been reached.[28]

The consolidation of power by the party's left wing was demonstrated in other ways as well. On nuclear energy, the SPD promised, if elected, to shut down all nuclear power plants within ten years, a move that disquieted some of the party's allies in the West German trade union movement. In elections to the SPD Executive Board (*Vorstand*) and other leadership positions, party moderates fared poorly. The extent of the breakup of the once powerful Schmidt "government" wing of the party was clear to all as one former Schmidt cabinet member (Georg Leber, Defense) lost his seat on the *Vorstand*, while another (Volker Hauff, Research and Technology), reversed his earlier support for nuclear power to become the prime spokesman for the party's antinuclear policies.[29]

In many ways, von Bülow and Hauff were symbolic of the leftward drift of the party since the Schmidt years. From having been ministers in a Schmidt government defending moderate policies, both men by the mid-1980s were in charge of important party commissions (Hauff was in charge of the environment and ecology commission) advocating radical shifts in policy. At the Nuremberg conference, Hauff declared that the future of atomic energy was past, while von Bülow's opening speech on security suggested a similar SPD preference for the future of NATO. Commenting on the demise of the once-powerful Schmidt faction and the left-wing victory at the Nuremberg conference, Hauff noted that "an historical era has ended."[30]

In addition to this shifting center of gravity within the party, different left-wing strands within the party were coalescing. Along with the moderate left wing led by Brandt, Bahr, and parliamentary leader Herbert Wehner (the *Verantwortungslinke*, or responsible left), there was also a more extreme left led by Eppler and Oskar Lafontaine (the *Gewissenslinke*, or conscientious left)[31]. During the Schmidt years, the "responsible" left, kept in line especially by Wehner, grudgingly went along with the Chancellor's policies, while the "conscientious" left was vocal in its opposition. Increasingly in the 1980s, however, these two left-wing strands came together, along with former centrists such as Hauff and von Bülow. The high point of this coalescing occurred at the Nuremberg conference, where delegates exhibited a sense of party unity and purpose not evident for many years.[32] The internal tensions that had plagued the SPD during the Schmidt years had abated, and in Johannes Rau, the SPD seemed to have a candidate for Chancellor who could appeal to a wide spectrum of voters. Thus there was cautious optimism regarding the January 1987 election, despite opinion polls showing the voters preferring the government coalition by a margin of 51 percent to 40 percent over the SPD.[33]

In the end, such optimism was short-lived. During the campaign, the moderate Rau (known as "Brother Johannes, the preacher's son from Wuppertal") found himself increasingly at odds with the leftist party leadership, which had strengthened its position in elections to the party presidium in the fall of 1986.[34] The party's Bundestag candidates drifted leftward as well, causing Rau to find himself in a bind between the party leadership at the national level and SPD parliamentary candidates at the district level.

More important than the situation within the SPD, however, was the strong political position of the incumbent government of Chancellor Helmut Kohl. Despite some political stumbling of its own in 1986, the Kohl government was able to capitalize on a fairly robust West German economy in its election campaign. On security issues, the resumption of U.S.-Soviet arms control talks and a lessening of East-West tensions from earlier years seemed to vindicate the Kohl government's policy of proceeding with deployment of the Pershing and cruise missiles in the face of widespread public opposition in 1983 and 1984.

Ultimately, what surprises there were in the January 1987 election had less to do with the two major parties than with the strong showing of Genscher's FDP and low voter turnout. The latter figure of 84.4 percent, the lowest since the first West German election in 1949, was due in part to bad weather, but also symbolized the lackluster nature and foregone conclusion of the campaign. This low voter turnout partially explains the disappointing showing for the CDU/CSU, whose share of the vote fell to 44.3 percent (from 48.8 percent in 1983). The result for the governing coalition, however, was little changed from 1983, as many CDU voters especially (some 800,000) gave their all important "second vote" (*zweite Stimme*) to the FDP, whose share of the vote increased from 7 percent in 1983 to 9.1 percent in the 1987 election. The SPD, meanwhile, also declined (from 38.2 percent in 1983 to 37 percent in 1987), with some of their support sliding left to the Greens, who remained a parliamentary force to be reckoned with, at 8.3 percent.[35]

Given the very unlikely possibility of a "red-green" coalition between the SPD and the Green Party, following the 1987 election the SPD faced the prospect of remaining out of power, at least until 1991, if not beyond. Despite the public's concern with foreign and security issues, most West German voters cast their votes primarily on economic and domestic issues. Moreover, something akin to an "iron law" still exists in West German politics, whereby the major political parties cannot afford to be perceived as being soft on defense and security issues.[36] Despite the tensions created by the INF issue and Reagan Administration policies, most West Germans continued to support West Germany's role in NATO strongly; were wary of changes in the NATO deterrent (as was evident following the Reykjavik summit); and also believed that the INF deployments had improved West German security (which explained West German skepticism of an INF arms control agreement).

Especially noteworthy was the fact that this last sentiment was shared by first-time German voters, aged sixteen to twenty-four. At the height of the Euromissile crisis in 1983, this age group thought the INF deployments would increase the likelihood of Soviet attack rather than improve West German security (by 54 to 18 percent), yet in 1984 the results of such polls were just the reverse (26 to 42 percent).[37]

The attitudes and beliefs of these younger voters are of crucial importance to the SPD. What appears to be happening is that the Green Party and the left wing of the SPD are appealing mainly to those in the thirty to forty-five age bracket; that is, those West Germans who experienced the West German student protests of the late 1960s or the environmental, single-issue politics of the 1970s; who were greatly affected by the explosion in the FRG university population in the 1970s; and who experienced difficulty in finding jobs during the recessions of the early and late 1970s. As is the case elsewhere in Western Europe and the United States, many of those born after the socially active 1960s are more conservative and concerned with issues of job security than their counterparts in the thirty to forty-five age bracket.

Polling data from the 1980 and 1983 elections seem to bear this out.[38] In 1980, the SPD won the votes of 49 percent of those aged eighteen to twenty-four, but this figure slipped to 39 percent in the 1983 election. The Green Party was the main beneficiary of this, increasing its share of this vote from 5 percent in 1980 to 14 percent in 1983. Yet the CDU/CSU also benefited, going from 34 percent in 1980 to 41 percent in 1983. Thus the

SPD lost the support of younger voters to both the Greens and the CDU/CSU; this trend must change if the party is to do well in future elections.

Because polling data and the realities of West German electoral politics suggest that the SPD will remain out of power—and free from the constraints of being the governing party—until the 1990s, the party can be expected to continue to push its "security partnership" concept vigorously. The extent to which it will stress the more unilateral aspects of its security policies, however, partially will depend not only on changes within the party, but also on the support it finds for such policies among its key political allies, such as the trade union movement, the Evangelical Church, and the activist core of the peace movement.

Continuity and Change in West German Politics

During the 1957–58 *Kampf dem Atomtod* movement, the SPD sought to make common cause in opposing Adenauer's nuclear weapons policy with three main groups: the German Trade Union Confederation (DGB), the Evangelical Church (EKD), and the grass roots peace movement. Outwardly at least, the situation in the 1980s has been quite similar, in that the party looks to the DGB and EKD to legitimize its policies with the West German electorate at large, while it sees the peace movement as a way to stimulate grass roots support for its policies. What is different, of course, is the changed nature of the West German political environment.

As noted previously, West German politics in the 1950s were dominated by the anti-Communist ideology and rhetoric of the Cold War. This made it risky for the SPD to advocate policies that could be portrayed as serving Soviet and East German aims. It was partly for this reason that the SPD tempered its support for the *Kampf dem Atomtod* movement in 1958 and ultimately dissassociated itself from the antinuclear campaign prior to its adoption of the moderate Bad Godesberg program.

In the 1980s, anti-Communism as an ideological force in West German domestic politics has largely been replaced by various strains of West German nationalism.[39] This process has been evolutionary, beginning with East-West détente and the FRG's *Ostpolitik* in the early 1970s, accelerating during the chancellorship of Helmut Schmidt, and finding perhaps its purest expression, in the SPD at least, during the 1983 election campaign, when the party's election slogan was "*Im Deutschen Interesse*" ("In the German Interest").

Within the SPD, as in the country at large, nationalist sentiments take many different forms. Some of the extreme left wing of the party speak contemptuously of West Germany's "complete dependence . . . without full sovereignty," when they attack U.S. policies. In advocating greater leeway for the FRG in pursuing a "third way" between the superpowers, Egon Bahr believes that the United States "is, in the end, but a power to be weighed on the scales of German national interest."[40] Somewhat more moderately, Willy Brandt casts his German nationalism in the sense of West Germany playing the role of mediator in alleviating East-West tensions and bringing about a more equitable economic order between the industrialized North and the underdeveloped South.[41] Central to these different strains, however, is the need for Germany to overcome the legacy of the Nazi past and to be in the forefront of seeking to reduce tensions in Central Europe. As Brandt has noted many times, German nationalist sentiments in the SPD, predicated as they are on establishing a new European peace order through political, nonviolent means, are far different than those that existed during either the Bismarck era or the Third Reich.

This parallel rise of German assertiveness and the deideologization of West German politics has given the SPD increased maneuverability in formulating its security policies. As can be seen by the extent to which a CDU/CSU government has continued the SPD's *Ostpolitik* practically unchanged, anti-Communist sentiments have little force in West German politics. Thus, the SPD is able to promote the security partnership concept and increased security consultations with the GDR as being legitimate national interests for the FRG.

Where the party runs into problems is the extent to which these policies are seen as conflicting with the country's Western interests and relationships with its NATO allies. As David Calleo has noted, by the late 1970s the three natural foreign policy spheres of the Federal Republic (the Atlantic, the European, and the Eastern) had become equally viable, necessitating difficult tradeoffs when they conflicted (e.g., U.S. criticism of Helmut Schmidt's support for the Soviet gas pipeline).[42] It is these tradeoffs that the SPD is attempting to reconcile through its East-West security partnership, on the one hand, and its adherence to the Atlantic Alliance and West European integration on the other. It is undoubtedly true that the party's commitment to arms control and to reducing tensions, even if the FRG must pursue unilateral policies to achieve these aims, is attractive to a great many West Germans who are skeptical of superpower efforts to ease East-West tensions. Yet, in seeming to give priority to its Eastern policy over West Germany's Atlantic and European interests, the

SPD has increased suspicions among its Western allies, portions of the West German electorate, and some of its traditional political allies (the trade unions in particular) that the party is undermining the FRG's western interests.

The SPD and West German Trade Unions

The most salient fact regarding political cooperation between the SPD and trade unions in the FRG is that, unlike France, Italy, or Great Britain, Germany has a long tradition of trade union independence from the left-wing political parties, whether socialist or Communist. This relative autonomy dates from the SPD party congress in Mannheim in 1906, when moderate trade union delegates, in blocking Rosa Luxemburg's call for greater use of the general strike as a political weapon, were able to establish the semi-independence of the trade union movement. The experience of the Weimar Republic, where political divisions between socialists and Communists greatly weakened the labor movement and helped facilitate Hitler's rise to power, was even more important in convincing trade union leaders in the late 1940s of the need to establish a clear position of autonomy from the West German political parties, to avoid being weakened by internecine disputes.[43]

Accordingly, organized labor in the early years of the Federal Republic concentrated its efforts primarily on economic issues to avoid becoming sidetracked by political issues not central to the welfare of the German worker. Wanting to avoid the ideological strife that weakened the Weimar labor movement, the German Trade Union Confederation (DGB) organized its dozen constituent unions in a confederal structure. With 20 percent of the rank and file usually voting Christian Democratic in national elections, the DGB maintains strong ties to the CDU/CSU, even though the DGB executive board itself is overwhelmingly made up of Social Democrats. This desire on the part of the DGB to tolerate ideological diversity within the labor movement and to work effectively with both SPD and CDU/CSU governments has meant that the DGB is judicious on those nonlabor issues where it confronts the government in power.[44] Even more, it means that the DGB is extremely cautious in advocating a general strike on anything but economic issues, and even then only when its member unions are in agreement. This caution was clearly demonstrated during the antinuclear protests in 1957–58, when the leaders of the DGB came out against mobilizing a general strike to oppose Adenauer's policies, even though West German public opinion was in favor of such a strike.[45]

The situation during the rise of the peace movement in the early 1980s and the mass protests against INF deployment has been similar. Although individual trade union leaders had gone on record as opposing the deployment of the Pershing and cruise missiles, and some of the more left-wing unions (e.g., the printers' union) lent organizational support to the peace movement, the DGB as a body avoided taking an active stand for fear of politicizing its membership and weakening its influence with the CDU/CSU government. Given the changes in business-labor relations brought about by the postindustrial and "microelectronic" revolution, with the composition of the German work force changing and state funding for social welfare policies harder to come by, the West German trade unions are interested primarily in establishing a *modus vivendi* with a Christian Democratic government that may be in power for another half decade or more.[46] While there will continue to be trade union sympathy, and in some cases, active involvement, with Social Democratic opposition to the government's policies, DGB interests will not always coincide with those of the SPD, especially regarding the future of civilian nuclear power.

Overall, then, the DGB will probably be a moderating force on SPD policies. Unlike the situation in Britain, for example, where the Trade Unions Congress (TUC) is organizationally represented within the Labour Party and seeks to push the party to the left, the DGB, to the extent that its leaders hold important positions within the SPD, will act as a brake on the implementing of the party's more radical policies when it returns to power.

The SPD and the Evangelical Church

The religious strife between Roman Catholics and Protestants that has characterized German history is now largely absent in the FRG, yet voting and political affiliation still breaks down along confessional lines. The CDU/CSU, for instance, is the successor to the Catholic Center Party of the Weimar period, and still draws heavily on the Catholic vote in Bavaria and the Rhineland, while the SPD has at times garnered as much as 65 percent of the Protestant vote.[47] Just as important, there is a strong tradition of active Church involvement in domestic politics, at least compared to the situation in the United States.

The 29 million Protestants in the FRG, of whom some 5 million are regular churchgoers, are represented by the Evangelical Church of Germany (EKD). Similar to the German trade unions, the EKD was scarred by its ineffective opposition to Hitler and the atrocities of the Third Reich. At its first major postwar conference in 1947, Church leaders vowed to "assume the enormous and difficult duty of playing a much greater part than before in influencing public life and especially the political community."[48] Yet, while the EKD saw its sphere of action as more broadly political than did the DGB, Church leaders were nonetheless wary of indulging in partisan politics and undermining Church unity. During the 1950s, for example, the EKD as a whole was strongly antimilitarist and provided both moral and organizational support to the campaigns against German rearmament and the deployment of nuclear weapons. Yet when prominent members of the Church, such as Gustav Heinemann and Pastor Martin Niemoeller, attempted to take the Church directly into the streets, they were removed from their positions in the Church hierarchy. As one commentator noted, this repudiation of Heinemann and Niemoeller by the EKD synod "marked the formal rejection of any attempt to transform German Protestantism into an active, partisan political force. . . . There would be no political crusades and no Protestant political army."[49]

Nonetheless, it is true that the EKD came much closer than the DGB to taking an organizational stand against Adenauer's nuclear weapons policies. In the late 1950s and early 1960s, the EKD remained in the forefront of the *Kampf dem Atomtod* campaign and the Easter peace marches, and many individual Church figures who were prominent in those debates are still active today in trying to shape SPD policy.

The Church exercises a great deal of influence on SPD policies at this level of individual contacts between the EKD and the SPD. For example, the physicist Carl Friedrich von Weizsäcker, one of the signers of the 1957 Göttingen appeal that helped launch the antinuclear movement, in 1983 was a security advisor to SPD chancellor-candidate Hans-Jochen Vogel (von Weizsäcker's brother, Richard, a Christian Democrat, is currently President of the Federal Republic). A second example, Erhard Eppler, is one of the leaders of the SPD left wing and a member of the executive board of the EKD. There are also numerous individuals who were active in both the *Kampf dem Atomtod* and the INF protests of the early 1980s, including Niemoeller and the Lutheran Pastors Helmut Gollwitzer and Heinrich Albertz (the latter a former SPD mayor of West Berlin).

More broadly, the EKD has been as deeply involved in the 1980s peace movement as it was in the 1950s. Though EKD synods still shy away from overtly supporting any political party, the Church has made common cause with large segments of the SPD in supporting the peace movement and stimulating grass roots activism on peace issues. In 1981, the EKD adopted the issues of peace and disarmament for its annual *Kirchentag* (Church Conference), drawing over 100,000 people to Hamburg. By the same token, however, the leadership of the EKD has also expressed discomfort with what it sees as an increasingly anti-American tone among many peace movement activists.[50]

Another important trend is the increasing attraction that the EKD holds, in part because of its criticism of nuclear weapons and nuclear power, for large numbers of younger Germans. In the same way that many young Germans are seeking alternative political vehicles in citizens-initiative and environmental organizations, so too are they finding an outlet in the Protestant Church. It is difficult to know how widespread this phenomenon of "internal emigration" is, but there is a sense that the Church is providing a spiritual haven for many young people from what they see as the "business as usual" atmosphere of West German politics and society. Reinforcing this trend is a similar pattern in the GDR, where the Protestant Church has taken the lead in mobilizing young East Germans in protests against nuclear weapons and the militarization of East German society. As one analyst has noted, "the large number of adolescents flocking to ecclesiastical synods in both Germanies does not signify a religious revival in the making. Rather, it is the Church's age-old tradition of providing sanctuary that has attracted these displaced flower-children born a generation too late."[51]

In sum, the EKD in the years ahead can be expected to continue its moral suasion against the nuclear arms race, as well as provide organizational support at the local level to the antinuclear movement. In both these ways, the Church can bolster those on the left wing of the SPD who argue for radically new measures to achieve disarmament in Central Europe and safeguard German security. To the extent that SPD leaders like Eppler can convince the EKD hierarchy to elaborate on its condemnation of nuclear weapons and superpower policies, the policies of the SPD will be strengthened. In the end, however, a concern for Church unity will likely mean that the EKD will confine itself to broad moral arguments on nuclear weapon issues, leaving the SPD, the CDU/CSU, the FDP, and the Greens to argue over which party has the most convincing political strategy for safeguarding the security of the German people.

The SPD and the Peace Movement

In many respects, the West German peace movement that coalesced in the early 1980s around the INF issue was little different in composition from the *Kampf dem Atomtod* movement of the late 1950s. As was the case in the 1950s, the 1980s peace movement was a diverse mix, spanning the political spectrum from Communists to clergymen, ecologists to military figures, the youth organizations of the SPD and FDP, and members of the labor movement and the media. A major difference, however, was in the central role played in the 1980s by both the Greens and a new constellation of security experts outside the government and political parties. This *"Gegenelite,"* centered in numerous West German peace research institutes and the media, continues to be a prime source of new security strategies (e.g., ''nonprovocative defense'' schemes) that have been adopted by activists in the peace movement, as well as the SPD left wing, in opposition to the pro-NATO policies of the CDU/CSU government and the Schmidt wing of the SPD. Thus, unlike the 1950s, when the Erler *et al.* "Gegenelite" of the SPD moved the party toward the adoption of pro-NATO policies, this new group of counterexperts is helping draw the SPD to the left.

A second difference in the relationship of the SPD to the peace movement has been that the central role played by the Greens has reduced the ability of the SPD leadership to influence the tactics and goals of the movement. In 1958, the *Kampf dem Atomtod* movement lost much of its momentum when the SPD began to withdraw its support of mass protests and switched to a strategy of challenging the constitutionality of Adenauer's nuclear weapons deployment decision. By contrast, the leaders of the current peace movement who identify with the Green Party have consciously tried to keep the SPD from gaining too much influence over the movement, in part out of fear of being coopted by the SPD.

There is yet a third difference worth mentioning, and that is the greater cooperation between the left wing of the SPD and the Communist-front organizations (e.g., the German Peace Union) associated with the peace movement. The deideologization of West German politics mentioned above has resulted in closer collaboration on the peace issue between the SPD left and the small German Communist Party (DKP). Consequently, SPD organizations at the local level are participating in the DKP-sponsored Easter Marches for the first time since the late 1950s. The reduced salience of anti-Communism in West German politics is not the only reason, however, that the SPD left wing has more room to maneuver in collaborating with Communist groups. Just as important is the changed perception of many in the SPD regarding the Soviet Union, where the USSR is now seen as less an ideological foe, driven by Marxism-Leninism, than as a hegemonic superpower whose goals actually differ little from those of the United States.[52] It is this increase within the SPD of seeing the two superpowers as "morally equidistant" which has given the Soviet Union greater scope for trying to influence SPD security policies, and which has also increased criticism of the SPD from Western critics in the United States, France, and elsewhere.

The SPD and the Soviet Union

Over the past decade, there has been a marked increase in contacts at the party level between the SPD and the CPSU, over and above the governmental relations that developed between the Brandt and Schmidt governments and Moscow. In part, this stems from Brandt's *Ostpolitik* and the "opening to the East," but there has been a fundamental shift as well regarding Moscow's attitude toward West European socialist and social democratic parties in general, and the SPD in particular.

Following the end of World War II, Soviet policy concentrated on building up the Communist parties in Western Europe and essentially regarded the non-Communist left in Europe as "social fascists" to be avoided and isolated. Because the German SPD was both anti-Communist (Adenauer's assertions to the contrary) and a major advocate of German reunification, Moscow regarded the SPD with special hostility. Moreover, the Eastern industrial regions of Germany had been a stronghold of the prewar SPD, so that Moscow and the East German regime were apprehensive about the effect that SPD-inspired reunification proposals could have on the stability of the GDR.

It wasn't until the Berlin Wall helped solidify the SED regime, and the entry into power of the Brandt government helped to normalize relations at the governmental level, that Moscow began to revise its attitude toward the SPD in particular and Western social democratic parties in general.

Since the mid-1970s, the SPD's relationship with Moscow has devloped over a wide range of issues.[53] In 1981, the Central Committee of the CPSU extended an offer of formal cooperation to West European socialist and social democratic parties on security issues; this was followed by the creation of institutional links between the CPSU and the Socialist

International's Advisory Council on Disarmament and Arms Control. With the fall of the Schmidt government in 1982 and the decreased influence of SPD moderates, these nongovernmental, party-to-party contacts have gained increased importance. At present, there are numerous such links between the SPD and CPSU, including working groups on arms control and defense issues; exchanges between the editorial staffs of the SPD journal, *Die Neue Gesellschaft*, and the CPSU journal, *Kommunist*; and frequent visits of party delegations. In addition, the Soviets have at the very least tolerated, if not actively supported, similar contacts between the SPD and SED in East Germany (see below), as well as with other East European Communist parties. An example of the latter that provoked some protest in the FRG occurred when Willy Brandt traveled to Warsaw in December 1985 to discuss the security partnership concept with General Jaruzelski, yet reportedly managed to avoid any mention of Solidarity during his stay.[54]

The extent to which the Soviets can use such contacts to actually shape SPD policy is probably quite limited. Nonetheless, Soviet receptivity to the SPD "security partnership" concept, as well as greater Soviet willingness to explore the feasibility of Nordic, Central European, and Mediterranean nuclear-free zones, as well as other arms control proposals, does represent an increased convergence on policy issues between the USSR and the SPD and other West European socialist and social democratic parties. When seen in the context of a broad range of Soviet efforts to influence Western public opinion (whether in the form of covert funding for the peace movements, greater access of Soviet spokesmen to Western media, or traditional disinformation campaigns), there is little question that the "deideologization" of West German politics referred to earlier does offer the Soviets greater opportunities than previously in the postwar period of capitalizing on divisions within NATO.[55]

The SPD and East Germany

It is hardly surprising that the current "security partnership" concept of the SPD can trace its origins to the *Ostpolitik* initiated by Willy Brandt when he became Chancellor in 1969. In tandem with U.S. efforts to promote superpower détente, the Brandt government concluded renunciation of force agreements with the USSR and Poland, and then the Basic Treaty with East Germany, in an attempt to normalize the FRG's relations with Eastern Europe.

In the beginning, this *Deutschlandpolitik* between the FRG and GDR focused primarily on issues of "low politics", that is, trade, transportation, energy, and common environmental concerns. More politically sensitive issues, such as West German recognition of GDR sovereignty, questions of German citizenship, access by West Germans to friends and family in the GDR, and the ability of East Germans to emigrate to the FRG, were discussed as well, but not resolved to the satisfaction of either state. It was only in the late 1970s that *Deutschlandpolitik* began, slowly and tentatively, to include common security concerns such as arms control and confidence-building measures that up until then had been handled primarily within the context of NATO and the Warsaw Pact.[56]

A breakthrough of sorts on security issues was achieved at the Schmidt-Honecker summit in December 1981, when the two heads of government agreed to try to formulate a joint initiative that could break the deadlock at the MBFR talks in Vienna on conventional forces.[57] The fact that Foreign Minister Genscher met in early 1982 with his East German counterpart, Oskar Fischer, to try to reach agreement on a common position was a departure from the usual FRG practice of entrusting such contacts to its Minister for Inner-German Relations (in this case, Egon Franke). By the same token, the GDR had usually avoided participating in talks with the FRG that went beyond strictly German concerns for fear of compromising its status as a sovereign state (considering that the FRG has refused to recognize the GDR as a sovereign, legal entity). In this case, however, the opportunity to deal directly with Genscher on an issue of such importance overcame East German hesitations.

Although no concrete proposals ever emerged from the web of contacts between disarmament officials of the two Germanys, the process itself was noteworthy, not only for inter-German relations, but for foreign perceptions of those relations as well. As one West German editorial writer commented, in evaluating Western reaction, increased contacts between the FRG and GDR "trip alarm bells in foreign capitals, as the world believes it can live more safely if the Germans are quarreling rather than agreeing."[58]

These attempts by the Schmidt government to open up lines of communication with East Berlin have since been continued by the Kohl government; they culminated in September 1987 with Erich Honecker's visit to the FRG, the first such visit by an East German head of state. At the same time, however, the SPD has been conducting its own bilateral talks with East German officials on a wide range of security issues. In March 1984, for instance, the SPD began a series of talks with officials of the East German Socialist Unity Party (SED) on ways to create a chemical weapons-free zone in Central Europe.[59] Strictly speaking, these "party-to-party" discussions were little different than the contacts the SPD had followed while in power, given the confluence of party and government in the GDR. At the conclusion of the fifth round of talks, in June 1985, the SPD and SED reached agreement on a draft proposal. Claiming this as a concrete expression of its security partnership policy, SPD spokesmen said the proposal, which included provisions for on-site inspection by an international commission, could provide the basis for formal governmental negotiations.[60]

Not surprisingly, the East German and Czechoslovak governments followed up quickly with a proposal to the Kohl government in September 1985 suggesting that the three countries begin negotiations on chemical weapons in Central Europe. The Kohl government demurred, saying it did not want to complicate the ongoing Geneva negotiations working toward a global ban on chemical weapons. As expressed by government spokesman Friedhelm Ost, the SPD-SED initiative was politely brushed aside, on the grounds that the Geneva negotiations should not "be circumvented through regional partial solutions."[61]

The fact that the SPD was negotiating directly with the SED (i.e., the East German government), an act that would have been an immense political liability in the 1950s, passed with little additional comment from the Kohl government. Nonetheless, the talks did raise political sensibilities within the United States and NATO (not least because the only chemical weapons in the FRG are American), implying that the party was undermining the Alliance through its independent initiatives. Similar efforts between the SPD and SED on nuclear weapons in Central Europe, as well as SPD talks with the Communist parties of the Soviet Union, Poland, and the GDR on ways to reduce defense expenditures, have added to speculation that the SPD would implement a more unilateral foreign policy if and when it returns to power.

Given that the SPD most likely will remain out of power until the 1990s, the significance of these bilateral contacts with Warsaw Pact states has been more symbolic than real. And it is even questionable how far a future SPD government would go in seeking to implement bilateral accords, given probable Allied and domestic opposition. At a minimum, however, this type of SPD-SED dialogue does focus attention on common German security concerns, while indirectly maintaining pressure on the Kohl government to preserve and expand the gains of *Ostpolitik*.

SUMMARY: THE LIKELY DRIFT OF SPD POLICY

Despite anxieties in the West that the SPD is sliding down the slippery slope of unilateralism toward fundamental opposition to NATO, the current situation within the SPD remains ambiguous. Opinions range from those of Oskar Lafontaine, who advocates a West German withdrawal from NATO's military command structure, to Willy Brandt, who is seeking a way of reducing East-West tensions in order to divert resources to what, for him, is the more important problem of North-South inequities. Others in the party, such as Karsten Voigt, argue that a West German role in the Western Alliance remains a necessary, but not an overriding, precondition for West German policy. If anything is clear about the evolution of SPD policy, however, it is that the moderate positions of Schmidt (who retired from the Bundestag following the January 1987 election), are on the decline, with little chance of regaining their former influence anytime soon.

One important factor influencing the direction of SPD policy arises from the changes in party leadership following Willy Brandt's resignation as party chairman in the spring of 1987. Hans-Jochen Vogel, who succeeded Brandt, is probably an interim caretaker at best, given his uninspiring performance as the party's candidate for chancellor in the 1983 election. More likely, the struggle over party direction will be played out between those party factions loyal to the two deputy party chairmen, Oskar Lafontaine and Johannes Rau. Although much will depend on the outcome of the 1988 special party conference and the new party program, the doubts that emerged during the 1987 compaign concerning Rau's ability to hold the party together,[62] have resulted in Lafontaine being well positioned to be the party's candidate for chancellor in the next election, scheduled for 1991.[63]

Whatever the outcome of this leadership struggle, the issue of U.S.-West German relations remains especially important in understanding current SPD security policy. While it is true that many in the party feel that the Schmidt years compromised basic SPD values and that a fundamental revision of the Bad Godesberg program is in order, the SPD debate on security issues has been influenced just as heavily by the defense and arms control policies of the Reagan Administration. Despite the (apparently) successful outcome of the U.S.-Soviet agreement on INF, many in the SPD remain suspicious of U.S. policies in general.

This is particularly true of the younger, postwar generation of SPD members whose attitudes toward the United States were shaped by

Vietnam and U.S. policies in the Third World, rather than by the Marshall Plan and European reconstruction. The attitudes of those aged twenty-five to forty are not necessarily anti-American, though they do tend more toward neutralism and deep mistrust of both superpowers. Rather, they are shaped by a desire for new initiatives on both European and global security issues that often conflict with U.S. policy. This will remain the case even though an INF agreement (including Chancellor Kohl's concession on dismantling the Pershing 1a missiles) and the improved prospects for a global ban on chemical weapons have stolen the thunder from SPD-inspired unilateral initiatives. Despite the progress in U.S.-Soviet arms control efforts, there will remain many policy issues (Central America, the Mideast, development policies) dividing the SPD from the United States.

By the same token, the current drift of SPD policies is causing concern elsewhere in the Alliance, especially in France. It is ironic, given the close Franco-German ties developed by Schmidt and Giscard d'Estaing, that at a time when France seems more amenable to coordinating its security policy with NATO and the FRG, the SPD is edging toward unilateralist policies that cause more alarm in Paris than anywhere else.

There is probably no issue that so differentiates the SPD from current American policy than that of the Strategic Defense Initiative (SDI). Beginning with President Reagan's speech of March 1983, the SPD has opposed both the goal of a space-based missile defense system and any form of West German participation in the SDI program. In October 1985, soon after Defense Minister Woerner called for a European ATBM effort to complement the SDI, the SPD participated with other European socialist parties in a "European Workshop on Space Weapons." SPD criticisms of the SDI at the conference ranged from Bahr calling "crazy" any attempt to find security in space, to calls by Vogel for the demilitarization of space, to Karsten Voigt saying that the FRG must not "participate in undermining the ABM Treaty" through collaboration of SDI projects. Any formal West German connection to the SDI was called "irresponsible," while Bundestag member Hermann Scheer criticized Wörner's ATBM proposal as being "more comprehensive, technologically more complex, and thus much more expensive than an SDI program."[64]

Summarizing the view that the SDI goal of a defense-dominant world is not only illusory but has complicated efforts to reduce offensive nuclear weapons (a position not unknown in the United States), Voigt called for: (1) unilateral disarmament measures by both East and West as a spur to negotiated settlements; (2) agreed-upon disarmament positions; and (3) a reform of NATO strategy.[65]

Voigt's third point was an additional issue on which the SPD has been increasingly vocal. In a speech to top Bundeswehr officers commemorating the thirtieth anniversary of West Germany's joining NATO, Hans-Jochen Vogel called for a reorientation of NATO strategy, citing in particular his party's opposition to "offensively oriented" strategies such as AirLand Battle and Follow-on Forces Attack (FOFA). Concerned above all with the implications of these strategies for the FRG's *Ostpolitik*, Peter Glotz criticized FOFA both for its effect on East-West relations and for being prohibitively expensive and of uncertain military value.[66] Not surprisingly, Samuel Huntington's concept of threatening conventional offensive retaliation by NATO ground forces into the GDR and Czechoslovakia in order to strengthen deterrence has been even more summarily dismissed by the SPD.[67]

The use of emerging technologies and precision-guided munitions to bolster conventional deterrence in Central Europe by threatening second-echelon Soviet forces and Warsaw Pact airfields, communications and transportation nodes, and command-and-control posts deep in Eastern Europe runs directly counter to the SPD preference for restructuring NATO along the lines of a "nonprovocative" defense. For Hermann Scheer, this means the denuclearization of Central Europe and the adoption of a defensive posture based on antitank belts along the inter-German border.[68] Erhard Eppler has amplified these themes, calling for a nuclear weapons-free zone extending from the Rhine to the Bug rivers, and within that a zone free of overtly "offensive" weapons (tanks and deep strike aircraft) that would cover most of the FRG, all of the GDR, and the western parts of Poland and Czechoslovakia (essentially an area bordered on the west by a line running from Bremen through Mainz to Lindau, and on the east by a line running from Gdansk through Katowice to Bratislava).[69]

Clearly, then, there has been no lack of alternative security proposals emanating from the SPD. In conjunction with security analysts from several West German peace research institutes (among the better known are Dieter Lutz, Gert Krell, and Albrecht von Müller), as well as activists in the peace movement and members of the West German media, the SPD is formulating new proposals and disseminating them to the West German public. To the extent that such proposals emphasize the need to protect the gains of *Ostpolitik* in a period of East-West tensions and stalemated arms control, they can be expected to find some resonance in the FRG. On the other hand, as noted above, polling data and the realities of West German electoral politics suggest that SPD attempts at finding a "third way" between the superpowers will remain untested until the party returns to power, sometime in the 1990s.

In the meantime, the SPD can be expected to maintain pressure on the Kohl government, and the United States, on issues of arms control and East-West relations. Especially on issues of high technology, such as SDI, the SPD will reiterate one of its major themes—that security dilemmas can only be solved through political accommodation, and not by technological fixes. Recalling the warning issued in 1889 by August Bebel, one of the founders of the German workers' movement, that "weapons technology . . . and a comprehensive revolution in the tactics of war . . . leaves little doubt that in the next war the devastation of civilians will reach a level never before experienced," Karsten Voigt and others in the SPD will continue to point to the security partnership concept as the only viable security policy for the FRG.[70]

In all likelihood, the special party congress scheduled for 1988 to discuss the revision of the Bad Godesberg program will provide a more solid indicator of where the party sees itself going in the 1990s, on both security and domestic issues. In the meantime, the SPD will undoubtedly search for ways to ameliorate East-West tensions, through the creation of a European peace order in a number of ways, including: increased contacts with Eastern Europe; through the Socialist International and its ties with Western European socialist and social democratic parties; and domestically in the FRG through the propagation of alternative security concepts for West Germany.

Given the fluid nature of current German politics, it is difficult to say how the West German public will respond to this SPD strategy. Domestically, one of the more important variables will be the long-term prospects of the Green Party in national politics, and whether the SPD will be successful in coopting large numbers of Green supporters. An ability of the SPD to make inroads with Green voters is all the more important as the current drift to the left of SPD policies makes it unlikely that the party will have the same appeal to FDP and CDU moderates that it had during the Schmidt years. Also important will be the general state of East-West relations and U.S. policies over the next few years. If the INF treaty falls prey to U.S. domestic politics during the 1988 election and there is a resumption of U.S.-Soviet tension, it is possible (though unlikely) that the SPD approach to safeguarding German national interests may find increased appeal within the FRG.

Whatever the course of German domestic politics and East-West relations, however, one thing seems certain. The SPD is nearing the end of that generational change in the party's outlook that has characterized SPD history since the late 1880s. In an attempt to deal with the complexities of safeguarding German national interests, both externally and domestically, the party is formulating new policies that undoubtedly have provided it with greater unity. What is less certain, however, is the extent to which the SPD can convince both the German electorate and the FRG's Western Allies that its security concepts provide the most viable means of reducing political tensions and military confrontation in Central Europe.

NOTES

1. For more on the early history of the SPD, see Helga Grebing, *Geschichte der deutschen Arbeiterbewegung* (Munich: Taschenbuch Verlag, 1979), pp. 108–120.

2. See especially Gordon A. Craig, *The Politics of the Prussian Army, 1640–1945*, 2d ed. (London: Oxford University Press, 1968), chap. 6.

3. Quoted in Karsten Voigt, *Wege zur Abrüsting* (Frankfurt: Eichborn Verlag, 1981), p. 142.

4. Wolf-Dieter Narr, "Social Factors Affecting the Making of Foreign Policy," in *Britain and West Germany: Changing Societies and the Future of Foreign Policy*, eds. Karl Kaiser and Roger Morgan (London, Oxford University Press, 1971), pp. 113–14.

5. Jeffrey Boutwell, "Politics and the Peace Movement in West Germany," *International Security* (Spring 1983): 74–75.

6. See especially Lothar Wilker, *Die Sicherheitspolitik der SPD, 1956–66* (Bonn-Bad Godesberg: Verlag Neue Gesellschaft, 1977), pp. 18–25.

7. The Bad Godesberg program is contained in *Grundsatzprogramm der Sozialdemokratischen Partei Deutschlands* (Bonn: SPD Presse und Information, November 1959).

8. As noted by Uwe Nerlich, these twin strands of détente "ensued more out of a parallelism of interests than out of a common strategy . . . the result of an accidentally favorable constellation." See Nerlich, "Washington and Bonn: Evolutionary Patterns in the Relations between the United States and the Federal Republic of Germany," in *America and Western Europe*, eds. Karl Kaiser and Hans-Peter Schwarz (Lexington, Mass.: Lexington Books, 1977), p.376.

9. For more on the SPD debate over the neutron bomb at the 1977 Hamburg party conference, see Jeffrey Boutwell, "External and Domestic Determinants of West German Security Policy: Adenauer, Schmidt and Nuclear Weapons" (Ph.D. dissertation, Massachusetts Institute of Technology, 1984), chap. 5 especially; to be published as *Nuclear Weapons and the German Dilemma* (forthcoming from Cornell University Press).

10. For more on the emerging security concepts of Brandt, Bahr, and SPD security expert Alfons Pawelczyk, see *Der Spiegel*, November 27, 1978.

11. As expressed by Erhard Eppler, a prominent left-wing party official, "The problem today is that no great issue exists which could integrate the party and make it stand out against the CDU. We are dealing almost exclusively with issues [e.g., INF, civilian nuclear power, arms exports] where the Union supports the government, while considerable parts of the SPD have growing doubts. I do not know for how long a party can live only with disintegrating issues." See *Der Spiegel*, February 9, 1981, pp. 23–25.

12. *Die Zeit*, December 7, 1979.

13. For a good analysis of the split between the "government" and "party" factions of the SPD, see the article by Gunther Gillessen in *Frankfurter Allgemeine Zeitung* [hereafter *FAZ*], February 7, 1979, p. 10. See also, "Eine SPD—Zwei Parteien," *Die Zeit*, February 19, 1982.

14. See Egon Bahr, "Sozialdemokratische Sicherheitspolitik," and Horst Ehmke, "Sicherheitspartnerschaft", in *Die Neue Gesellschaft*, February 1983. According to Bahr, the "security partnership" concept is predicated on the fact that war in the nuclear age is no longer winnable; thus the notion of security must be reciprocal, and this applies as much to the FRG and GDR, or France and Poland, as to the United States and Soviet Union.

15. David Conradt, "The 1983 Elections: A Data Analysis," paper presented at the 1983 American Political Science Association Annual Meeting, September 1–4, 1983, Chicago.

16. Helmut Schmidt was one of only 14 party delegates, out of some 400, who voted in favor of the NATO decision at the SPD party congress in Cologne; see *Die Zeit*, December 2, 1983.

17. For more on changes in West German domestic politics in the 1970s, see Bernd Guggenberger, *Bürgerinitiativen in der Parteiendemokratie* (Stuttgart: Kohlhammer, 1980).

18. *The German Tribune*, January 17, 1982. See also Richard Löwenthal, "Reflections on the 'Greens': Roots, Character, and Prospects," *German Studies Newsletter*, Harvard University, Center for European Studies, February 1985.

19. The von Bülow report is entitled *Strategie vertrauensschaffender Sicherheitsstruckturen in Europa: Wege zur Sicherheitspartnerschaft* (Bonn: SPD, September 1985).

20. For CDU/CSU criticism of the von Bülow report, see *FAZ*, September 11, 1985, p. 4, and also Wolfgang Pordzik, "Aspects of the West German Security Debate," *German Studies Newsletter* (Center for European Studies, Harvard University, November 1985). For reports of the Bundestag parliamentary debate, see *Foreign Broadcast Information Service: Western Europe*, September 13, 1985, pp. J1–J4.

21. *Neue Ruhr-Zeitung*, September 9, 1985.

22. *FAZ*, September 11, 1985.

23. Wilhelm Bruns, *Der Beitrag der beiden deutschen Staaten zur Sicherheits- und Entspannungspolitik* (Bonn: Friedrich Ebert Stiftung, January 1986).

24. See 6 draft of "Peace and Security: Policy of the Social Democratic Party of Germany," (Bonn: Social Democratic Party, April 28, 1986).

25. See ibid., pp. 1–4 especially.

26. Manfred Wörner, "A Missile Defense for NATO Europe," *Strategic Review*, Winter 1986. For more on ATBMs, see Donald Hafner and John Roper, eds., *ATBMs and Western Security: Missile Defenses for Europe* (Cambridge, Mass.: Ballinger Publishing Co., 1988).

27. "Peace and Security", p. 5.

28. James Markham, "Militants Show Muscle as Bonn Socialists Meet," *New York Times*, August 31, 1986.

29. For more on the antinuclear sentiments expressed at the Nuremberg conference, see *Der Spiegel*, September 1, 1986, pp. 19–21, and *FAZ*, August 28, 1986.

30. Quoted in *Der Spiegel*, September 1, 1986, p. 24.

31. *FAZ*, February 7, 1979.

32. Erhard Eppler, for one, commented that "four years ago I wouldn't have dreamed that we could adopt this program" (quoted in *Der Spiegel*, September 1, 1986, p. 24). In an editorial, the *Süddeutsche Zeitung* noted that the Nuremberg party conference was characterized by a positive unity regarding the election platform, as opposed to the "negative consensus" on nuclear weapons and nuclear power issues that dominated the 1983 Cologne and 1984 Essen party conferences; see *Süddeutsche Zeitung*, August 30/31, 1986.

33. *The Economist*, August 30, 1986, p. 40.

34. For a profile on one of the new left-wing members of the Presidium, Heidi Wieczorek-Zeul (former chair of the Jusos and a member of the European Parliament), see *Der Spiegel*, September 8, 1986, pp. 22–24.

35. For a good postelection analysis, see Gordon Smith, "The Changing West German Party System: Consequences of the 1987 Election," *Government and Opposition*, Spring 1987, pp. 131–44.

36. See Josef Joffe, "All Quiet on the Eastern Front," *Foreign Policy* (Winter 1979–80), pp. 161–75.

37. Poll results can be found in Gebhard Schweigler, "Anti-Americanism in Germany," *The Washington Quarterly* (Winter 1986): p. 81.

38. See Joachim Hofmann-Gottig, "Die Jungen Wähler 1983—Ein Stimmungs-Barometer," *Die Neue Gesellschaft*, June 1984, p. 527. For more on the growing conservatism of West German youth, see *New York Times*, January 19, 1986, p. 1. For a different perspective, see Ronald Inglehart, "Generational Change and the Future of the Atlantic Alliance," *Political Science*, Summer 1984, pp. 525–35.

39. One of the most important expositions of this view from an SPD-perspective is Peter Bender, *Das Ende des ideologischen Zeitalters* (West Berlin: Severin und Siedler, 1981).

40. Quoted in *Die Zeit*, January 18, 1980.

41. See, for example, the reports of the Independent Commission on International Development Issues, chaired by Willy Brandt: *North-South: A Program for Survival* (Cambridge, Mass.: MIT Press, 1980) and *Common Crisis* (Cambridge, Mass.: MIT Press, 1983), as well as Brandt's *Arms and Hunger* (Cambridge, Mass.: MIT Press, 1986).

42. David Calleo, *The German Problem Reconsidered: Germany and World Order, 1870 to the Present* (New York: Cambridge University Press, 1978), p. 177.

43. For more on the role of the DGB in West German politics, see Otto Kirchheimer, "West German Trade Unions: Their Domestic and Foreign Policies," in *West German Leadership and Foreign Policy*, eds. Hans Speier and W. Phillips Davison (Evanston: Row, Peterson and Co., 1957).

44. See Richard J. Willey, "Trade Unions and Political Parties in the Federal Republic," *Industrial and Labor Relations Review* (October 1974).

45. See Gerard Braunthal, "West German Trade Unions and Disarmament," *Political Science Quarterly*, 73, no. 1.

46. See Josef Esser, "State, Business, and Trade Unions in West Germany after the Political 'Wende'," *West European Politics*, April 1986.

47. For more on the role of the Catholic and Protestant Churches in current West German politics, see *Der Spiegel*, August 18, 1986, p. 24.

48. Frederic Spotts, *The Churches and Politics in Germany* (Middletown, Conn.: Wesleyan University Press, 1973), p. 128.

49. Spotts, *Churches and Politics in Germany*, p. 128.

50. See "The Preservation, Promotion and Renewal of Peace," A Memorandum of the Evangelical Church in Germany, 1981.

51. Joyce Marie Mushaben, "Anti-Politics and Successor Generations: The Role of Youth in West and East German Peace Movements," *Journal of Political and Military Sociology* (Spring 1984): 181.

52. Erhard Eppler, for one, believes that the Soviet Union does not want world domination (*Weltherrschaft*), which he says the United States is actually better positioned to achieve, but only a condominium and equality of rights with the United States. See his "Handfest und Sentimental" (a review of the book *Neutralität für Mitteleuropa: Das Ende der Blöcke* by Jochen Loser and Ulrike Schilling), in *Die Neue Gesellschaft*, September 1984, pp. 816–19.

53. See in particular John von Oudenaren, "Soviet Policy Toward Western Europe: Objectives, Instruments, Results," *RAND Project Air Force Report R-3310-AF*, Santa Monica, February 1986.

54. For more on Brandt's trip to Warsaw, see *Die Zeit*, December 20, 1985, p. 2.

55. One example of Soviet covert funding of antinuclear protests in the FRG comes from Stanislav Levchenko, a KGB officer who defected to the West

in 1979, who has said that Moscow provided $200 million to the campaign in Western Europe against the neutron bomb; see *New York Times*, July 26, 1983. Also, Klaus Rainer Rohl, former editor of the left-wing magazine *Konkret* (and former husband of Ulrike Meinhof), has testified to receiving approximately a million D-marks from East Berlin and Prague for the magazine; see *Human Events*, September 26, 1981.

56.   For a fuller discussion of the evolution of *Deutschlandpolitik*, see Jeffrey Boutwell, "The German Search for Security," in *Securing Europe's Future*, eds. Stephen J. Flanagan and Fen Osler Hampson (London: Croom Helm Ltd., 1986).

57.   *Foreign Broadcast Information Service: Eastern Europe*, February 10, 1982, p. E2.

58.   *Frankfurter Rundschau*, January 19, 1982.

59.   Karl-Heinz Lohs, a member of the East German delegation, provides a summary of the GDR position in his "Pros and Cons of a Chemical Weapons-Free Zone in Europe: The Genesis of a Concept," paper presented to the 35th Pugwash Conference on Science and World Affairs, Campinas, Brazil, July 3–8, 1985.

60.   The SPD delegation included Karsten Voigt, Egon Bahr, and Hermann Scheer, while the SED delegation included Lohs, Hermann Axen (SED Politburo member), and Klaus-Dieter Ernst from the GDR Foreign Ministry. The final proposal was published by the SPD under the title "Chemische Abrüstung: Modell für eine chemiewaffenfrei Zone in Europa," *Politik* Nr. 6, (Bonn: SPD, July 1985). See also *Die Zeit*, June 28, 1985.

61.   *Foreign Broadcast Information Service: Western Europe*, September 17, 1985, p. J6.

62.   During the campaign for the 1987 election, Rau felt continually undermined by party chairman Brandt and party manager Peter Glotz, while Klaus Bölling, former FRG representative to the GDR, openly doubted Rau's leadership abilities. See *Die Zeit*, August 22, 1986.

63.   In discussing the need for a revised party program, Lafontaine has stressed many of the "post-industrial" issues raised by the Greens, especially quality of life issues relating to the workplace and the environment; seminar at the Center for European Studies, Harvard University, September 26, 1987.

64.   *FAZ*, October 2, 1985.

65.   For Voigt's views on SDI, see his "12 Theses on the SDI Concept from a European Perspective," unpublished paper, 1985.

66.   Peter Glotz, "Der Schritt in die falsche Richtung—FOFA und die deutschen Moglichkeiten," *Die Neue Gesellschaft*, December 1984, pp. 1112–14.

67. Samuel Huntington, "Conventional Deterrence and Conventional Retaliation in Europe," *International Security* (Winter 1983–84), pp. 32–56.
68. Hermann Scheer, "Denuklearisierung und konventionelle Defensivstruktur," *Die Neue Gesellschaft*, September 1984.
69. Erhard Eppler, "Handfest und Sentimental," *Die Neue Gesellschaft*, September 1984, pp. 815–19.
70. Quoted in Karsten Voigt, "Schrittweiser Ausstieg aus dem Rüstungswettlauf," *Die Neue Gesellschaft*, January 1980, p. 49.

5 ARMS CONTROL AND THE FREE DEMOCRATIC PARTY

For over two decades, the Free Democratic Party (FDP or Liberals) has been instrumental in shaping Bonn's foreign policy, exercising an influence disproportionate to its small size. Since 1949, it has participated in all but two cabinets at the national level, and has served to check the more extreme factions of its larger coalition partners. Moreover, the FDP has been assured a decisive input into the foreign policy-making process through its sustained control of the Foreign Ministry; since 1969, the FRG's foreign minister has been an FDP politician, first Walter Scheel, then Hans-Dietrich Genscher.

The FDP's power derives from its unique role in the postwar German political system. Though the party has continually sought a more substantive profile, the FDP's political and electoral support has been achieved less from its program than from its perceived and actual function as coalition-maker, safety valve and corrective. Though the party continues to espouse liberal themes—free-market economic principles and individual rights—the FDP has long recognized the electoral advantages that accrue from its image as guarantor of stability, continuity, and moderation. This image neatly matches the German electorate's apparent preference for avoiding drastic departures from the status quo, whether the radical change was proposed by the left of the SPD or the hardline ideology of the Christian Democrats' rightwing.

The FDP's continued participation in national governments is matched by continuity in its attitudes on security and arms control. Its fairly unwavering support of arms negotiations is rooted in its overall perception of the desirable condition of East-West relations, and is evidence of the controlling hand of Hans-Dietrich Genscher within the party. Without exaggeration, one can assert that Genscher's policy is FDP policy. Under

Genscher's leadership, continuity and predictability have become the catchphrases of FDP foreign policy. As in the days of the social-liberal coalition (1969–82), the FDP sees strong ties to the West and NATO (*Westpolitik*) and cooperation with the East (*Ostpolitik*) as two indispensable and complementary components of West German foreign policy. The party has supported Genscher's initiatives to bring about substantive progress in arms negotiations and European security conferences, along with his calls for a vigorous European and German role in the East-West dialogue.

The FDP's influence has been inextricably linked to its power as the swing party, its access to crucial leadership positions, and Genscher's long tenure as Foreign Minister. Whether the FDP can continue to play this corrective role will depend both on the evolution of the party in the post-Genscher period and on developments in the West German political system on the whole. Since 1982 and the FDP's realignment with the CDU/CSU, the party has been in a state of transition. A large turnover in membership and leadership has left the FDP without potential leaders that are well-versed in foreign affairs and security issues. Genscher's strategy appears to be to stay in power as foreign minister long enough for this next generation of leaders to acquire the necessary expertise to ensure continuity of the party's current policy. But struggles over leadership succession within the FDP, an intensifying conflict with the CSU, or a usurpation of the FDP's traditional functions by the Greens as a result of the next election could undermine Genscher's efforts. The combined effects of these factors make it unlikely that the post-Genscher FDP would exercise as great an influence in the formulation of Bonn's security policy as it has in the past.

THE FDP IN THE WEST GERMAN POLITICAL SYSTEM

The FDP owes its continued existence at the national level both to the peculiarities of the West German electoral system and the support of German voters who see the party as playing a critical role in the political system. Parliamentary elections in the FRG are decided through a system of modified proportional representation. Half of the representatives in the Bundestag are elected by plurality vote in single-member districts, half by proportional representation from state party lists. A voter may cast two ballots, the first for a district candidate, the second for a party. Under this system, a voter may choose to "split the ticket" and "lend" the second vote to the coalition partner; the second vote is then used to determine the final percentage of parliamentary mandates which a party receives.[1] If a party is unable to win three district contests, it must capture at least five percent on the second ballot to gain access to the Bundestag. Though the FDP has usually registered less than ten percent of the second vote since 1949, the incidence of ticket splitting has been frequent enough to keep the party in parliament at both the national and the local levels.[2]

In the West German political system the three functions seemingly allotted to the FDP are coalition-maker, safety valve, and corrective.[3] By forming coalitions with the SPD and, more recently with the CDU, the small FDP has gained control over key positions and a voice in the formulation of government policy. With the exception of the CDU/CSU between 1957 and 1961, no German political party has been able to win an absolute majority at the national level. As a result, the votes of the FDP have been required to enable one of the larger parties to form a government. In fact, the FDP has served in all but two national governments since 1949. The FDP's willingness to enter into these coalitions has given it a degree of bargaining power disproportionate to its relative size. The greater its percentage of votes in any election, the more negotiating power the FDP has been able to bring to bear in determining the distribution of ministerial seats. When the FDP made a weak showing, its hold on ministerial posts has been more tenuous, as in 1983 when the FDP was forced to relinquish the interior minister's slot to the CSU. Since 1969, the Liberals have been able to retain control over two key posts: the Foreign Office and the Economics Ministry.

Conversely, the FDP's role as "pivot" party also gives it the power to bring down governments. It was the FDP that ended two decades of CDU participation in national governments in 1969 by signalling a willingness to join the SPD in coalition. Similarly, the FDP's shift from the SPD to the CDU in the fall of 1982 resulted in the downfall of Helmut Schmidt's government.

The FDP also serves as a "safety valve," a way for the public to express dissatisfaction with the policies of the major parties. By shifting either to the right or to the left in tune with changing political trends and moods, the FDP has been able to garner support from voters dissatisfied with the major party's policies but for whom a switch to the alternate major party would be too extreme.[4] A vote for the FDP is thus a means of registering disapproval of the larger parties' policies.

The FDP may also be seen as providing a necessary "corrective" to the policies of the major *Volksparteien*, keeping them tied to a more or less consensual middle course. In the years of the social-liberal coalition (1969–82), the corrective function was initially more important with regard to economic and fiscal policies, and only later on foreign policy. During the debate over the NATO dual-track decision, Genscher and the FDP were a visible check on the demands of the SPD's left wing. In the current government, the FDP has cast itself as a counterpoint to the Union's right wing and the Bavarian CSU, most notably Franz Josef Strauss. Genscher has resisted the tendency to view the world strictly along ideological lines and has countered the influence of adamantly pro-American factions in the CDU/CSU. Genscher and the FDP have not failed to recognize the benefits of appearing the guarantor of moderation, as seen in numerous statements by FDP leaders during the months preceding the national elections in January 1987, such as Genscher's declaration: "We (the FDP) are the factor of stability and reliability in the government."[5]

The FDP has sought a more substantive or programmatic profile to appeal to voters.[6] It has combined diverse strands of German liberal tradition, championing the principles of free market economy, civil liberties, and the German system of codified law. In recent years, foreign policy and inter-German policy (*Deutschlandpolitik*) have figured increasingly in the FDP's attempts to differentiate and distance itself from the Christian Democrats. Adherents of different factions within the FDP disagree about the relative importance of the party's programmatic elements. One faction, including former Economics Minister Otto Graf Lambsdorff and the party's general secretary, Helmut Haussmann, focuses almost exclusively on the propagation and implementation of free market economic principles. A more traditional social-liberal faction, on the other hand, including FDP treasurer Irmgard Adam-Schwaetzer, Gerhard Baum, and Hildegard Hamm-Bruecher, would like to see some return to civil libertarian causes. Still, programmatic causes have usually proven less important to party officials than pragmatic political considerations. And, on foreign and security policy, the factions largely agree.

This legacy of divisions never fully resolved gives the FDP its unique profile. At the national level, it is a heterogeneous collection of locally diverse parties, weak organizationally, and dependent on the unifying power of a few strong leaders that maintain a high profile. The party's core support of loyal voters has always been a tiny minority, usually hovering around 3 to 4 percent of the electorate. On average, however, its members have a higher social, economic, and educational status than members of the CDU/CSU or SPD.[7]

FDP ARMS CONTROL POLICY

The FDP's attitudes toward arms control are rooted in the original elements of the social-liberal coalition's program: maintenance of a firm foundation in NATO coupled with dialogue and cooperation with the East. Over time, this prescription has undoubtedly been shaped by Genscher's own perspectives on the requisites of German foreign policy. The result has been a view of arms control and, more generally, of East-West relations that has been largely unchanged over the past two decades. Only the nuances of emphasis have altered, with an increasingly important role assigned to a European pillar within the Alliance as a counterweight to the influence of the United States. While Genscher emphasizes the importance of Alliance and German-American cooperation, he also has attempted to preserve the fruits of détente, including the inter-German dialogue. The recurring themes of continuity, predictability, continuing cooperation and dialogue with the East, and substantive progress in European security have been the hallmarks of Genscher's tenure as Foreign Minister. They have also become mainstays of the FDP's foreign policy agenda.

The FDP's attitude toward arms control is related to its support of and involvement in the early phases of Bonn's *Ostpolitik*. The building of the Berlin Wall in 1961 provoked a gradual reassessment of the party's original adherence to the goal of national unity and an uncompromising stance vis-à-vis the East. The FDP subsequently supported the more flexible policies of CDU/CSU Foreign Minister Gerhard Schroeder against more conservative members of the Union. Three of its leaders, Wolfgang Mischnick, Wolfgang Schollwer, and Hans-Wolfgang Rubin, even advocated de facto recognition of the GDR and normalization of relations with the East.[8] By 1969, the party had abandoned its adherence to the goal of reunification of Germany as a national state, an important concession given the fact that this objective had long been an integral part of German liberalism. The FDP advocated the full normalization of relations with Bonn's Eastern neighbors, a policy stance that was also supported by business and industry interests within the party who may have hoped to benefit from increased opportunities for trade with the East.[9]

The initiation of Willy Brandt's *Ostpolitik* and its further implementation under Helmut Schmidt were fully supported by the FDP. But at the same time, the party continued to emphasize the importance of a firm alliance with the West. The FDP sought to maintain a balance between the two facets of Bonn's foreign policy, and was aided in this task by its continued control over the Foreign Ministry.

Though the FDP has since changed coalition partners, its attitudes on arms control and East-West relations have remained virtually unchanged, which may be the clearest evidence of Genscher's overall impact on FDP attitudes. Genscher's statements and interviews reflect the views of a man committed to NATO but also equally adamant about the necessity of broad-based cooperation with the East, including but not limited to arms control. Genscher has made virtues of continuity and predictability. In Genscher's view, the FRG cannot afford to leave its neighbors in East and West in doubt about its policies or intentions, a belief that has led him to criticize the SPD's policies. In dealing with the Soviet Union, he preaches constancy and firmness, asserting that "foreign policy must be conducted" with a steady hand "and continuity."[10]

Though apparently firmly wedded to the Alliance, Genscher has by no means passively endorsed the strongly pro-American line of the Christian Democrats, insisting instead on a more autonomous European voice. While acknowledging that the superpower relationship is decisive in East-West relations, Genscher also has spoken of a "European mission of peace" (*europaische Friedensaufgabe*) and, moreover, of the Germans' "national obligation" to strive for improvement in East-West relations and progress in arms control.[11] Consequently, he assigns great importance to European security conferences, such as the CSCE process and the Stockholm Conference on Confidence Building and Disarmament in Europe; Genscher views these conferences as a means by which the smaller and medium-sized European states may also bring influence to bear, bolstering European interests against the great powers' predominance. Through conferences and consultations, Genscher would have the Europeans and Germans play a "compelling role" in arms control. In the Foreign Minister's words, "We (the Europeans) want to be more than just spectators of international politics."[12]

The European emphasis of Genscher's foreign policy was clearly evident in the negotiation of the U.S./FRG agreement on German participation in the Strategic Defense Initiative. Upon Genscher's insistence, the agreement dealt only with economic issues, not military ones, was negotiated on the German side by Economics Minister Martin Bangemann, and made no provision for governmental support of the program. Genscher insisted that the strategic implications of the SDI be considered only within the NATO context. The shape of the resulting agreement clearly reflects Genscher's priorities and his triumph over the

CDU's right wing (and the CSU). Within the FDP, only Lambsdorff seemed to favor SDI.

The purpose of European endeavors, in Genscher's scheme, is continuing and expanding cooperation with the East, above and beyond arms control negotiations. Such broad-based cooperation is necessary, in Genscher's view, because security can no longer be guaranteed unilaterally, but only through cooperation. And while Genscher has not gone so far as to use the SPD's term "security partnership," he has spoken of a "survival partnership" (*Ueberlebensgemeinschaft*) and of the goal of creating global and European "cooperative security structures." Further, while he does not echo the Social Democrat's call for a "second phase of détente," Genscher has expressed his hope for a "new phase of East-West relations, of détente."[13]

The European framework is also the only permissible context for German initiatives. In this vein, Genscher rejects unilateral actions by Bonn, arguing that Bonn should work together with its European allies for progress in arms control. Genscher supports efforts by the two German states, within their respective alliances, to improve East-West relations, promote cooperation, and accelerate progress in disarmament and arms control. But he draws the line at unilateral initiatives, such as the SPD's ongoing dialogue with the East German Socialist Unity Party (SED). He has cautioned the SPD against going beyond the limits of party activity and intruding upon governmental prerogatives or undermining the defense consensus. But he has tempered his condemnation of the SPD's "parallel foreign policy" (*Nebenaussenpolitik*) by welcoming the comprehensive exchange of information.[14] It is not an inter-German dialogue per se that Genscher seemingly rejects, but the attempt to pursue negotiations with the GDR outside the existing alliance system, as reflected in Genscher's comments on his duties as Foreign Minister:

> For someone who was born in what is now the GDR, as Foreign Minister of the Federal Republic, one will naturally always be acutely aware of the responsibility which one has both for Germany's fate, and for what the Germans in the Federal Republic and in the GDR must do in the future. Before every decision I consider the fact that Germans like us live in the GDR, and I never forget that Europe is more than the European community. At times, that results in a bit more reflection and prevents one from oversimplifications, or from painting everything in black or white or seeing the world clearly divided into good and evil.[15]

The FDP's recent party programs bear the stamp of Genscher's views and agenda. The FDP listed as its major foreign policy objectives the continuation of détente policy, improvements in inter-German relations, and creation of a European union. Arms control plays an integral part in the cooperative process, and the party has been very specific in its goals, calling for the following steps to be taken:

- Agreement on confidence-building and security measures at the Stockholm conference;

- Gradual achievement of a balance in conventional forces in Central Europe through an agreement at the Vienna MBFR negotiations;

- Elimination of all chemical weapons in Europe as part of a global agreement to ban chemical weapons, which, in the party's view, could be completed by fall 1987;

- An immediate halt to all nuclear tests and the completion of a comprehensive test ban treaty;

- Agreements on the gradual dismantling of nuclear weapons in order to achieve the goal, proclaimed by the United States and the Soviet Union, to prevent an arms race in space and end the global arms race;

- Inclusion of tactical and intermediate-range nuclear weapons in arms control negotiations;

- Strict adherence to the ABM Treaty in its narrowest interpretation and the continued complete application of the SALT II limits.[16]

CHANGES IN FDP POLICY

Given the marked continuity in the FDP's security policy over more than two decades, any change in the party's attitudes on arms control would likely be linked to the party's further evolution, particularly after Genscher's departure. The FDP has recently gone through a period of great upheaval. In the months preceding the coalition change in 1982 and immediately thereafter, the party lost approximately 20,000 members, many of whom were dissatisfied with the rightward drift of theparty or the manner in which the transition was handled. By March 1983, the FDP had managed to attract some 6,000 new members, drawn predominantly from the old and new middle classes (self-employed and independent professionals and administrators), but by 1984, the party still had barely 70,000 members. The party reached a low point in 1985, when it was excluded from all but five *Landtage* and regional governments.[17]

The membership turnover was mirrored by changes at the leadership level. Since 1982, a new, largely unknown and untried generation of leaders has emerged at the local and state (*Land*) level, leaving the party with a very small pool of expertise on which to draw, particularly with regard to foreign policy or defense issues.[18] Moreover, one of the FDP's few prominent members, Otto Graf Lambsdorff, was forced in June 1984 to resign his post as Economics Minister after being indicted.[19] He was succeeded by Martin Bangemann. Genscher himself was severely criticized for his management of the realignment and, in February 1985, after sustained pressure from state level FDP leaders, Genscher relinquished his post as the FDP's chairman to Bangemann. Genscher only regained his earlier standing in the party as the FDP's political fortunes began to improve and his strong advocacy of an INF arms control agreement won him new recognition.

The party appears to have recovered from the turmoil that followed the 1982 realignment. The party's gains in the January 1987 national elections (from 7.0 to 9.1 percent of the second vote) have put the FDP on firmer footing. During the national election campaign, the FDP appealed successfully to voters on the basis of familiar economic and social themes and, additionally, on its experience and moderation in foreign policy. In the end, Strauss's vitriolic campaign against the FDP and Genscher's conduct of foreign affairs hurt the Union, as conservatives "lent" their support to the smaller coalition partner.[20] The Liberals' strengthened position in the coalition allowed the party to retain control over the Foreign Ministry. As a consequence, the party also acquired a decisive influence over arms control policy, as was seen in 1987 when Kohl used the FDP to counter pressure from Strauss and the CSU, as well as from more conservative members within the CDU who opposed an INF agreement.

The party's outlook beyond 1987 is more uncertain. During the months preceding the national elections, party chairman Martin Bangemann seemed intent on situating the FDP firmly in the more conservative of what he called the "two camps" of German politics. Bangemann's support of the FDP's alliance with the CDU first began in 1975. Shortly after he became general secretary in October 1974, Bangemann began to argue that the FDP should be open to a realignment in coalition. After barely a year in office, Genscher sent him to Strassbourg to serve in the European Parliament. In 1984, when the FDP failed to win 5 percent in elections to the European Parliament, Bangemann returned to Bonn. His return was opportune, coinciding with the party's search for new leaders. As party chairman, Bangemann has had ample opportunity to propound on his theory of the "two camps" of German politics. According to Bangemann, the German political system was divided into a reliable center-conservative bloc and an unstable alliance on the left of Greens and Social Democrats. The FDP, Bangemann stressed, should remain firmly wedded to the CDU/CSU.[21]

In contrast, Genscher has resisted a permanent alignment of the FDP with the conservatives. He has cautioned against thinking in terms of blocs or camps.[22] Despite the FDP's preelection commitment to continuation of the center-right coalition, Genscher gave some indication that for the future he would like to leave a door open to the left, providing the SPD returned to a more center course, and left no uncertainties as to its commitment to NATO. When asked specifically about the FDP's alignment, he affirmed the party's coalition commitment for the 1987 general elections, but beyond that, he commented, one would have to look at things from a new perspective. Genscher's stance is hardly surprising, since it is the FDP's ability and willingness to cooperate alternately at the national or regional level with parties of the left or the right that has ensured its survival. This fact helps to explain why other FDP leaders, Bangemann included, began in 1987 to distance themselves from the "two-camp" theory. Following a prolonged period of conflict between the CSU and FDP over domestic and foreign policy issues, and a series of CDU setbacks in regional elections, FDP general secretary Helmut Haussmann described the Liberal party as a "party of the center," a description echoed by party chairman Bangemann at the FDP's annual convention in September 1987.[23]

The FDP is attempting to create a broader and more secure voter base by taking advantage of social and political changes in the FRG. Analyses of national and regional elections in the 1980s point to a growth in the pool of floating voters, who feel no strong allegiance to any major political party. This trend in the past has favored the two smaller parties, the FDP and the Greens. Moreover, the FDP is trying to take advantage of socioeconomic changes in voting structure; its championing of tax reform, civil liberties, and East-West dialogue are designed to attract support from the growing numbers of educated workers employed in service industries—the new middle classes.[24]

The FDP's future stance on security issues similarly depends on developments at the party's leadership level. Until now, Genscher's influence over the Liberals' arms control policy has been virtually exclusive. There are a number of possible successors to Genscher, but few if any would be able to wield as much influence, either in the party or vis-à-vis a coalition partner, as Genscher. Figuring into the equation are the ambitions of former Economics Minister Otto Graf Lambsdorff, cleared in July 1986 of charges of bribery and now free to pursue his political career. The party's general secretary, Helmut Haussmann, has also hinted at designs on the Foreign Minister's position. The capabilities or arms control preferences of this new generation of state leaders are an unknown quantity. It may indeed be part of Genscher's strategy to remain in office long enough to train a new generation of like-minded younger party leaders to succeed him as the FDP's foreign policy architect. In this vein, it is significant to note the appointment in 1987 of a member of the younger guard, Dr. Irmgard Adam-Schwaetzer, as deputy minister in the Foreign Office.

The ability of the FDP to influence policy, however, will not only depend on the internal evolution of the party, but on broader developments in the political system as well. In the early 1980s, the FDP's traditional role as coalition-maker and corrective was challenged increasingly by the Greens. Between 1982 and 1985, the Greens replaced the FDP in six state parliaments and, in Hesse, even took over the Liberal's role of coalition-maker, as they formed a government with the Social Democrats. The FDP owes its continued existence and political influence to the support of German voters who may be uneasy with the prospect of two large political parties completely dominating the political system and who thus perceive the FDP as fulfilling a positive function. The appearance of the Greens on the national and local political scene has redefined German politics. While most Germans would not view the Greens as a viable functional substitute for the FDP, the Liberals can no longer take for granted their continued presence in governing coalitions. As long as the Greens exist as an alternative to the FDP pivot, the Greens have the potential, albeit a limited on, to usurp the FDP's traditional role.

CONCLUSIONS

The FDP's attitudes on arms control and its ability to influence governmental policy will depend on the party's leadership in the post-Genscher period and on its ability to retain its function in the German political system. The party must first find successors to current leaders who, in turn, may determine whether the party would later realign itself with the SPD or remain firmly allied to the CDU/CSU. The party's attempt to appeal to voters on the basis of program rather than solely as a safety valve may or may not be successful. The further evolution of the Greens is a factor beyond the FDP's control, but one which may bear on its political future.

Though the questions of leadership and future alignment remain open, there are few indications that the party's attitudes on arms control, East-West relations, or defense will undergo drastic changes. The party has displayed remarkable continuity in its policies, with the only change being greater emphasis on the European component of arms control as an alternative to a more unquestioning pro-American line. The party's program in the 1980s, in fact, reads much like the original proposals and goals of the early foreign policy of the social-liberal coalition. It is a moderate course with familar elements.

The FDP's emphasis on moderation, continuity, and predictability in foreign policy may prove to be one of its strongest assets in its fight to retain its function in the German political system. The FDP's steady but independent course in foreign policy is likely to appeal to German voters who are wary of both the strident ideologies of the right and the radical departures from the status quo advocated by the left. And the FDP has proved itself adept at playing on these fears, depicting the FDP as a factor of stability, an advocate of arms control, a promoter of European cooperation, and watchdog of the inter-German dialogue. The portrayal of the FDP as loyal ally to Bonn's European partners and the United States, but one with an independent and forceful voice as well, may carry enough electoral appeal to secure the FDP's future as kingmaker and corrective, and safeguard its channel for influencing arms control policy.

NOTES

1.   The seats that any party wins in the district contests are subtracted from the number of mandates that a party would be entitled to under a system of pure proportional representation. The remainder gives the number of party mandates from *Land* lists. See David P. Conradt, *The German Polity* (New York: Longman Inc., 1982), pp. 117–19.

2.   Christian Soe, "The Free Democratic Party," in *West German Politics in the Mid-Eighties: Crisis and Continuity*, eds. H.G. Peter Wallach and George K. Romoser (New York: Praeger, 1985), pp. 113–14.

3.   Ibid., pp. 113–18.

4.   The argument has been made by Elisabeth Noelle-Neumann. Cited in Soe, "The Free Democratic Party," pp. 180–81.

5.   " 'Mehrheiten nur mit der FDP': *Spiegel* Interview mit Aussenminister Hans-Dietrich Genscher," *Der Spiegel*, June 16, 1986. p. 33.

6. See Soe, "Free Democratic Party," pp. 118, 123–6.

7. Ibid., pp. 125, 171; David Broughton and Emil Kirchner, "Germany: The FDP in Transition—Again?," *Parliamentary Affairs* 37 (Spring 1984): 187–90.

8. Helga Haftendorn, *Security and Détente* (New York: Praeger, 1985), p. 299, n. 67. See also Soe, pp. 128–32. Soe notes that both Mischnick and Schollwer, as well as Genscher, began their political careers in the early postwar years as members of the Liberal Democratic Party in the East German zone.

9. Soe, "Free Democratic Party," pp. 126–30.

10. Genscher has voiced these views on a number of occasions. See, for example, Claus Gennrich, "Balancegang bei der Waehlerwerbung," *Frankfurter Allgemeine Zeitung* (hereafter *FAZ*), July 2, 1986.

11. "Genscher sieht seiner Reise nach Moskau 'hoffnungsvoll' entgegen," *FAZ*, July 15, 1986.

12. "Paper Reports on Genscher's Agenda for U.S.," *Foreign Broadcast Information Service* (Western Europe), April 14, 1986. pp. 2–3; *Der Spiegel*, June 16, 1986; " 'Auf keinen Fall Oel ins Feuer'," *Die Zeit*, September 27, 1985.

13. *FAZ*, July 15, 1986; Claus Gennrich, "Genschers Schutzschild," *FAZ*, July 18, 1986, *Die Zeit*, September 27, 1985. The phrase also appears repeatedly in resolutions passed at the FDP's party congress in May 1986. See "Parteitagsbeschluesse: Schwerpunkte liberaler Aussen-, Deutschland-, Sicherheits-, und Entwicklungspolitik," *Die Neue Bonner Depesche*, no. 6 (June 1986): 48–53.

14. "Genscher on SDI Agreements, East-West Relations," *Foreign Broadcast Information Service* (Western Europe), April 9, 1986, pp. J1–2; *Die Zeit*, September 27, 1985.

15. *Die Zeit*, September 27, 1985.

16. "Parteitagsbeschluesse," pp. 48, 50. Similar themes were sounded at the FDP party congress in September 1987 in Kiel.

17. Soe, "Free Democratic Party," pp. 171–72.

18. Ibid. pp. 172–73; "FDP: Jetzt folgt das Schaulaufen," *Der Spiegel*, June 4, 1984, pp. 13–19; "Der Maerchenprinz," *Der Spiegel*, January 14, 1985, pp. 25–6; "Nur noch eine Huelle," *Der Spiegel*, October 28, 1985, pp. 93–4.

19. Lambsdorff was subsequently cleared of all charges and has again become an active and vocal participant in party affairs.

20. "Strauss fordert einen Wechsel im Auswaertigen Amt nach der Bundestagswahl," *FAZ*, August 4, 1986.

21. "Bangemann spricht ein Machtwort fuer die Koalition. Ein verlaesslicher Partner auch nach der Wahl," *FAZ*, July 1, 1986; *FAZ*, July 15, 1986; Gerhard Spoerl, "Nur drei Punkte?," *Die Zeit*, January 11, 1985.

22. *FAZ*, July 1, 1986, July 15, 1986; "FDP: 'Wir koennen auch anders'," *Der Spiegel*, June 30, 1986, pp. 19–21.

23. Claus Gennrich, "Die Freude der FDP ueber die Wahlerfolge ist getruebt," *FAZ*, September 15, 1987.

24. Election analyses point to the increasing influence of this group of voters. See "In den Revieren des neuen Mittelstandes werden Wahlen entschieden," *FAZ*, February 2, 1987.

6 ARMS CONTROL AND THE GREEN PARTY

The Greens are a small, fractious party born of protest movements, whose policies are viewed, at best with skepticism, at worst with derision and ridicule, by mainstream German voters. The party's fairly unified stance on "peace policy" still leaves it outside the bounds of any well-established consensus on such postwar givens as the Atlantic alliance, German-American cooperation, or, more recently, the arms control process. Viewed as unpredictable and largely lacking credibility, the Greens are unlikely to make major inroads into the defense establishment nor affect actual policy on arms control.

Since the party's creation at the national level in January 1980, the Greens of West Germany have operated mostly outside the parameters of establishment party politics. Both the party's agenda and decentralized structure reflect its origins in earlier protest movements and political activist organizations, which also give the party its left-utopian orientation. Until now, the Greens have used parliament less as a means of affecting actual policy than as a forum to criticize or propagate their worldview. But the Greens are increasingly divided over the continuation of this strategy as well as the relative weight to be given to ecological themes versus socio-economic change.

The Greens pacifist-neutralist prescription for security policy—disarmament, withdrawal from NATO, and dissolution of the bloc system in Europe—is based on the party's programmatic commitment to the principle of nonviolence. Arms control, along with deterrence and defense policy, are typically not addressed directly: conventional policies are considered bankrupt strategies that have failed to advance humanity toward the ultimate goal—a disarmed, demilitarized global community.

The future ability of the Greens to advance their views will depend on the successful reconciliation of essential differences among the diverse groups and interests that make up the party. The division between fundamentalists and realists over strategy and political agenda may be irreconcilable, and may eventually splinter the party or lead to its demise at the national level.

Still, regardless of how they fare in future national elections, the Greens are likely to remain a political force in West German politics, if only at the state and local level. From here, the Greens, who sometimes claim to be the "better, more moral Germans," will not hesitate to articulate positions that clearly link arms reduction, survival, and national autonomy. By articulating these extreme positions within the political debate, Green pronouncements on defense and security issues may have some limited effect on the security debate in the SPD, and eventually, perhaps, on governmental decisionmaking. By legitimizing certain less extreme policies that would still require major departures from the status quo, the Greens may also have some direct impact on public opinion and, thus, on German politics. In this regard, however, it is unclear whether the primary effect is to increase support for left-wing positions or, both by frightening voters into the arms of the CDU/CSU and by siphoning support away from more centrist elements in the SPD, to decrease the probability of a left-wing government in Bonn.

ORIGINS OF GREEN SECURITY POLICIES

The Green's agenda and evolution into a political party reflect the uneasy and often tenuous alliance between its diverse and competing constituent groups. The roots of Green security policy may be traced back to the party's historical antecedents, including: (1) the protests against German rearmament and the first antinuclear campaign in the 1950s; (2) student rebellions in the 1960s; (3) citizens' initiatives and the antinuclear power movement of the 1970s; and (4) the German peace movement of the early 1980s. As the Greens evolved from protest movement to political party, and ever more groups were brought under the Green umbrella, the scope of their political platform broadened. The Greens owe many of their ideas, strategies, and members to these earlier protest movements and citizens groups.

In the 1950s, two waves of protest erupted, the first opposing German rearmament and entrance into NATO, the second against the deployment of nuclear weapons on German soil. The *ohne mich* and *Kampf dem Atomtod* campaigns mirrored a lingering aversion to militarism that followed the Nazi period and the reemergence of a German military force. This first German peace movement raised many of the same issues of peace and survival in the nuclear age that were to be echoed by the West German peace movement of the 1980s.

Many Green members and key leaders have been drawn from a second precursor: the student protest movement and extraparliamentary opposition of the 1960s. Led by the German Socialist Student Association (SDS), the movement was antiauthoritarian and leftist; the targets of protest are middle-class values, the increasing anonymity of modern society, and the central authority of the state. By 1968–69, the student movement had been radicalized, due in part to the lack of any sizable parliamentary opposition during the years of the Grand Coalition (1966–69) and thus the lack of spokesmen for these views within the government. The culmination of the campaign was the merging of protest groups into an "extraparliamentary opposition movement" (APO). By 1970, however, the SDS had splintered into several factions, including the Communist "K-groups" (dogmatic Marxist-Leninist groups); Maoist groups; and antiauthority and anarchist groups, such as the "Spontis."[1] A number of these would later be involved in the creation of the Green party, and are responsible for the party's leftist orientation. One former student activist and "Sponti," Joschka Fischer, has become a prominent member of the Greens, and was the first Green member to serve as a minister in a regional government.[2]

In the early 1970s, a growing concern for environmental protection gave rise to a number of locally based citizens' initiatives (*Buergerinitiativen*) which organized to achieve limited, single-issue objectives. The nuclear energy issue was rallying point and catalyst for the movement, but an additional source of motivation may have been a growing perception in the late 1970s that the political system had calcified and that the parties were largely unresponsive.[3] In this view, traditional political processes could not represent the common interests of the people adequately nor prevent an ecological crisis. By 1977, approximately 1,000 citizens' groups existed.[4] They banded together at the national level to form the Federal Association of Environmental Citizens' Initiatives (*Bundesverband Buergerinitiativen Umweltschutz-BBU*), which proved for the first time that grass-roots political action could be translated into a national political force. The Greens were to benefit from the organizational support of the citizens' initiatives and the BBU. Much of the Greens' ecological program is drawn from the agenda of these citizens' groups. The Greens' notion that traditional politics is a bankrupt process and must either be revitalized or radically changed can be traced back to the *Buergerinitiativen*, as well.

A counterculture developed in West Germany, parallel to the rise of the citizens' initiatives. The *Alternativen* reject the perceived consumerism and materialism of modern society, and advocate a return to more spiritual values, a holistic worldview, and concern with the notion of community. What separates the alternative subculture from mainstream German society is not a political schism along traditional left-right lines but a divergence in values, with the alternatives adhering to "postmaterialist" values. The utopian components of the "alternative" worldview resurfaced in the Greens' program. Moreover, holders of "postmaterialist" values have been a strong source of electoral support for the Greens.

The peace movement that developed in response to the 1979 NATO two-track decision was the final source of Green supporters and ideas. The Greens and the peace activists are not one and the same; the antinuclear movement of the 1980s was much broader based and included women's and pacifist groups, some Communist organizations, and many church and religious organizations as well. But much of the Greens' "peace policy" platform, discussed below, echoes the demands of the peace movement.

Drawing on these varied groups and ideas, the Green movement passed through a number of phases on the way to becoming a national political party. The consolidation began between 1977 and 1979 at the local community and state (*Land*) level, and reflected the different concerns in different parts of the country. In the Hamburg and Berlin Green parties, for example, "alternatives" and leftists predominated; two of Hamburg's unorthodox Marxists, Thomas Ebermann and Rainer Trampert, would go on to play a decisive role at the national level. In contrast, the Green party in Baden-Wuerttemberg was formed around a coalition of conservative environmentalists and independent nationalists.[5] In each case, the local and regional political constellation determined the profile of the party, a characteristic that continues to be a hallmark of the Greens. The movement toward greater consolidation led to the formation of a Green party at the national level in January 1980. The final step was taken when the Greens captured 5.6 percent in the March 1983 election and entered the Bundestag.

The party proclaims adherence to four basic principles: its program and actions are to be ecological, social, nonviolent, and congruent with the ideal of participatory democracy.[6] From the beginning, most Greens agreed that the party would be a supplement to, but not a substitute for, extraparliamentary activity. But just how far those parliamentary, supplementary activities were to extend was left unresolved; it is an issue that continues to plague the Greens.

In essence, Green party members have never been clear on whether they want to be, or should be a party at all. At every level of organization, Greens are divided over goals (the predominant are ecological or socioeconomic issues) and strategies (fundamental opposition versus acceptance of governmental responsibility and coalition with the SPD). These fundamental divisions are exacerbated by the structural organization of the party. The principle of participatory democracy and a commitment to decentralization have blurred the relationships between grassroots support (*Basis*), national executive committee (*Bundesvorstand*), and parliamentary party group (*Fraktion*), resulting in an ongoing tug-of-war between competing components.

To their credit, the Greens enjoy a relatively more stable existence in city, county, and even state governments. Between 1980 and 1987, the Greens gained entrance to seven of ten state parliaments and were active in many city and council political bodies. Generally speaking, the Greens have done well in Northern Germany, in Protestant areas, in urban regions, and in university cities. They have garnered less support in the South, in Catholic and rural areas, and in heavy industrial areas such as the Saar and Ruhr. The average Green voter is young (nearly 70 percent of Green voters are under thirty-five), middle-class, urban, and well-educated.[7]

While it is possible to profile an average Green voter, it is more difficult to describe a typical Green party member. Though the boundaries between factions are fluid and therefore hard to define, the Greens can be divided roughly into four groups: two groups of "fundamentalists"—the "red-Greens" or "ecosocialists," and "ecological fundamentalists" or "fundamentalist oppositionists"; and two groups of "realist/reformists"—the "Green-red realists," and reform ecologists.[8] A profile of each faction, its goals and notions on political strategy, is presented below.

The fundamentalists ("fundis") are bound by a commitment to what could be termed "no compromises, no coalitions." The red-Greens or "ecosocialists" include former members of the K-groups, and orthodox and unorthodox Marxists. This faction is strongest at the *Land* level in the Berlin Alternative List (AL) and the Hamburg Green Alternative List (GAL) and predominates on the Green national executive committee. Two of its more noted representatives are Thomas Ebermann and former executive committee spokesperson, Rainer Trampert. As traditional socialists, red-Greens see ecology as only one issue among many and are more passionately devoted to bringing about radical change in the political-economic system. On security issues, they tend to be anti-American and take a relatively benign view of the Soviet Union. The red-Greens view parliament as another tool in the struggle for change; they adamantly oppose any coalition with the SPD, though some favor an approach to the trade unions.

The red-Greens are joined in their uncompromising stance by the "fundamental oppositionists," such as Petra Kelly and Jutta Ditfurth, who has gained national prominence in her capacity as executive committee spokesperson. For the fundamental oppositionists, human survival is the overarching criterion of all political activity, taking precedence over class struggle and socioeconomic change. This faction of "fundis" consequently condemns atomic energy, nuclear deterrence, and the "waste" of the modern economy. Though its members do not reject parliamentary democracy out of hand, they demand that the Greens remain uncompromising critics of traditional politics. The Greens, in their view, should remain an "antiparty party" and shun governmental responsibility and coalition with the SPD.[9]

The realists/reformists, in contrast, are more willing to enter the sullied realm of compromise and politics, believing that it offers the only chance of achieving any reform at all. The largest faction, the "Green-red realists" or "Green reform Socialists," is best represented by such persons as the former environmental minister in Hesse, Joschka Fisher, Otto Schily, and former executive committee spokesperson, Lukas Beckmann. The Green-red realists give precedence to ecological issues over socialist ones, but, in contrast to the "fundis" are prepared to accept political responsibility, enter coalitions and governments—in short, to utilize the tools of traditional politics in order to bring about small changes wherever possible. In the "realos" view, limited cooperation—even coalition—with the SPD should not be excluded. Cooperation may call for formal coalition, as in Hesse, or a pledge to "tolerate" an SPD-led government. In either case, the Greens should aspire to be a leftist, reformist party, an "uncomfortable but indispensable partner," corrective of the SPD.[10]

The Green-red realists are joined by a smaller group of reform ecologists, who tend to be more conservative, middle-class conservationists. They are most strongly represented in Baden-Wuerttemberg, Lower Saxony, and, to a lesser extent, in Northrhine-Westphalia. The reform ecologists focus on environmental issues and are willing to participate constructively in parliament and accept political responsibility.[11]

The already existent ideological splits within the Greens are magnified by the party's commitment to participatory democracy and a decentralized structure. Local, regional, and state party organizations enjoy a significant degree of autonomy, and the party is organized to protect such autonomy.

The statewide assembly (*Landesversammlung*) meets semi-annually to settle policy and strategy questions, and to elect a state executive committee which carries out administrative tasks. In those states in which the Greens are represented in the *Landtag*, a parliamentary party group (*Landtagsgruppe*) also exists. The lines of responsibility between executive committee and parliamentary group are not clearly drawn, however; the latter tends to view itself as a parallel, autonomous organization, not one subject to committee dictates.[12]

A similar structure and blurring of responsibility occurs at the national level. Delegates to the national assembly are elected directly from the local level, (not by the states). Like its counterpart at the state level, the national assembly decides policy and strategy. The national executive committee is composed of eleven members, with three designated as presiding officers and spokespersons. The question of ultimate control and authority, and the relationship between local organization, executive committee, and *Fraktion* has yet to be defined. On a daily basis, leadership at the national level by default falls to the Bundestag parliamentary caucus, since most members of the executive are only part-time politicians.[13] Sometimes the executive committee may reassert itself, as it did at the national assembly in May 1986.

The consequence of the Greens' ideological heterogeneity and political practice is an ongoing struggle for dominance between the fundamentalists and realists. When it comes to the Greens, in the view of one analyst, there simply is no authoritative speaker.[14] The "realos" seem to be strongest at the local level and are gaining in the Bundestag parliamentary group, but the executive belongs to the "fundis," as evidenced by a failed vote at the May 1986 party congress to unseat the two most adamant oppositionists from the executive committee, Ditfurth and Trampert, and the election of a fundamentalist majority to the executive committee in spring 1987.[15] In 1987, heated disputes between the Greens' national executive committee and *Fraktion* executive committee received national press attention, as the two groups struggled for control over the future course of the party.[16] Depending upon the governmental level or changing political fortunes, one or the other faction may gain the upper hand; the outcome of this process may well be crucial to the Greens political future.

THE GREENS AND SECURITY ISSUES

As its political agenda has evolved, only one issue area has galvanized the party into a somewhat unified whole: "peace policy," disarmament, and alliance politics. The Greens' positions on defense and arms control are firmly rooted in the party's principle of "nonviolence" that often is indistinguishable from programmatic pacifism. Security policies are related as well to the Green vision of ecological utopia—a decentralized, demilitarized world in which security is achieved through "political means." A number of alternatives to conventional defense arrangements, ranging from strictly defensive forces to "social defense," have been proposed in this context. But in each case, the Greens operate outside the existing defense and security consensus in the Federal Republic. Their views therefore do not find broad acceptance among most German voters. Nevertheless, the Greens' alternative security policies may help to shape public security concerns, or influence perceptions of threats to German security. Additionally, the Greens' emphasis on participatory democracy—even for security policy decisions—constitutes a source of continuous pressure on the government to be accountable to its citizens' fears and concerns.

The guiding principles of Green security policy are nonviolence, peace, and disarmament; together they provide a contextual framework to understand the Greens' specific proposals on NATO and the arms control process. The Greens are fundamentally opposed to the use of force between nations, declaring in their party program that an "ecological foreign policy is nonviolent policy." They similarly reject all things connected with the possible use of violence: domestic and foreign militarism, the arms race, and, above all, nuclear weapons, which, they argue, have made war the equivalent of murder and a "crime against life."[17]

In lieu of traditional defense policy, the Greens advocate an "active peace policy," whose goal is global disarmament, a demilitarized world, and a "peaceful and cooperative living together." In the Greens' view, law must replace violence; all nuclear, biological, and chemical weapons should be destroyed; and all "foreign troops should withdraw from foreign territories" (a phrase clearly applied to Eastern and Western Europe as well). The Greens argue that the Germans have a particularly strong motivation for adopting their "peace policy," pointing out that in a crisis, the use of nuclear weapons would occur on German soil, costing German lives. The Green program thus links national autonomy to questions of disarmament and survival.[18]

The Greens' attitude toward arms control must be viewed within this broader contextual framework. The Greens categorically reject deterrence. The arms control process, as part and parcel of conventional notions of defense and security, is similarly dismissed; indeed, there are few specific pronouncements on ongoing arms control negotiations. Instead, the Greens tend to restrict themselves to broad slogans or catchphrases.

To move the world toward demilitarization, the Greens in their party programs have suggested a number of far-reaching measures, including:

- West German withdrawal from NATO and the dissolution of both NATO and the Warsaw Pact.

- The creation of a common European "peace order," with the goal of achieving concrete results in all deadlocked arms control forums. Bonn should take the first step by rejecting all new weapon systems and beginning to disarm unilaterally.

- Global disarmament negotiations.

- Removal of all NATO and Warsaw Pact theater nuclear weapons.

- Creation of a weapons-free zone in Eastern and Western Europe.

- Withdrawal of all "foreign troops" from "foreign territories."

- Dismantling of the Bundeswehr and border patrol.[19]

To replace traditional defense structures, a variety of proposals have been suggested. The Greens draw on the work of a number of analysts, including Horst Ahfeldt's concept of area defense and a Bundeswehr restructured into defensive "technocommando units," and Theodor Ebert's notion of "social defense" or security through "political means."[20] As with other aspects of the Greens' policies, there is not total agreement on the degree of "nonviolence" that is desired. At its extreme, society is to be reorganized in alternative, decentralized structures, and citizens reeducated to civil courage and the will to resist. In theory, such measures would make it clear to any potential aggressor that the cost of occupation would be greater than any conceivable gain.

The Greens' program for security is utopian and largely confined to sweeping statements or slogans. For the most part, specific problems of security or arms control are not addressed. On those occasions when a specific response to a particular arms control issue is appropriate, Green parliamentarians have tended to make sweeping statements on the inadequacy of limited arms control negotiations. In August 1987, for example, Helmut Lippelt and Alfred Mechtersheimer criticized the conditional nature of Chancellor Kohl's pledge not to modernize West German Pershing 1 missiles, and urged the government to take unilateral steps toward disarmament. On other issues, while the Greens oppose SDI, they do not engage in technical arguments about its feasibility. Rather, the focus of debate on SDI or other issues is the morality of policy measures, the bankruptcy of traditional security approaches.[21]

THE FUTURE OF THE GREENS

The future impact of the Greens on West German arms control policy or any other issue depends largely on the future of the party itself. The conflict between "fundis" and "realos"—rooted in the Greens' evolution from protest movement to party—is unresolved, the definitive answer to the coalition question still forthcoming. The differences may be irreconcilable, threatening the party's continued survival after 1987 at the national level.

The coalition question may yet prove the Greens' nemesis. In the view of a number of analysts, the acceptance of political responsibility advocated by the "realos" is both opportunity and threat. It is an opportunity because it offers the Greens the chance to achieve some reform; it is also a threat, however, because many of the fundamentalists would rather split the party than compromise and dirty their hands in the world of politics.[22]

There are some indications that the realists among the Greens may be ascending. The practice of rotating Green representatives in the Bundestag has been abolished. Moreover, setbacks in a series of state elections provoked some rethinking of Green strategy. In the Saar (March 1985), the Greens were "out-Greened" by SPD candidate Oskar Lafontaine, who successfully usurped Green themes in the election campaign. In Northrhine-Westphalia (May 1985), the Greens' refusal to consider a coalition with the SPD may have contributed to their losses. Even in Lower Saxony (May 1986), where the Greens won 7.1 percent of the vote, the results were viewed by some as a loss, because of higher expectations. In the aftermath of the Soviet Chernobyl nuclear disaster, the Greens had been expected to capture 8 to 9 percent of the vote.[23] Some Greens have drawn the appropriate lessons. In November 1985, for example, the "realists" of the Green party in Northrhine-Westphalia succeeded in pushing through a resolution committing the party to "utilization of all opportunities in the parliament, including participation in the government." At the Baden-Wuerttemberg party congress in July 1986 a coalition of "realos" and moderate feminists outvoted and outmaneuvered the party's "fundis," including prominent Green member Jutta Ditfurth. In fall 1987, the spokesman of the Baden-Wuerttemberg caucus, Fritz Kuhn, proposed in a lengthy working paper that the Greens adopt a policy of "shifting majorities," including cooperation with the CDU.[24]

Nevertheless, in other party forums, the fundamentalists retain the upper hand. The party's fundamentalist faction reasserted itself at the Greens' Duisburg conference in spring 1987 and elected an executive committee dominated by members from their ranks. Fundamentalist critics also cite the collapse of the Hesse "red-Green" experiment as proof that the realist course is doomed to failure.[25]

But the Greens' continued existence at the national level will also depend on a number of external factors. The party may have reached or be reaching the limits of growth. First-time voters—those entering the eighteen to twenty-five age bracket—may be returning to more traditional values and political preferences.[26] More important, the Greens must also face the German voters' deep-seated aversion to the specter of instability that the Greens conjure up. As Theo Sommer points out, the German voter does not want chaos, but clarity and predictability.[27]

CONCLUSION

Given the perhaps fatal divisions among the Greens, and their uncertain future as a political party, at least at the national level, it is tempting to dismiss entirely the impact of this small party. But even though their positions are unacceptable to a substantial majority of West Germans, the Greens may exercise a limited influence on three aspects of the broader context of West German security policy: the SPD security debate; the governmental decisionmaking process; and public threat perceptions and attitudes toward the United States and Soviet Union. Even if the party drops below the requisite 5 percent of the national vote in future elections, its presence at the local or state levels is fairly secure, ensuring that Green views on security issues will be given a public hearing.

Though difficult to assess, the very existence of a party to the left of the SPD may serve as a source of pressure on the Social Democrats' policies. The leaders of the SPD may be moving the party toward the center as part of an election-winning strategy, but the existence of a Green party, espousing policies potentially attractive to the SPD's left wing or younger members, may check the party's drift in this direction. The Greens' policies—though more radical departures from the established defense consensus than those advanced by the SPD—do display points of similarity, including the notion of an "European peace order," and the proposal for weapons-free zones in Europe. The Greens could conceivably exercise a subtle "leftward tug" on the policies of the SPD.

The Greens may diminish the chances for victory by a left-leaning government at the regional or national level. Voting analyses do not reveal a clear trend, but there are indications that moderate SPD voters or, even more likely, voters dissatisfied with conservative coalitions may be scared away from voting for the Social Democrats because they fear a "red-Green" coalition. For such voters, the Hesse experiment offers proof that the Greens would be an incalculable and unpredictable coalition partner. The Greens' continued espousal of absolutist goals at the Hanover party congress in May 1986 and their support of antinuclear power demonstrations that later turned violent may have played a role in the Greens' failure to win the projected 8 to 9 percent of the vote in the Lower Saxony elections. Less clear is whether the Greens' policies and the possibility of an SPD-Green coalition robbed the SPD of votes as well. On the other hand, the CDU has recognized the electoral value of scare tactics. Verbal attacks on the Greens during the 1987 national election campaign, such as Heiner Geissler's reference to the Greens as the "*Volkssturm* of the SPD" clearly were intended to heighten fear of the red-Green specter among moderate voters.[28]

True to their commitment to direct democracy, the Greens will likely exert sustained pressure on government decisionmaking. In this vein, the Greens supported the call for a referendum on the NATO decision to deploy Pershing and cruise missiles, arguing that such a fundamental, "life-or-death" decision could not be left to elected officials (or foreign governments) but should reflect the will of the people. Though the referendum campaign failed—as other such attempts to "democratize" the process are likely to do—the call to greater accountability may not be entirely ignored.

Further, the Greens' perceptions of the threat to West German security—the arms race, militarism, and the tensions inherent in the East-West bloc system—may have some limited impact on public attitudes toward the Soviet Union, the United States, and East-West relations in general. The Green tendency either to treat the United States and Soviet Union as moral equals or level greater criticism against American policies may affect the views of non-Green voters as well.

Finally, though a small but vocal minority, the Greens have given vent to deep-seated fears about environmental threats, the arms race, national survival, and national autonomy, issues by no means confined to Green party ranks. The numbers of groups and individuals that the peace movement as a whole successfully mobilized, particularly among younger West Germans, is one indication of the reservoir of feeling tapped by the Greens. In this sense, while more conservative German voters would undoubtedly dismiss the call to withdraw from NATO or unilaterally disarm, the underlying concerns articulated by Green spokesmen may be shared to a lesser degree by other West German voters.

NOTES

1. Gerd Langguth, *The Green Factor in German Politics*, trans. Richard Strauss (Boulder, Colo.: Westview Press, 1986), pp. 1-4.
2. Fischer was environmental minister in Hessen from October 1985 to February 1986.
3. Horst Mewes, "The West German Green Party," *New German Critique* 28 (1983): 51–4.
4. Langguth, *Green Factor*, p. 7.
5. Mewes, "Green Party," pp. 56–59.
6. Die Gruenen, *Das Bundesprogramm* (Bonn: Die Gruenen Bundesgeschaeftsstelle, 1981), pp. 4–5.
7. Alfred Rothacher, "The Green Party in German Politics," *West European Politics* 7 (July 1984): 113–14.
8. This classification scheme is based on the analysis of Gerd Langguth, *Green Factor*, pp. 57–61. Other authors have suggested alternative groupings. See, for example, Mewes, "Green Party," pp. 69–71; Gertrud Schruefer, *Die Gruenen in Deutschen Bundestag: Anspruch und Wirklichkeit* (Nuremberg: Pauli-Balleis-Verlag, 1985), pp. 76–82.
9. Langguth, *Green Factor*, pp. 58, 60–61; Mewes, "Green Party," p. 69.
10. Langguth, *Green Factor*, pp. 58–59; Gerhard Spoerl, "Ein Sponti spielt Vabanque," *Die Zeit*, December 13, 1985.
11. Langguth, *Green Factor*, pp. 59–60.
12. Fritjof Capra and Charlene Spretnak, *Green Politics* (New York: E.P. Dutton, Inc., 1984), pp. 230–32.
13. Ibid., pp. 232–34; Rothacher, "Green Party in Politics," pp. 110–11.
14. Rothacher, "Green Party in Politics," p. 111.
15. Horst Bieber, "Die Reifepruefung steht noch bevor," *Die Zeit*, May 15, 1987.
16. Following elections in September 1987 in Bremen and Schleswig-Holstein the two committees even held separate press conferences. Each offered its own evaluation of the election's significance for the Greens. See "Kohl:

Streit in der Union kostete Stimmen. Strauss: Kohl trifft nicht den Kern der Sache," *Sueddeutsche Zeitung*, September 15, 1987; "Historische Chance verpasst," *Frankfurter Allgemeine Zeitung* [hereafter *FAZ*], September 15, 1987.

17. Die Gruenen, *Bundesprogramm*, pp. 5, 18–19.

18. Ibid.

19. Ibid.

20. Works often cited include Horst Ahfeldt, *Verteidigung und Frieden: Politik mit militaerischen Mitteln* (Munich: C. Hanser, 1976); and Theodor Ebert, *Soziale Verteidigung* (Waldkirch: Waldkircherverlagsgesellschaft, 1981).

21. Kim Holmes, "Eco-Peace Movements and the Security Consensus in West Germany," paper presented at Ninth Annual Conference of the German Studies Association, Washington, D.C., October 4–6, 1985.

22. See, for example, Horst Bieber, "Beide Flügel Werden gebraucht," *Die Zeit*, December 20, 1985; and Gerhard Spörl, "Ein Spartic spielt Vabanque," *Die Zeit*, December 13, 1985.

23. A number of very optimistic Greens had hoped to win 10 percent of the vote. See Matthias Nass, "Wir haben einen Elfmeter vergeben," *Die Zeit*, June 27, 1986.

24. "Schoenste Nebensache," *Der Spiegel*, November 11, 1985, pp. 22–23; "Jedem Stalinisten eine Freikarte fuer einfache Fahrt nach Albanien," *FAZ*, July 7, 1986. On Kuhn's suggestions, see "Wenn's dem Cleverle nicht reicht, hilft's Dummerle aus," *FAZ*, September 15, 1987.

25. In 1984, the SPD premier of Hesse, Helges Boerner, could win reelection only with the support of the Greens. After much internal debate, the Greens agreed to form a coalition and assume governmental responsibilities. Joschka Fischer was sworn in as environmental minister, the first Green to serve in a cabinet.

26. See, for example, "Vorwaerts zurueck," *Der Spiegel*, February 11, 1985, p. 34. Others might argue that it is too early to tell whether this is evidence of a long-term shift in young voters' preferences. More recent poll information is unclear on the point. See "Rot-gruene Mehrheit bei Waehlern unter 40," *Der Spiegel*, June 30, 1986, pp. 36–45.

27. Theo Sommer, "Gruent Gruen oder welkt Gruen?" *Die Zeit*, March 22, 1985.

28. Rolf Zundel, "Ein Sieg der Machttechniker," *Die Zeit*, June 27, 1986.

7 WEST GERMAN PUBLIC ATTITUDES ON ARMS CONTROL

Stephen F. Szabo

Any study of public attitudes on issues as esoteric as arms control must have limited ambitions. The West German public is interested in arms control only as part of a larger conception of security, not as an end in itself. Germans have remained in favor of the general objective of disarmament and arms control since the 1950s, but have always been unclear about and uninterested in the specifics of arms control issues. Consequently, general patterns of consistency underlay more detailed contradictions and indifference. Germans are concerned about their security, but not about the details of negotiations or proposals on arms control.

Yet, the study of public attitudes often reveals patterns and trends in images of security. Arms control serves as a seismograph in this regard, monitoring structural changes below the surface. The reader thus should be interested in questions relating to long-term continuity and change and should not place much weight on the responses to individual items—polls are pieces of a mosaic rather than the whole.

Mass opinion may not even be the most important aspect of public opinion to examine. As a study of German elite opinion in the 1960s concluded, "If past experiences are an indication, mass opinion (will) follow the lead of elite opinion."[1] Given these limitations, this chapter will offer an examination of the levels of public interest in, and knowledge of, arms control issues, as well as a consideration of the factors shaping West German attitudes on security policy. It concludes with a survey of public views on important specific arms control issues.

The views expressed in this chapter are solely those of the author and do not necessarily reflect the views of the U.S. Department of Defense.

WEST GERMAN PUBLIC ATTITUDES ON ARMS CONTROL

West German public opinion on arms control and related issues is part of a conception of security that has been shaped by two broad approaches, the *Westpolitik* of the Adenauer period and the *Ostpolitik* of the Social-Liberal coalition of 1969–1982. The first stressed the importance of the Federal Republic's integration with the West for security. The Social Democrats (SPD) did not fully accept this approach until the Bad Godesberg party congress of 1959.

The second element of security policy was added by the Brandt-Scheel government (SPD-FDP) between 1969 and 1974 and consolidated by the Schmidt-Genscher coalition of 1974–1982. The *Ostpolitik*, along with the Harmel Report of NATO, which added to defense the elements of détente and dialogue with the East, was accepted by the opposition Christian Democrats no later than the election of 1983.

Both official and public views on arms control reflect these two phases in the German definition of security. Arms control was viewed in the 1950s and 1960s with reservation and skepticism by government elites. Integration into NATO and the buildup of the German military contribution to the Alliance then took clear precedence over arms control measures, which were thought to imply consolidation of the status quo in Europe and permanent recognition of the division of Germany.

A major study of German elite opinion in the 1960s described attitudes on arms control at the time. "Armament rather than disarmament had been the major preoccupation of the German Federal government and effective deterrence of Soviet aggression, rather than arms control, the principal argument of its spokesman regarding international stability and world peace."[2]

After *Ostpolitik*, however, arms control came increasingly to be viewed as a means of defusing East-West confrontation and promoting détente and the German-German relationship.[3] The process is now seen as a symbol of conflict management and a limitation on superpower conflict. No German government can afford to be unconcerned about arms control. The government deployed Intermediate Range Nuclear Forces (INF) successfully in the early 1980s in the face of substantial public opposition; this occurred, in part, because the government was able to maintain and even enhance the German-German dialogue while deploying the missiles.

Given this general background, a closer look at public awareness and knowledge of arms control issues follows.

Arms Control and the German Public

Throughout the West, public opinion on foreign and defense policies tends to be less informed and intense than opinion on domestic issues. The latter are seen to affect individuals' standard and quality of living directly and to be subject to national political control. Foreign policy issues, in contrast, are much more remote from everyday life and are believed to be largely beyond the control of the individual or even the national government. This remoteness is especially pronounced in European opinion with its long tradition of viewing defense and foreign policy as an elite preserve managed by distant bureaucracies.

The West German case fits within these general parameters. National surveys have shown consistently that the German public is almost always primarily concerned with economic and social issues. Unemployment, inflation, terrorism and, more recently, environmental protection are consistently listed as the most important problems facing the nation. Concerns related to defense or foreign policy, such as the problem of inadequate defense, the threat of war, or even the continued division of the German nation, are seldom listed by more than 10 to 20 percent of the adult population as key problems for the country.[4] Even during the height of the debate on INF, for example, only 20 percent of a national sample chose INF stationing as one of their two greatest concerns. About two-thirds of the respondents, on the other hand, chose unemployment and one-third chose crime, as their major concerns.[5]

A lack of interest in security issues is characteristic of all Europeans but has been reinforced in the Federal Republic by the limited German autonomy in security issues caused by West German dependence on the U.S. security guarantee and its integration into the NATO command structure. The small size of the West German strategic community, the general consensus on security policy prevalent through most of the postwar period, and the highly bureaucratized nature of the security policy process have also limited public involvement.[6]

As is illustrated in the Harris survey summarized in Table 7–1, the West German public was far less concerned about security issues than were other European publics. In the survey, respondents reporting the threat of war

Table 7-1. Major Public Concerns in Western Europe.

"Which of the following are your greatest concerns for yourself and your country today?"

	France	FRG	Britain	Italy	Norway	Switzerland
Unemployment	78%	52%	60%	69%	64%	85%
Threat of war	47	14	40	56	30	40
Nuclear weapons	26	15	43	39	31	33
Crime	30	10	36	58	12	34
Social injustice	27	12	23	28	15	32
Inflation	39	9	18	38	3	20
Excessive government spending	21	5	12	19	4	13
Poor political leadership	24	7	19	25	9	4
Energy crisis	15	4	15	19	1	13
Inadequate defense	7	2	11	7	4	5
Other/no answer	2	5	1	3	3	—

Source: The Atlantic Institute for International Affairs–Louis Harris Poll *Security and the Industrial Democracies* (April–May 1984). Coordinated and centralized by Louis Harris–France, Paris.

to be one of their greatest concerns ranged from 30 percent in Norway to 56 percent in Italy—but only 14 percent of West German respondents. Similarly, whereas one-third or more of respondents in most surveyed nations cited nuclear weapons as one of their greatest concerns, only 15 percent of the German respondents made such claims.

Arms Control and the Attentive Public

As security and foreign policy issues have not been *salient* for most Germans, their awareness of them has been very limited. Awareness is represented by the percentage of people who state that they follow international affairs "very closely," a fraction known as the *attentive public*.

Interest in arms control issues increased in the 1980s as compared to the 1950s and 1960s. The Deutsch study of opinion in the 1960s previously cited concluded that both elites and publics were uninterested in arms control and disarmament. Those issues were viewed as technical in nature and out of German hands in any case. The authors noted, "It seems that passions and controversy which rearmament and nuclear testing aroused in the 1950s have yielded to a mood of apathy, indifference and cynicism about disarmament."[7]

USIA data from the earlier period, for example, revealed that only about one-third of a national West German sample in 1954 had heard of or read about a then recent Soviet proposal for disarmament. This was no longer the case by the early 1980s. From 55 to 60 percent of Germans surveyed had heard about SALT II and up to 75 percent were aware of the INF negotiations in the early 1980s.[8]

Polls conducted in four West European countries, including the FRG, between 1979 and 1983 indicated that the level of awareness on national security and foreign policy issues remained in the 7 to 22 percent range of the adults sampled throughout the period.[9] In West Germany, however, the attentive public is somewhat larger; its share increased from 6 percent in 1979 to 28 percent in 1984. West Germany was the only European country to register a major sustained increase in its attentive public over this period. In the other European countries, interest in security affairs peaked in 1982–83 and then declined by 1984 to pre-INF levels.[10]

Knowledge in the Federal Republic tends to be greater than the European average. About one-third of the German public chose the correct description of SALT II from a multiple choise list, while less than 20 percent in the other European states did so. On the politically intense issue of INF, roughly 60 percent in a 1981 West German survey knew that the Euromissiles would be deployed in other NATO states, as well as in the FRG. About one-half knew that the INF systems were nuclear. Only less than one-third did not know enough to respond to knowledge tests about INF.[11]

Although important distinctions should be made between attentives and better educated elites, most surveys do not break down data between these groups.[12] Data is most often categorized by party, age, educational level, and sex. In short, the opinions of educated individuals are easier to analyze than those of the attentives.

The best educated in West Germany are defined as those who have received at least the secondary academic training of the *Gymnasium* and have attained the qualification to attend a university, the *Abitur*. This group is no longer as elite as it was in the early 1960s: in 1970 approximately 14 percent of students attended a *Gymnasium*: by 1983 that proportion had increased to 25 percent.[13]

In general, better educated West Germans tend to be more concerned about security issues. During the height of the Euromissile controversy in April 1983, for example, only 22 percent of the public listed the stationing of the missiles as a leading issue confronting the nation. The better educated were twice as likely to be concerned over the issue, with 40 percent of this group listing the missile issue as a major one. For them, the missiles were second only to unemployment. Similarly, better educated West Germans tend to be more aware of security issues; about one-half of those with a basic education had heard of the NATO double decision, while almost all of those with an *Abitur* had.[14]

In addition to educational level, both partisan affiliation and age tend to be related to attentiveness. Generally, arms control issues have been the concern of affluent middle-aged males. During the INF debate, a substantial politicization of the issue occurred wherein the most active and attentive tended to be the better educated young (under thirty-five) who identified with either the SPD or the Greens. This group tended to believe that INF was a major issue and were committed opponents. Those who were uncertain or unconcerned about INF were more likely to be women, to have only an elementary education, to support the CDU/CSU, to be over thirty-five years of age, to have low incomes, and to live in small to medium-sized towns.[15]

The better educated may have been the most involved but they were not always better informed. Ideological preconceptions often distorted their view of the facts. They were less informed when it came to knowledge about the Soviet INF monopoly, for example, and they were more likely to believe that the FRG had INF systems deployed prior to December 1983.[16]

The German better educated, in short, were highly critical of the INF decision and of U.S. policy in general and were much more favorably inclined toward the "peace movement" than was the general public. This better educated group may be the harbingers of long-term change. In the 1960s, it was this same intellectual elite, then politically marginal, that "favored a change in the status quo in the form of détente in Central Europe."[17] That view emerged as the new popular consensus, however, by the late 1970s.

There are some signs that this group has been less critical on a number of post-INF arms control issues than they were on INF. Polls on the desirability of retaining SALT II restraints taken in July 1985 found that the better educated were more supportive of maintaining the treaty than were the less informed, but not more likely to be either pro-United States or pro-Soviet Union in their views of violations. Similarly, polls on attitudes toward SDI indicated that while the better educated were somewhat more critical of the program, their views again were not as distinctive as they were on INF. No clear association between demographic variables and attitudes on SDI was apparent.[18]

Did the INF debate "inoculate" the public against nuclear issues or did it "sensitize" it to them? Was it anticlimax or prologue?[19] It is likely that INF reflected a longer term change in West German society that has resulted in a larger potential attentive public on security issues. This changing social context includes an expanded level of secondary and higher education, changing social values and views of authority, the development of an adversial media on security policy, as well as of a network of peace research and strategic studies institutes. The emergence of the Greens as a partisan alternative to the major parties, combined with the coming of age of a large postwar generation socialized in this new environment, augur a long-term secular trend.

While arms control issues since the initial deployment of INF in late 1983 have had less resonance with the wider public, it would be a mistake to conclude that the attentive public has returned to the old postulates of German security policy. The attentive public of the 1980s remains larger than it was before the Euromissile debate, and it has been sensitized to the broader aspects of West Germany's security policy, especially its dependence on the United States. The previous common assessment drawn by the Deutsch study and others that a general indifference and consensus characterized West German public attitudes on arms control is no longer valid.[20]

The Electoral Impact of Arms Control

In spite of these important changes, it is clear that arms control issues specifically and security policy generally were not decisive factors in the federal elections of January 1987. In this sense the 1987 election was consistent with the traditions of postwar German voting behavior. Elections in West Germany have hinged on economic issues and performance or on the general competence of the chancellor and the ruling coalition. The one major exception to this rule was the 1972 federal election that centered on *Ostpolitik* and the Eastern treaties.

A thorough survey analysis of voting behavior in the January 1987 election found that economic issues dominated the electorate's concerns and that the Christian-Liberal coalition was viewed as the most competent in dealing with these issues. The study by *Forschungsgruppe Wahlen Mannheim* found that unemployment was listed by 81 percent as a very important issue facing the country followed by the environment (68 percent), securing pensions (65 percent), and then arms control (59 percent).[21]

When this list is compared to a similar one compiled for the 1983 election it is clear that in both elections economic concerns dominated, but that the environment and probably arms control (which was not offered to the voters as a choice in 1983) were of more importance in 1987 than in 1983. Relations to the East and to the United States ranked near the bottom in both elections, cited by a quarter of the voters.

In both elections the SPD was viewed as more competent to deal with arms control, the environment, and relations with the East, while the CDU-FDP coalition was viewed as more competent in dealing with the United States. The relatively low salience of these foreign policy issues, however, limited their electoral impact.[22]

Arms control was listed as a very important issue by Green voters (81 percent) and SPD voters (67 percent), but only by 53 percent of CDU-CSU voters and a similar proportion of FDP voters. Similarly, Green and SPD voters were more likely to list relations with the USSR or the GDR as very important issues compared to CDU-CSU and FDP voters who stressed relations with the United States.[23]

In conclusion, arms control issues have been overshadowed by economic concerns for the majority of German voters. However, a surprisingly large number did cite arms control as very important in 1987; by itself the issue tended to help the SPD. The Christian-Liberal coalition did not allow much daylight between itself and the SPD on its commitment to the principle of arms control. In a closer election, arms control issues could be more significant, as, in fact, they apparently were in the state election in Rhineland Palatinate in the spring of 1987. This election occurred during a time of dissension within the CDU-CSU over whether to accept the double-zero proposal of INF. The FDP gained important votes through its clear commitment to the proposal.

However, in the state election in northern Schleswig Holstein held in September 1987, only two weeks after Chancellor Kohl agreed to scrap the German Pershing 1a missiles as part of an INF agreement, the pro-arms control position did not benefit the CDU, which dropped nine points from its previous performance. Unemployment and agricultural issues were much more salient than arms control.

SOURCES OF WEST GERMAN ATTITUDES ON ARMS CONTROL

Having set the general context of attitudes, a closer examination of the key factors associated with West German attitudes on arms control follows.

Perceptions of threat, images of security and of the major German ally, the United States, as well as the role of inter-German relations on West German attitudes will be explored, as will attitudes toward nuclear deterrence and other aspects of current Western strategy. Finally the impact of partisan and demographic variables on these attitudes will be discussed.

Threat Assessment and the Military Balance

One of the most dramatic changes in West German strategic culture over the past decade has been the steady muting of the perception of a Soviet military or political threat. The postwar security consensus rested the foundation of a strong concern over the threat posed to German security by the USSR. This view has been altered substantially over the past decade.

Although the West German public has always had a negative image of the Soviet Union as a society, the image of the Soviets as a military or political threat has diminished. The data in Table 7–2 provide a picture of the declining perception of the Soviet threat. While specific events that have involved the use or threatened use of Soviet military power (i.e., events in Hungary, Czechoslovakia, Afghanistan) have resulted in short-term increases in these threat perceptions, the long-term secular trend has consistently reasserted itself after a period of a few months to a year.

The result is that by the mid-1980s, only 9 to 16 percent of West Germans felt the Soviets would attack Western Europe in the next five years.[24] A SINUS survey conducted in the fall of 1986 found that 31

Table 7–2. Changing West German Perceptions of the Soviet Threat.

"Do you think that the USSR (East) is a threat to us or don't you think so?"

	7/52	3/58	11/64	9/69	4/71	2/80	5/82	5/83
Serious threat	66%	51%	39%	32%	28%	10%	44%	44%
Not so serious threat/No threat	15	27	37	55	46	35	55	49
Don't know, No answer	19	22	24	13	26	14	1	8

Source: Adapted from Hans Rattinger, ''The Federal Republic of Germany,'' in *The Public and Atlantic Defense*, ed. Gregory Flynn and Harns Rattinger (Totawa, New Jersey: Rowman and Allanheld, 1985), p. 118.

percent of West Germans felt the FRG was militarily threatened while 44 percent did not and 25 percent were unsure.[25]

The Germans tend to be somewhat less concerned than the British and French about the Soviets as a military and political threat. A December 1985 USIA-commissioned survey found that 16 percent of West Germans were "very" or "fairly" concerned about a Soviet attack within the next five years, compared to 28 percent of the French and the British. The Italian and Dutch publics were even less concerned than the Germans.

Similarly, only 28 percent of the West Germans were concerned over the prospect of Soviet intimidation while those concerned in the Netherlands, Italy, and the United Kingdom were in the 33 to 36 percent range. In fact, more West Germans were concerned about American pressures on their nation's policies than they were about Soviet pressures.

This diminishing perception of threat has occurred in a military environment that is perceived to be far less favorable to the West than it was in the 1960s. The data in Table 7–3 outline the changing West German public view of the military balance. By the early 1970s, more West Germans consistently believed that the Warsaw Pact was superior militarily. The Reagan defense buildup tended to shift perceptions in the early to mid-1980s; by the end of 1986 there had been substantial erosion of the Soviets' perceived lead (although 20 to 25 percent still viewed the Soviets as ahead). As the data in Table 7–4 suggest, the recent trend reflects increasing numbers of West Germans who believe that there is rough parity between East and West.

Moreover, West Germans, as do West Europeans in general, tend to prefer a state of parity to one of U.S. superiority. The 1986 SINUS poll, for example, asked which condition was desirable from the West German perspective and found that only 24 percent favored U.S. superiority compared to 63 percent who favored military parity. This represents a marked change from the 1950s when 73 percent preferred the United States to be militarily stronger than the USSR.[26] Parity is seen as a more stable condition, one conducive to arms control, while the superiority of one side is viewed as an incentive for an arms race.

This does not mean that the Soviet military buildup has been ignored by West Germans. As the data in Table 7–5 illustrate, the military buildup by the Soviet Union was viewed in 1984 as the factor creating tensions. While the West German public is relatively hawkish on the Soviets as compared to other Europeans, they are also the most critical public concerning the U.S. buildup. In fact, fewer West Germans mention the

Table 7–3. West German Views of the NATO-WTO Military Balance.

"What do you think: which bloc is militarily superior at present, NATO or the Warsaw Pact (East Bloc)?"

	NATO	Warsaw Pact	Both Equal	Don't Know
1962	37%	8%	26%	29%
1967	27	20	41	12
1968	17	28	37	18
1969	24	21	39	18
1971	15	25	55	4
1972	23	23	37	17
1973	17	27	39	17
1974	14	27	42	17
1975	17	35	32	16
1976	13	35	34	18
1977	19	28	40	14
1978	14	35	47	4
1979	16	31	49	4
1980	15	39	43	3
1981	16	41	42	2
1982	20	32	46	1
1983	12	34	51	3
1984	13	39	na	na

Source: Press and Information Office, Federal Ministry of Defense, *Hinweise fuer Offentlichkeitsarbeit*, Mr. 7/79 (Bonn: September 14, 1979) and "Meinungsbild zur Wehrpolitischen Lage," surveys for the Ministry conducted by EMNID; and Gebhard Schweigler, *West German Foreign Policy: The Domestic Consensus* (Beverly Hills, Calif.: Sage Publications, 1983), p. 118.

Table 7–4. Public Perceptions of the Military Balance.

"Who is stronger militarily?"

	1981	1982	1983	1986
NATO and the Warsaw Pact on a par	24%	27%	37%	40%
NATO stronger	20	25	13	13
Warsaw Pact stronger	42	32	36	31
Unsure/Don't know	14	16	13	17

Source: SINUS, "Amerika and die Deutschen" (Munich:SINUS, mimeograph, undated).

extension of Soviet influence as a factor creating tensions than mention aggressive American policies toward the USSR.

Table 7–5. European Views of the Sources of International Tension.

"Which of the following things do you feel are most responsible for current international tensions?"

	France	FRG	Britain	Italy	Norway	Switzerland
Soviet military buildup	31%	50%	47%	37%	54%	42%
U.S. military buildup	20	41	37	26	27	47
Superpower activities in the third world	29	32	32	20	31	27
Insufficient unity in Western Europe	25	32	19	26	8	15
Extension of Soviet influence	24	19	20	14	5	7
U.S. interest rates and the role of the dollar	38	26	10	22	1	18
U.S. aggressive policies toward the USSR	12	26	36	25	9	26
West European governments too willing to give in to the USSR	12	12	10	7	2	2
Growing popularity of neutralism and pacifism in West Europe	10	6	10	4	7	4
Other/No answer	19	14	11	25	9	17

Source: The Atlantic Institute for International Affairs – Louis Harris Poll, *Security and the Industrial Democracies* (April-May 1984). Coordinated and centralized by Louis Harris–France, Paris.

Coexisting with these assessments is a continued negative stereotype of Soviet society. The German popular view of the Soviets as an antimodel in societal, political, and economic terms remains unchanged. The Soviets are viewed as secretive, overly bureaucratic, and repressive.

These attitudes carry over to the West German image of the Soviet Union as an international actor. Majorities or pluralities have believed from the 1950s right through the mid-1980s that the Soviets were seeking military superiority. Germans remained skeptical of both Soviet intentions in pursuing détente and of Soviet goodwill. Yet, the public seems to believe that the imperatives of peace and stability override these concerns and that the Soviets can and must be dealt with in negotiations. In the public view, the Soviets remain the key to improved relations with the GDR.

Strategies for Dealing With the Soviets

As one analyst of European affairs has noted, "It is possible to see the Soviet Union as a threat without presumably seeing cruise missiles as the best remedy to the problem."[27] Although the West German image of the Soviets remains generally negative and distrustful, the German public has drawn the conclusion that the best policy is one that stresses cooperation and dialogue with the East. As the noted West German historian Hans-Peter Schwarz has observed, "Despite a majority's basic mistrust of the Soviet Union, there is still a marked desire for fairly harmonic relations with the East."[28]

Poll data bear out the juxtapositioning of German skepticism with support for détente. A major survey on the mood of the nation commissioned by *Der Spiegel* in the fall of 1981 disclosed that close to three-fourths of those questioned believed that the Soviets were seeking military superiority and only a quarter believed they would be satisfied with a military balance.[29] Another poll the following spring found that close to 60 percent of those surveyed agreed with the statement that "Moscow misuses our wish to reach an understanding in order to expand its own power," although 40 percent believed that the Soviets were sincere in their desire for détente.[30] And as the data in Tables 7–6 and 7–7 indicate, skepticism about *Ostpolitik* increased during the 1970s.

However, support for the continuation of *Ostpolitik* remained unaffected. Surveys throughout the early 1980s found that three-quarters of those questioned believed that Germany should continue the policy of détente and a majority believed the *Ostpolitik* to be worth the effort.[31] While the Federal Republic is clearly European in many of its attitudes on arms control issues, it remains distinctive, of course, because of the impact of the continuing division of the German nation. The legacy of *Ostpolitik* and of substantial détente with the GDR has been profound. The German public seems to have accepted the SPD's view that a climate of détente is a prerequisite for movement on the German question and that arms control is an important part of this process.

The revival of the national question has also meant its transformation. The old goal of reunification has lost its saliency, as it is replaced by the more modest, and realistic, objective of lowering barriers between the two states in hopes of improving the living conditions of East Germans. While the East German regime and its leadership retains its negative image for West Germans, a general agreement exists that tensions between the two

Table 7–6.   Who Profits Most from Ostpolitik?: 1973–1980
(Total West Germans, 16 and Older).

"Who do you think has profited most from the improvement in
German-Soviet relations—the Soviet Union or West Germany?"

	1973	1977	1980
Soviet Union	45%	44%	55%
West Germany	9	6	6
Both equally	31	33	25
Impossible to say	15	17	14
	100	100	100

Source: Institut fuer Demoskopie, *The Allensbach Report* (Allensbach: Institut fuer Demoskopie, 1980), p. E/4.

Table 7–7.   Russian Attitude toward Détente: 1976–1980
(Total West Germans, 16 and Older).

"Here two men are having a conversation about Russia. With
which of them would you tend to agree?"

	1976	1977	1980
"I think the Russians abuse our willingness to reconcile with the East. They use our willingness to come to an agreement in order to further expand their power in the world."	62%	60%	68%
"I think the Russians are serious about the politics of détente. They don't abuse our trust in order to expand their power in the world."	19	20	13
Undecided	19	20	19
	100	100	100

Source: *The Allensbach Report*, (Allensbach, West Germany, Institut fuer Demoskopie, 1980) p. E3.

Germanys need to be lowered to enhance increased contacts and lower the
level of repression in the GDR. Honecker's use of the term "damage
limitation" and Kohl's "community of responsibility" are code words in
this context.

This special stake in the national question has not compromised the
Western orientation of the Federal Republic; however, the almost
exclusively Western orientation of the 1950s and 1960s has been modified

by the *Ostpolitik* and the *Deutschlandpolitik*. A poll commissioned for the SPD in the fall of 1983, for example, found that 86 percent agreed that the two German states should continue to pursue a policy of détente even if relations between East and West worsened; only 14 percent gave priority to relations with the United States and NATO. The 1986 SINUS survey found that 43 percent believed that the policies of the government relied too much on Allied policies with the United States and neglected détente.[32]

West German public prescriptions to ensure security in the future emphasize arms control and dialogue with the USSR, although one-third typically still mention the need for a military balance with the USSR. Polls find that such concepts as nuclear-free zones, no first-use policies, arms control, confidence-building measures, and mutual renunciations of force agreements receive substantial public support.[33]

Images of the United States

The early to mid-1980s demonstrated a growing tendency toward what has been described as "equidistancing," a "Europe between the superpowers" view of German security, or what the SINUS study labeled "skeptical realism."[34] This growing propensity among West Germans to view both superpowers as equivalent in their foreign policy behavior reflects a delinking of the images of U.S. and Soviet domestic societies from images of the great powers' foreign policy behavior.

Anti-Americanism, defined as antipathy to American society, is only common among a small fraction of West Germans. More general views perceive both superpowers as tending to intervene in the affairs of and seek to dominate other states, both superpowers as paying little heed to the interests and views of allies and smaller states, and both superpowers as imposing their ideological conceptions upon others. As already noted, both the United States and the USSR are viewed as contributing to the arms race and international instability by their striving for military superiority.[35]

These tendencies are fed by the fear of war and by conflicts between German views of détente and those of the post-Afghanistan American Administrations. Since Afghanistan, the general West German consensus on détente has come into direct conflict with an American approach that stressed the need to redress the military balance and that gave priority to defense modernization over arms control. One result of this divergence has been a sharp decline in German public confidence in American foreign policy. The data in Figure 7–1 chronicle that decline through the

Figure 7–1. Net Favorable Confidence in U.S. Foreign Policy: 1981–1984.

Net favorable: Percent who express "great deal" or "fair amount" of confidence minus percent "not very much" or "none at all."

Question: In general, how much confidence do you have in the ability of the (U.S./Soviet Union) to deal responsibly with world problems—a great deal, a fair amount, not very much, or none at all?

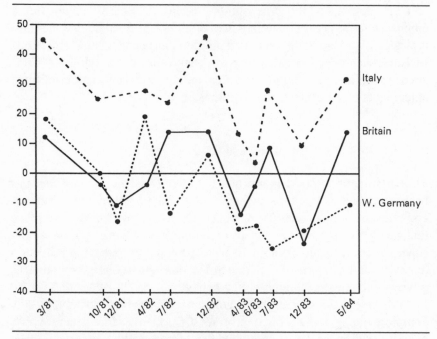

Average net scores for confidence in U.S. foreign policy were:
  1960–75: Britain +18, West Germany +33, Italy +35
  1981–84: Britain +1, West Germany –7, Italy +25
There were 13–14 measurements in the first period, 11 during 1981–84, and none between May 1975 and March 1981.

Source: USIA, *Research Memorandum*, October 3, 1984.

mid-1980s and indicate that the level of confidence in U.S. foreign policy is lower in the Federal Republic than in either Italy or Britain.

This drop in confidence in U.S. leadership has been accompanied by a growing tendency to differentiate between German and U.S. security interests, and to seek to mediate between the superpowers on arms control and other issues. In the 1950s and early 1960s, from 56 percent to 81 percent of West Germans believed that German interests were in agreement with those of the United States. By 1982, the proportion seeing West

German and American interests in agreement had fallen to 35 percent, with 53 percent regarding the interests of the two countries as different.[36]

The manifestations of these trends in arms control are discussed in the section dealing with attitudes on specific arms control issues.

Attitudes Toward Nuclear Deterrence

As Europe's major nonnuclear power, the FRG has been especially sensitive to its dependence on the extended deterrence of the American nuclear umbrella. Combined with its exposed geostrategic position and its commitment to forward defense, the FRG has relied on a close coupling of the regional deterrent to U.S. central systems and on the threat of early use of nuclear weapons. German concerns on the nuclear issue have swung between fears of abandonment to concern about the dangers of too close a tie to the American deterrent.

Underneath these swings has been an unsurprisingly consistent reluctance to sanction nuclear first use. A comparison of the results of a four-nation survey in 1955 on the question of nuclear first use, shown in Table 7–8, with responses to a similar question in the 1980s presents a study in continuity.

The German public in the mid-1980s, while divided, continues to support the concept of deterrence. Even after the long debate and deployment of INF, the 1986 SINUS survey found that a plurality of 44 percent continue to believe that the generation of peace in Europe has been due to nuclear weapons and that without them conventional war would be more probable.[37]

The INF debate brought many latent concerns to the surface with nuclear *Angst* peaking during 1982–83. While fear of nuclear war has receded somewhat over the past three years, longer term anxieties remain. Less than 20 percent in 1985 favored the first use of nuclear weapons. The number of nuclear pacifists (those who reject any use of nuclear weapons) increased from 29 percent in 1979 to 44 percent in 1984. These levels were the highest of any of the seven European nations polled. Close to one-half of West German respondents either favor unilateral nuclear disarmament or reject the deployment of more nuclear weapons in the FRG even in response to the introduction of new weapons by the Soviets.[38]

Although the concept of nuclear deterrence still finds a narrow plurality of supporters in West Germany, there is substantial doubt that deterrence will continue to work in the future. Close to 90 percent favor nuclear-free

Table 7–8. European Attitudes toward Nuclear Weapons in the 1950s.

"If Western Europe were attacked without the use of atomic or hydrogen bombs, would you approve or disapprove of the use of such bombs on enemy cities?"

	FRG	Italy	Great Britain
Approve	6	5	10
Disapprove	85	75	71
Don't know	9	20	19

Source: "Part II—The USIA Data Collection" in *Western European Perspectives on International Affairs*, Richard L. Merritt and Donald J. Puchala, Eds. (Praeger Publishers, New York, 1968), p. 381.

zones and a no first-use agreement by both sides. While support for deterrence is obviously fragile, no clear alternative is apparent. Polls also indicate little support to increase defense spending or to spend more on conventional forces in order to raise the nuclear threshold. These surveys reflect, in part, a general satisfaction with the state of the conventional balance in Europe.[39]

The erosion of support for nuclear deterrence seems to be most noticeable among the better educated, the young, and partisans of the left.[40] The increase of nuclear anxieties can be traced, in part, to the upsurge of technological pessimism catalyzed by the Greens. More fundamental is the relationship of such anxieties to German reliance on the American deterrent. Attitudes toward nuclear weapons have always been a barometer for confidence in American policy; as trust in that policy has declined, concerns about deterrence have increased.[41]

The Political Demographics of Perceptions

Partisan affiliation, in association with age and educational level, provides the great divide on security issues. The impact of partisan affiliation on security attitudes is especially significant. CDU/CSU supporters, in general, are more likely to feel threatened by the Soviet Union and to be pessimistic about the nature of Soviet intentions and of the state of the military balance. They tend to see a great deal of compatibility between U.S. and West German interests and are confident in America's ability to lead the Alliance. SPD and especially Green supporters tend toward the

Table 7-9..   West European Opinion on Use of Nuclear Weapons by NATO.

"There are different opinions about the use of nuclear weapons in Europe by NATO. Which one of the following is closest to your own?

A. NATO should not use nuclear weapons of any kind under any circumstances.
B. NATO should use nuclear weapons only if the Soviet Union uses them first in attacking Western Europe.
C. NATO should use nuclear weapons to defend itself if a Soviet attack by conventional forces threatened to overwhelm NATO forces."

	Britain		Germany		Italy		Belgium			Netherlands			Denmark	Norway
	7/82 (967)[a]	5/84 (1131)	7/82 (923)	5/84 (1033)	7/82 (1053)	5/84 (1040)	10/81	7/82	5/84 (1018)	10/81	7/82 (1287)	5/84 (1219)	5/84 (978)	5/84 (929)
A. Not under any circumstances	30%	24%	38%	44%	38%	41%	47%	51%	35%	50%	37%	36%	43%	30%
B. Only if Soviets use them first	45	51	33	42	40	44	26	28	34	31	32	30	35	48
C. Against an over-whelming conventional attack	19	18	16	11	14	9	16	14	14	11	16	16	7	11
Don't know	6	7	13	2	8	5	10	7	17	8	15	17	15	10

a. Numbers in parentheses refer to the size of the national samples.

Source: USIA, Research Memorandum, September 19, 1984.

converse. Table 7–10 summarizes the issues in which the differences among party supporters were especially pronounced in the surveys.

The areas of consensus among the supporters of the three major parties, however, are broad and include a desire for dialogue with the Soviets, a rejection of unilateral nuclear disarmament, support for the presence of U.S. troops in the FRG, and support for a range of arms control and other measures to reduce tensions in Europe. Table 7–11 summarizes some areas of interparty consensus among partisan identifiers.

On specific issues, supporters of the CDU/CSU and the SPD tend to agree on most proposed arms control measures. For example, although the CDU-led government has rejected the inclusion of British and French systems in the INF talks, both CDU and SPD supporters feel that U.K. and French systems are for national, and not German, defense, but nevertheless should be included in the INF talks. The CDU public, more supportive of the zero option than was the leadership, pulled the leadership to eventual acceptance of the double-zero option.

In summary a broad consensus is apparent on détente and a general agreement exists on a strategy toward the Soviet Union. The area of dispute is the nature of the future relationship with the United States. The continuing elite fragmentation on this cluster of questions is likely to reinforce the partisan and generational divisions apparent in the data. The debate will likely be more heated regarding the nature of the relationship with the United States than it will regarding policy toward the Soviet Union.

ATTITUDES ON SPECIFIC ARMS CONTROL ISSUES

Given this general context in which West German public opinion is shaped, the final section of this chapter presents a look at public opinion on specific arms control issues, viewing them as case studies in the German view of security.

Historical Background: 1950s and 1960s

Data describing West German public opinion on the relatively esoteric issues of arms control and disarmament prior to the late 1970s is scarce. What is available indicates that at least since the early 1960s, West

Table 7–10. Selected Areas of Dissensus among the Parties (15 Percentage Point or More Difference between the Major Parties).

Percent Believing	CDU/CSU	SPD	Greens
Feel threatened by the East	69%	49%	36%
Need for a sufficiently armed West to deter the East	63	43	20
Welcome INF as a counterweight to Soviet missiles	42	19	6
Soviet buildup primarily responsible for global tensions	63	48	58
U.S. buildup primarily responsible for global tensions	33	48	69
Favor military alliance with U.S. rather than neutralism	69	49	—
Must cooperate closely with the U.S.	60	34	21
Must cooperate closely with the U.S. and the USSR	31	51	59
FRG too concerned about NATO to the detriment of détente	12	49	64
U.S.-FRG basic interests in agreement	79	59	—
Have confidence in U.S. policy (August 1983)	51	26	—
Use of nuclear weapons unacceptable under any circumstances	23	41	59
Introduce enough nuclear weapons to balance the USSR	50	27	6
INF promotes deterrence	32	9	3
Favor nuclear free zone in Europe	49	67	84

Reprinted by permission of the publisher, from *Evolving European Defense Policies*, edited by Catherine M. Kelleher and Gale A. Mattox (Lexington, Mass.: Lexington Books, D.C. Heath and Company, Copyright 1987).

Germans consistently have favored the goal of disarmament but have been pessimistic about the prospects for any real progress.

As the data in Table 7–12 suggest, the West Germans have been in the European mainstream in their support for disarmament, with only the British demonstrating some reserve about the proposition of general and

Table 7–11.   Selected Areas of Agreement among the Parties (Less Than a 15 Percentage Point Difference between the Major Parties).

Percent Believing	CDU/CSU	SPD	Greens
Need for continuing dialogue with the USSR	41	43	57
Believe Soviets will attack within five years	8	9	3
Military balance important to Western security	38	27	17
Confident U.S. will defend Europe	35	27	11
NATO can defend Europe conventionally	52	60	48
NATO essential to German security	94	85	–
U.S. troops in Europe deter attack	87	77	64
Favor unilateral nuclear disarmament	17	29	54
Reject chemical and biological weapons	81	89	88
Favor nonaggression pact with East	81	88	88
Favor development of space based defense by the U.S.	24	12	1
Conventionalize rather than enhance nuclear deterrent	43	44	45

Reprinted by permission of the publisher, from *Evolving European Defense Policies*, edited by Catherine M. Kelleher and Gale A. Mattox (Lexington, Mass.: Lexington Books, D.C. Heath and Company, Copyright 1987).

complete disarmament. Over three-fourths of those surveyed in a 1961 poll, for example, strongly supported the West's efforts to reach a disarmament agreement. Even in 1963, just two years after the building of the Berlin Wall, polls found large majorities supporting such agreements.[42]

Widespread support for the goal of disarmament was not accompanied by much optimism for the prospects of an agreement, however. Only 28 percent of the 1961 sample believed it likely that the United States and the Soviet Union would reach an agreement on disarmament within five years, while 55 percent remained pessimistic.

During this period, the West German public laid the blame for lack of progress primarily on the Soviets. Surveys throughout the 1950s and 1960s found that Germans believed that Americans were more serious in their efforts toward disarmament than the Soviets. In 1961, for example, 72 percent believed the Americans wanted some agreement, while only 33

Table 7–12.   European Attitudes toward Disarmament in the Early 1960s.

"What are your feelings in general about disarmament? Are you for general and complete disarmament throughout the world, for some partial limitations on arms, or for no limitations on arms?"

	France		FRG		Italy		United Kingdom	
	6/61	*2/63*	*7/61*	*2/63*	*7/61*	*2/63*	*6/61*	*2/63*
General and complete disarmament	73%	80%	70%	70%	73%	84%	43%	56%
Partial limitation	15	14	18	15	7	11	35	28
No limitation	3	2	2	1	1	—	2	—
Qualified/Don't know	9	4	8	12	17	4	9	9

Source: "Part II—The USIA Data Collection" in *Western European Perspectives on International Affairs*, Richard L. Merritt and Donald J. Puchala, Eds. (Praeger Publishers, New York, 1968), p. 363.

percent felt the same about Soviet intentions. Conversely, 46 percent believed the Russians wanted no limitations on arms, compared to 12 percent holding this view of the Americans. Similarly, in 1963, 62 percent believed the United States to be working fairly or very hard to obtain some degree of disarmament, compared to only 9 percent believing this of the Soviets.[43] This German skepticism of Soviet intentions was the highest of the four West European publics surveyed.

Figure 7–2 provides an overview of West German perspectives on the seriousness of Western (not just American) interest in disarmament over two and a half decades. It provides a stable profile, showing only slight increases of skepticism about Western seriousness in the late 1970s and early 1980s.

While the United States still tends to get the benefit of the doubt concerning the sincerity of its intentions in arms control negotiation, the gap between it and the Soviet Union on this question narrowed considerably in the 1980s. Surprisingly, not only is American seriousness in arms control negotiations now questioned more frequently, but even American willingness to observe arms control agreements is questioned.[44]

SALT II/START

The SALT II treaty and the public debate over the production and deployment of enhanced radiation warheads (ERW, or the neutron bomb)

Figure 7–2.   Is The West Interested In Disarmament?:
1956–1981 (Total West Germans, 16 and Older).

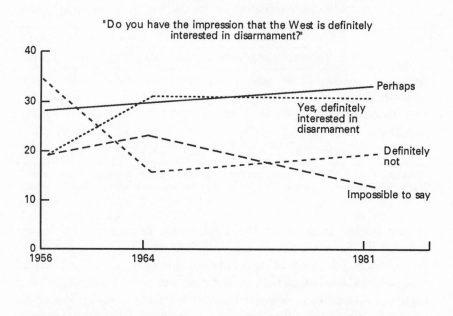

"Do you have the impression that the West is definitely
interested in disarmament?"

Source: Institut fuer Demoskopie, "American-German Relations as Seen by German Public Opinion"
(Allensbach: Institut fuer Demoskopie, October 7, 1981), p.40.

marked the beginning of renewed public interest in security and arms
control issues. This renewed interest began in 1977 with the advent of the
Carter Administration, the Schmidt speech on arms control and the
Eurostrategic balance to the IISS in October 1977, and the decision of
President Carter to cancel production of ERW.

Public interest in SALT II was limited compared to concern over INF,
and the implications of the proposed treaty were largely an elite concern,
typified by the Schmidt IISS speech to an audience of specialists. A survey
conducted in 1979 found that 60 percent had heard of SALT II, but only
24 percent said that they followed the talks very or fairly closely.[45] This
placed the German public at about the middle of the European spectrum
of public attentiveness on SALT II in 1979.

The issue did not gain a greater audience in the 1980s. Only 26 percent
of a national survey in September 1985 stated that they had read or heard

a great deal or fair amount about SALT II; this poll followed the Reagan Administration's decision to continue observing SALT II restraints. (However, 45 percent of the better educated in the 1985 poll did follow the issue.) [46]

About one-third of the German public was able to choose the correct description of SALT II as dealing with intercontinental systems; this proportion was somewhat higher than those in other European countries. Although the German public was generally ill-informed about the particulars of the treaty, they supported the treaty by margins of five to one in polls taken in 1979; only 12 percent disapproved. These approval levels were similar to those found in polls taken in Britain and France at the same time.[47]

Support for SALT II is consistent with the general West German support for disarmament found already in the early 1960s. The main reasons listed in polls for supporting the agreement were that SALT II would promote parity and thus would help to control the arms race and reduce the chances of war. These findings underline attitudes revealed in polls in the early 1980s that demonstrated a strong German public preference for parity. The Germans were more optimistic in this regard than either the French or the British, with twice as many (43 percent) likely to believe that SALT II would restrain the arms race. The Germans (41 percent) were also much more likely to believe that the agreement would reduce prospects of Soviet political pressure being applied to Western Europe.

The main dissatisfaction with SALT II was that it did not go far enough; a majority continued to believe that the treaty would not affect the nuclear arms race. Only about 10 percent wished to reduce defense spending after the treaty's ratification; the majority favored maintaining defense spending at current levels. It cannot be argued, convincingly therefore, that the public was swept up in a wave of illusions or euphoria over SALT.

German public attitudes, rather, were shaped by a deep skepticism about Soviet intentions, coupled with a fear of the consequences of confrontation and escalation and a strong desire to maintain the arms control process in order to salvage détente. Polling done within a month of the Soviet invasion of Afghanistan found that public trust in the Soviets had declined, with a clear majority having no confidence in talks with the USSR. Yet 74 percent wanted détente to continue and 66 percent favored a Schmidt-Honecker meeting. Elite surveys as well found that although they were lukewarm about the treaty because of decoupling fears, the elites supported its ratification out of concern that tensions would escalate if the treaty were not ratified.[48]

Skepticism about Soviet adherence to SALT II has not translated into demands to scrap the treaty. Surveys in July 1985, for example, found that 43 percent believed that the Soviets had violated the SALT II agreement, while only 9 percent felt that they had observed it; 26 percent believed the United States had stuck to the agreement, while 25 percent had the view that the United States had violated it. However, there was substantial approval for the U.S. decision to continue to observe the treaty. A plurality also felt the United States should continue to observe the agreement even if Soviet violations were discovered. The better educated portion of the public was the most supportive of continued observance.[49]

Similar attitudes prevail regarding the START talks. In a 1982 poll, for example, the majority was pessimistic that the talks would succeed in reducing ICBM levels over the next two to three years; only 20 percent were optimistic. The better educated were even more pessimistic.

However, in the case of START, the tendency toward distancing had become more pronounced. Both superpowers were blamed for the impasse in the talks. About 46 percent believed that the cuts proposed by the United States would be unfair to the USSR, while 47 percent did not accept that proposition. The Germans were the most skeptical of American proposals, by a wide margin, of all the Europeans polled. However, a majority of Germans also believed that the Soviets were unwilling to make ICBM cuts to bring their inventory down to U.S. levels.

Public attitudes on strategic arms limitation in West Germany can thus be summarized as supportive of the effort, but pessimistic about the potential for success. Negotiations are viewed as important as part of the détente process and as a tool of East-West conflict management. The Soviets remain untrusted and American concerns about verification are believed to be justified. Still, overwhelmingly, West Germans believe the strategic balance of power is one of rough parity and, therefore, that the larger process of détente should not be jeopardized over minor violations. The Soviets are believed to be interested in arms control out of self-interest.

What is new in German public attitudes, beginning in the early 1980s, is a growing skepticism about the American commitment to arms control and to general parity. The divergence between the Administration's view of the military balance and that of the German public has led to a perception in the Federal Republic that the Americans want superiority and are uninterested in arms control.

INF

The dual-track INF decision, which linked arms control to deployments, was a concrete expression of the impact of détente on German thinking on security. Arms control negotiations early were recognized by the German public as a prerequisite for INF modernization. Germans clearly believed that arms control was a better way to enhance their security than force modernization. A survey conducted for *Der Spiegel* in the fall of 1981, for example, found that 65 percent felt the arms control track was the most important one, while only 35 percent believed that deployment should take priority because of the need to restore the balance in Central Europe.[50] Less than 10 percent of respondents in surveys conducted in the 1981–1984 period would have accepted INF deployments without arms talks. Conditional supporters (i.e., those who supported deployment only if arms talks were in progress or had failed) ranged from 40 to 50 percent, while unconditional opponents (those who opposed deployment irrespective of the arms talks) ranged from 26 to 36 percent.[51]

This support for talks either before deployments or simultaneous with them held despite a general pessimism that the talks would succeed or that the Soviets and, to a lesser extent, the Americans were sincere in their negotiating efforts. Pessimists concerning the outcome of the talks numbered in the 60 percent range, while only 20 percent were optimists.[52]

Germans tended to be divided over the seriousness of Soviet intentions in the talks. While the figures fluctuated over the INF years, anywhere from a plurality to a majority tended to believe that the Soviets were not serious in the negotiations. Up to two-thirds in a October 1982 poll, for example, believed the Soviet goal was to keep all of its nuclear forces while preventing the United States from building up its own nuclear strength in Western Europe. Furthermore, up to two-thirds of respondents in June 1983 believed that the USSR was seeking military superiority rather than equality.

Immediately following the Soviet walkout of the Geneva talks in December 1983, German public confidence in Soviet interest in arms control fell sharply. By mid-1984, only 25 percent believed that the Soviets were making genuine efforts to reach an agreement. The Soviet image, however, recovered by the end of 1985 and a plurality (39 percent) again felt the Russians were making genuine efforts to reach an agreement.[53]

The proportions believing in the sincerity of the United States in seeking an agreement were always much higher, but at times German opinion was almost equally divided on this issue. There was also an almost equal division over the question of whether the American government wanted an agreement or if it was using the negotiations to stall for time in order to build up its own nuclear forces.

There was also a growing tendency to view the U.S. objective as military superiority, rather than parity; the decline in confidence in U.S.

foreign policy became increasingly marked as the negotiations dragged on. This decline in confidence was especially noticeable among the better educated. About two-thirds of the better educated had little or no confidence in U.S. policy, as compared to about one-half the general public. In a June 1983 poll, for example, 38 percent believed that U.S. policies increased the risk of war while only 31 percent felt they promoted peace.[54]

The U.S. image improved after the Soviet walkout in Geneva. By the end of 1985, 57 percent believed the United States was making serious efforts to reach an agreement, and only 18 percent doubted American intentions. However, serious doubts existed about the American commitment to any agreement that might be achieved. A majority in late 1985 were not confident that the United States would observe the terms of an agreement. Three-quarters also doubted the Soviets on this score, and almost everyone agreed with the U.S. insistence on verification.[55]

There was a widespread belief in the early 1980s, prior to the U.S. deployments, that both NATO and the USSR already had deployed INF systems in Europe, with the better educated the most likely to believe this. A majority believed that the United States had INF deployed, and up to three-quarters named the French systems in this category. While slightly less than one-half believed that the British and French systems were intended solely for national defense, a majority (by a five to one margin) favored including them in the INF negotiations.

When respondents in polls were told that the Soviets had an INF monopoly, support for deployments increased moderately (by less than 10 points). This information did not have a greater impact because of a sanguine view of the military balance, a declining belief in the deterrent value of the U.S. INF systems, and the muted perception of a Soviet military or political threat. The prospect of negotiations had a greater positive impact on support for INF than did efforts to stress the Soviet threat.

The legacy of INF for German public attitudes on arms control was profound and probably lasting. First, the Euromissiles sensitized unprecedented numbers of the German public to security policy and arms control. This sensitizing impact was especially significant for the postwar generations.

Second, INF established a dual-track precedent that will link further nuclear and chemical modernization projects to an arms control track. It is likely to be politically unacceptable for West German governments to ignore the arms control track in the future.

Third, the German principle of nonsingularity was established, meaning that future NATO deployments cannot occur solely on German soil, but will have to take place in other NATO states as well.

Fourth, the tendency toward distancing among key elements of German opinion crystallized during the long years of debate. America lost what was left of its halo in the arms control arena and came to be viewed with growing skepticism regarding its commitment to arms control agreements. Conversely, the Soviet image fluctuated but gradually improved in relative terms in the arms control area, opening up greater opportunities for its public diplomacy, opportunities which were seized upon with alacrity and skill by Mikhail Gorbachev.

Finally, arms control gained a priority higher than that afforded to military measures in the public's view of security. Defense spending and an emphasis on military balance became secondary to negotiations and dialogue.

It is too soon to say whether INF was a unique event or a watershed that shaped the attitudes of a generation. INF was a unique issue in terms of public attention, as much a domestic as a foreign policy concern. It was concrete in that it involved the stationing of foreign-controlled missiles in one of the most densely populated countries in Europe. The debate over deployment became part of a larger discussion about the compatibility of German and American security interests, on the almost total dependence of West Germany upon the United States for its security, and on the wisdom of the U.S. approach to the Soviet Union. INF also became part of a larger cultural conflict over the nature of the West German identity and of a growing technological pessimism. SALT, START, SDI, and the ABM Treaty also touch on these dimensions but have not mobilized public opinion and political action as INF did. They lack the immediacy of INF: they do not involve the deployment of foreign-controlled weapons on West German soil. Even chemical weapons have remained far more an elite issue than INF.

SDI and ABM

The Strategic Defense Initiative and the cluster of issues that surround it became a major arms control concern on the agenda of West German elites. Public attitudes on SDI in the Federal Republic remain unformed and largely untested. Only a few USIA-commissioned surveys exist on

European opinion concerning SDI. The existing data indicate that SDI remains largely an elite issue that has not caught the public's imagination.

As with other arms control issues, public interest in and information about SDI and ABM-related issues is very limited. About a third of the public in 1985 identified from a multiple choice question the goal of SDI as defense against an attack by enemy missiles. Only one-third reported having heard of or read "a fair amount" about SDI. More specifically, only about 17 percent believed that SDI would be nonnuclear. While a majority knew of Soviet SDI research and only 5 percent thought the Soviets had not been conducting research into antimissile defenses, fully 45 percent did not know. Only about one-quarter knew that the Soviets had deployed ABM systems.[56]

The impact of these low levels of information and interest is apparent in the large numbers of "don't know" responses to specific questions. Slightly more than one-third of the German public supported SDI research in May 1985, as compared to 22 percent who thought it was a bad idea. However, 41 percent were undecided on the issue. By the end of 1985 the proportion supporting the research had fallen to 31 percent, while opposition increased to 30 percent. Again, the undecideds remained a high 40 percent.

The limited poll data available suggests that those West Germans favoring participation in SDI research did so primarily to ensure that if such systems were deployed they would protect Western Europe, not just the United States, and because they believed it would help West Germany to acquire the latest technology. Few supported research on the grounds that it would reduce dependence on nuclear weapons, perhaps because most did not believe it was a nonnuclear system.

Opposition to research concerned the diversion of funds from other projects and fear that it would accelerate the arms race. Between 42 and 48 percent of the German sample viewed SDI research as a bargaining chip that could be bartered for a nuclear arms control agreement. Only a quarter believed it was too important to relinquish. More than one-half of the supporters of SDI research would trade the program for an arms control agreement.

By the end of 1985, a plurality (42 percent) believed that SDI would tend to make the United States more likely to come to European defense than not (27 percent disagreed, 30 percent thought it would make no difference). Similarly, only about a quarter believed an SDI system would only cover the United States, while 47 percent thought it would also cover Western Europe.

No clear correlation between attitudes on SDI and age, education level, or party preference were apparent, unlike the clear associations of these variables with attitudes on INF. This is another indication of SDI's low saliency. INF was a catalyst for a range of values related as much to domestic politics as to foreign policy. SDI lacks the concreteness of the placement of foreign-controlled missiles on German soil.

SDI may become a serious issue at the elite level, however. As Chancellor Kohl's points on SDI of February 1985 indicate, the German elite is concerned about the possible decoupling effects of SDI, its impact on the arms race and arms control, and its technological consequences for German industry.[57] SDI raises again the renewed specter of making Germany safe for a conventional war, and may impose new obstacles to agreements on strategic systems.

The SPD is united in its opposition to SDI, and thus it is likely to remain a divisive elite issue. As Elizabeth Pond has concluded, "It is inconceivable that any West German government would endorse a unilateral American violation or abrogration of the ABM treaty or be able to mobilize the silent majority to accept the U.S. position."[58]

CONCLUSIONS

The Deutsch study of elite and public German opinion on arms control in the 1960s reached a number of conclusions. The authors found a widespread consensus that allowed the government to "continue its policies of aloofness on general disarmament and *immobilisme* on arms control in Central Europe."[59] They also found a large silent majority that neither craved nor categorically rejected nuclear weapons. German leaders were characterized as "comparatively ignorant and indifferent" about arms control proposals and likely to consider their influence over developments in this area as "nonexistent." Arms control negotiations were viewed as putting the cart before the horse because they could only follow an improvement in the overall polical climate. They concluded that "mass opinion would follow elite opinion."[60]

When data from the 1980s are compared with these data and with other studies of that period, it is clear that fundamental changes have occurred in German public opinion on arms control over the past two decades. The elite and public consensus is not as widespread as it was in the 1960s. The elite fragmentation has been both cause and effect of the growing attentive public. Elite fragmentation, in turn, fed further division and enhanced the growth of a critical, attentive public.

By the mid-1980s, German leaders could no longer afford to take a passive position on arms control or leave the negotiations solely to the Americans. They increasingly had to demonstrate to their public that they were asserting German interests and pushing for dialogue. Arms control has become too important to be left to the diplomats, generals, and the Americans. Why?

In part, because German definitions of security have changed. Arms control is no longer seen as placing the cart before the donkey, but has become part of an ongoing process of dialogue with the East that has become part of the new German consensus. It has become a symbol for a more self-assertive West Germany, particularly for a new generation that increasingly differentiates its interests from those of the Americans. It is the arena where Germans can have an impact and can pressure the United States.

It is also a prism through which long-term changes in the German-American relationship can be viewed. The trend toward distancing, for example, is apparent particularly in the growing skepticism about American leadership and sincerity in the negotiations.

Future trends in West German attitudes will depend, to some extent, on what happens in the East-West relationship. Arms control and dialogue with the East seem to be essential components for obtaining German public support for security policy. A dual-track approach that somehow links modernization with arms control negotiations will be an essential part of any future modernization package, as will the German insistence on nonsingularity.

Arms control agreements and renewed détente will lessen pressures on the arms control front but, as the concern of conservative German elites over the impact of the double-zero proposal demonstrated, could revive fears of decoupling and of superpower condominium. Still, the impact of the postwar generation on public attitudes will increase with the passage of time, and fears of decoupling are likely to be subordinated to the "détente imperative."

Arms control is likely, consequently, to remain at the fulcrum of U.S.-German-Soviet relations for the foreseeable future. Public opinion in the Federal Republic will become a key target in what promises to be an intensified public diplomacy campaign.

NOTES

1. Karl W. Deutsch et al., *France, Germany and the Western Alliance: A Survey of Elite Attitudes on European Integration and World Politics* (New York: Scribner, 1967), p. 209.
2. *Ibid.*, p. 186.
3. Helga Haftendorn, *Security and Détente: Conflicting Priorities in German Foreign Policy* (New York: Praeger, 1985), pp. 31–68, 83–157.
4. See, for example, *Der Spiegel*, February 7, 1983, p. 90 and October 30, 1984, p. 40; Karl Heinz Reuband, "Ist der sicherheitspolitische Konsensus zerbrochen?" in W.R. Vogt, ed., *Militaer als Gegenkultur?* vol.1 (Leverkusen: Leske und Burdrich, 1985), pp. 32–33.
5. *Der Spiegel*, February 7, 1983, p. 90.
6. See Helga Haftendorn, "West Germany and the Management of Security Relations," in *The Foreign Policy of West Germany*, eds. Ekkehart Krippendorff and Volker Rittberger (Beverly Hills, Calif.: Sage, 1980)., pp. 7–32.
7. Deutsch et al., *France, Germany and the Western Alliance*, p. 188.
8. Richard L. Merritt and Donald J. Puchala, eds., *Western European Perspectives on International Affairs* (New York: Praeger, 1968), p. 363; *Der Spiegel*, November 23, 1981, p. 57.
9. Kenneth P. Adler, "Polling the Attentive Public," *The Annals* 472 (March 1982): 148.
10. See also Stephen F. Szabo, "European Opinion After the Missiles," *Survival*, November/December, 1985, pp. 265–66.
11. *Der Spiegel*, November 23, 1981, p. 57.
12. Adler, "The Attentive Public", pp. 143–54.
13. Similarly, there has been an expansion in the number of university students from 210,000 in 1960 to 976,000 in 1983. Emil Huebner and Horst-Hanek Rohlfs, *Jahrbuch der Bundesrepublik Deutschland 1985/86* (Munich: Beck, 1985), pp. 161, 172. Werner Voss, *Die Bundesrepublik Deutschland: Daten und Analysen* (Stuttgart: Kohlhammer, 1980), p. 120.
14. *Der Spiegel*, November 23, 1981, p. 57.
15. Gunther Schmid, "Zur Soziologie der Friedensbewegung und des Jugendprotestes," *Aus Politik und Zeitgeschichte*, June 19, 1982, p. B24; *Der Spiegel*, November 23, 1981, pp. 65–68.
16. USIA surveys, April–June, 1983, summarized in USIA "Research Memorandum," September 12, 1983; hereafter referred to as USIA-RM.
17. Deutsch et al., *France, Germany and the Western Alliance*, p. 204.
18. Kenneth P. Adler, "West European Opinion on the Strategic Defense Initiative," USIA-RM, September 1985.

19. Elizabeth Pond, "The Security Debate in West Germany," *Survival* (July/August 1986), p. 335, fn. 1.

20. Deutsch, et al., *France, Germany and the Western Alliance*, pp. 206–9.

21. Forschungsgruppe Wahlen Mannheim, *Bundestagswahl 1987* (Mannheim: January 28, 1987), p. 38.

22. Forschungsgruppe Wahlen Mannheim, *Bundestagswahl 1983* (Mannheim: March 9, 1983); *Bundestagswahl 1987*, especially pp. 38–44.

23. *Bundestagswahl 1987*, p. 39.

24. Hans Rattinger, "The Federal Republic of Germany: Much Ado About Almost Nothing," in *The Public and Atlantic Defense*, eds. Gregory Flynn and Hans Rattinger (Totawa, N.J.: Rowman and Allanheld, 1984), pp. 116–18; David Capitanchik and Richard C. Eichenberg, *Defense and Public Opinion* (London: Routledge and Kegan Paul, 1983), p. 59; USIA survey, December 1985.

25. SINUS, "Amerika und die Deutschen" (Munich: SINUS, mimeographed, undated), p. 68. The survey of 1,800 eligible voters was conducted at the end of September and the beginning of October 1986.

26. SINUS, "Amerika und die Deutschen," p. 70; *Der Spiegel*, November 23, 1981, p. 57; Merritt and Puchala, *Perspectives*, p. 209.

27. Edwinea Moreton, "Images of the Soviet Union: A More Typical Adversary," in *Public Images of Western Security*, ed. Gregory Flynn et al. (Paris: The Atlantic Institute, June 1985), p. 27.

28. Hans Peter Schwarz, "The West Germans, Western Democracy and Western Ties in the Light of Public Opinion Research," in *The Federal Republic of Germany and the United States*, ed. James Cooney et al. (Boulder, Colo.: Westview, 1984), p.68.

29. *Der Spiegel*, November 23, 1981, p. 57.

30. *Der Spiegel*, April 2, 1982, p. 3.

31. Institut fuer Demoskopie, *The Allensbach Report 1980*, (Allensbach: Institut fuer Demoskopie, 1980), p. E4; SINUS, "Sicherheitspolitik, Buendnispolitik, Friedensbewegung" (Munich: SINUS, October 1983), pp. 25–28.

32. SINUS, "Sicherheitspolitik," p. 31: and SINUS, "Amerika und die Deutschen," p. 72.

33. SINUS, "Sicherheitspolitik," pp. 25–27; Louis Harris and the Atlantic Institute, "Security and the Industrial Democracies" (Paris: May 1986, mimeographed) and also summarized in the *International Herald Tribune*, June 7, 1984.

34. Moreton, "Images," p. 28; SINUS, "Amerika und die Deutschen," p. 50.

35. Elisabeth Noelle-Neumann, "Breite Mehrheit," *Capital* (August 1981): 87–94; SINUS, "Amerika und die Deutschen," pp. 3–41, 50–60. See also Siegfried Knauer, *Lieben Wir Amerika?* (Hamburg: Stern, 1987) for a summary of this survey.

36. USIA-RM, September 19, 1984.
37. EMNID, "Meinungsbild in der Bundesrepublik Deutschland zur Sicherheitspolitik" (Bonn: Ministry of Defense, October 1984, mimeographed); Capitanchik and Eichenberg, *Defense and Public Opinion*, pp. 61–64; SINUS, "Sicherheitspolitik," pp. 34–36 and "Amerika und die Deutschen," p. 79.
38. Capitanchik and Eichenberg, *Defense and Public Opinion*, p. 63; Rattinger, "The FRG," pp. 132–37; *Die Zeit*, June 8, 1984, Mathias Schoenborn, "Perceptions of National Security of the U.S. and the Federal Republic of Germany," paper presented at the annual conference of the American Association for Public Opinion Research, May 28–31, 1981, pp. 132–37.
39. USIA-RM, September 19, 1984; SINUS, "Sicherheitspolitik," pp. 26–27.
40. Merritt and Puchala, *Perspectives*, pp. 367–71; USIA, "Foreign Opinion Note," January 17, 1986; *Der Spiegel*, November 23, 1981, pp. 56–70; Institut fuer Demoskopie, Allensbach, "Pazifistische Stroemungen in der Bundesrepublik," May 1982; Schmid, "Soziologie."
41. Christoph Bertram, "Europe and America in 1983," *Foreign Affairs: America and the World 1983*, vol. 62, no. 3, p. 619. A 1984 survey provides some empirical evidence for this linkage; 47 percent of those Germans with a great deal of confidence in U.S. policy also were nuclear pacifists, compared to 57 percent who had no confidence in U.S. policy. This indicates that although more is at work than just confidence in U.S. policy, it remains a factor in explaining attitudes on nuclear weapons. Infratest Sozialforschung, "Security Survey" (1984), USIA commissioned survey, question 26.
42. Merritt and Puchala, *Perspectives*, pp. 364, 366.
43. *Ibid.*, pp. 369–71.
44. *Ibid.*, p. 255; Leo Crespi, "Long Term Trends in Some General Orientations Toward the U.S. and the USSR in West European Public Opinion," Research Report, USIA Office of Research, July 1983, p. 17.
45. USIA, SALT II poll, 1979.
46. USIA-RM, September 25, 1985.
47. USIA, SALT II poll, 1979.
48. USIA, "Research Report," May 14, 1980, p. vi.
49. USIA-RM, September 25, 1985.
50. *Der Spiegel*, November 23, 1981, p. 59.
51. USIA-RM, September 19, 1984.
52. USIA-RM, September 12, 1983.
53. USIA, "Foreign Opinion Note," January 17, 1986.
54. USIA-RM, October 3, 1984.
55. *Der Spiegel*, November 1985.
56. Adler, "SDI."

57.   Pond, "Security Debate," p. 375.
58.   *Ibid.*
59.   Deutsch et al., *France, Germany and the Western Alliance*, p. 206.
60.   *Ibid.*, p. 208.

Appendix:
Biographies of Key Actors in FRG
Decisionmaking on Arms Control

Adam-Schwaetzer, Irmgard (FDP)

Current position

Deputy Minister in Foreign Office (1987–present)

Background

Birth date: 1942 in Muenster

Education: Studied pharmacology at Universities of Pasau, Muenster, and Bonn

Previous positions: Member of FDP since 1975; General Secretary (1982–84); Federal Treasurer (1984–87)

Bahr, Egon (SPD)

Current positions

Director, Hamburg Institute for Peace Studies and Security Policy (1984–present); Member of SPD's commission on security policy; Head of SPD Delegation in negotiations with East German Socialist Unity Party (SED)

Background

Birth date: 18 March 1922, in Treffort, Thuringia

Education: Abitur, degree in Journalism

Previous positions: Journalist (1945–59); Special Ambassador in Chancellery (Dec. 1972–May 1974); Member of Palme Commission

Positions on security issues

Bahr is one of the primary proponents of the SPD's concept of "security partnership." Bahr has also been involved in negotiation with the GDR of a draft treaty to create a chemical-free weapons zone, hardly surprising given Bahr's central role in the negotiation of Bonn's Eastern treaties in the early 1970s. Bahr is strongly opposed to SDI.

Relationships to other key figures

Bahr is one of Willy Brandt's closest associates; the two have worked together since their days in Berlin (1960). Bahr is also widely recognized as the "architect" of Brandt's *Ostpolitik* and directed the policy's implementation from Brandt's chancellery, largely bypassing the Foreign Office. The Brandt/Bahr wing of the party also includes a number of younger SPD members, including Karsten Voigt.

Miscellany

Bahr's Hamburg Institute has been involved in research on a space-based defense strategy.

Bangemann, Martin (FDP)

Current positions

Minister of Economics; Chairman of Free Democratic Party (FDP)

Background

Birth date: 15 November 1934, in Wanzleben, Saxony

Education: Studied law at Universities of Tuebingen and Munich

Previous positions: Bangemann became a Member of the FDP in 1963, originally belonging to the left wing of the party; Vice Chairman (1969), then Chairman (1973) of FDP in Baden-Wuerttemberg; Member of Bundestag (1973–79); General Secretary of FDP, until fired by Genscher (October 1974–75); Member of European Parliament (1979–84).

Positions on security issues

Bangemann's statements on security policy reflect the official position of the FDP. On SDI, Bangemann favored a framework agreement, and was involved in the negotiation of the terms of participation.

Relationships to other key figures

Bangemann is said to be on good terms with leading figures in the CDU/CSU, including Franz Josef Strauss. Within his own party, Bangemann seems on good enough terms with Genscher, but probably sees himself as second fiddle to Genscher, though he has taken over the position of party chairman. Next to Genscher, the biggest threat to Bangemann's position in the party is Lambsdorff; since resigning as Economic Minister, Lambsdorff has continued to issue statements and directives on economic policy, undermining Bangemann's authority on economic issues.

Miscellany

Bangemann is said to be cheerful and buoyantly self-confident, but also erratic and lacking in the necessary expertise to direct the Economics Ministry. *Speigel* also reports that other FDP members find him "unusually stubborn and injudicious." Other in the party and Economics Ministry have complained about Bangemann's "rhapsodic operating style."

Brandt, Willy (SPD)

Current position

Honorary Chairman of SPD (1987–present)

Background

Birth date: 18 December 1913, in Luebeck, Schleswig-Holstein

Education: Gymnasium (Luebeck), studied history at University of Oslo

Previous positions: Lord Mayor of Berlin (1957–66); Foreign Minister (1966–69); Chancellor (1969–74); Chairman of SPD (1964–87)

Positions on security issues

> Brandt and Egon Bahr generally are credited with developing the concept of a "security partnership" with the East.

Relationships to other key figures

> Brandt's closest associate in the party is Egon Bahr. Among the SPD's successor generation, Brandt appears closest to a number of state leaders, including Oskar Lafontaine (left wing of SPD) and Gerhard Schroeder (SPD leader in Lower Saxony). Brandt's influence on the SPD's foreign policy is still considerable.

Miscellany

> Brandt spent 1933–45 in exile, working as a journalist in Scandinavia.

Buelow, Andreas von (SPD)

Current positions

> Member of Bundestag (since 1969); Chairman, SPD Committee on Security Policy

Background

> Birth date: 17 July 1937, in Dresden

> Education: Studied law at Universities of Heidelberg, Berlin, Munich, and Paris

> Previous positions: Parliamentary State Secretary, Ministry of Defense (1976–80); Minister of Research and Technology (1980–82); Member of SPD since 1960.

Positions on security issues

> Von Buelow authored the SPD security commission's September 1985 draft report, which outlined a number of steps to give substance to the party's notion of "security partnership": the creation of a 300-km wide nuclear-free zone in central Europe; drastic cuts in the

number of short-range nuclear weapons; withdrawal of chemical weapons from East and West Germany; and restructuring of the Bundeswehr.

Relationships to other key figures

Von Buelow is part of a group of younger members in the SPD who challenge pro-NATO orthodoxy, including Alfons Pawelczyk, Hermann Scheer, Karsten Voigt, and Erwin Horn. Buelow's report for the security commission, however, was not well-received by the SPD's executive committee. According to some reports, von Buelow published the report, hoping to feather his own political nest and enhance his standing in the party.

Dregger, Alfred (CDU)

Current positions

Member of Bundestag (1972–present); Chairman of CDU/CSU parliamentary party group (*Fraktion*) in Bundestag (1982–present)

Background

Birth date: 10 December 1920, in Muenster, Westphalia

Education: Studied law at Universities of Marburg, and Tuebingen

Previous position: Member of state parliament, Hesse (1962–72)

Positions on security issues

Dregger represents the views of the more conservative wing of the CDU. He was critical of the NATO dual-track decision, and opposed the link between deployment and arms control, arguing that deployment of INF was necessary for military security. Dregger supported the speedy conclusion of a state-to-state military agreement on German participation in SDI. On the whole, Dregger takes positions that favor military security over détente; in his view, arms control should not be at the expense of the requirements of stable deterrence. Dregger's positions are supported by CDU nationalists and expellees' groups.

Relationships to other key figures

> Dregger's policy stances usually put him in alliance with Juergen Toedenhoefer, Franz Josef Strauss, and the CSU. Dregger and other conservatives in the *Fraktion* have been critical of "Genscherists" in their own ranks, above all Deputy Chairman of the CDU, Volker Ruehe.

Ehmke, Horst (SPD)

Current positions

> Member of Bundestag (since 1969); Chairman of SPD Working Group on Foreign and Security Policy, Inter-German, European and Development Policy; Vice Chairman, Friedrich-Ebert-Foundation; Deputy Chairman of SPD *Fraktion* (1977–Present)

Background

> Birth date: 4 February 1927, in Danzig

> Education: Studied law, economics, political science, history at Universities of Goettingen and Princeton. Doctorate and professorship at University of Freiburg

> Previous positions: State Secretary, Ministry of Justice (1967–69); Minister of Justice and with Special Portfolio and Director of Chancellor's Office (1969–72); Minister for Research and Technology, Post and Telecommunications (1972)

Positions on security issues

> Ehmke is one of the proponents of the SPD's "security partnership" concept.

Relationships to other key figures

> Ehmke works closely with the Brandt/Bahr faction of the party.

Eppler, Erhard (SPD)

Current positions

President of German Protestant Church Conference (1981–present); Member of Executive Board of Evangelical Church of Germany (EKD)

Background

Birth date: 9 December 1926, in Ulm, Wuerttemberg

Education: Studied English, German, history at Universities of Frankfurt a.M., Bern, and Tuebingen

Previous positions: Member of Bundestag (1961–76); Member of State Parliament, Baden-Wuerttemberg (1976–82); Minister for Economic Cooperation (1968–74) (resigned)

Positions on security issues

At the SPD's 1979 party convention in Berlin, Eppler was the only one to vote against INF deployment. After that, Eppler was actively involved in the peace movement. His arguments are often cast in moral terms; he emphasizes the link between development and disarmament. On the U.S.-FRG relationship, Eppler has said, "Either we are allies or we are satellites." Eppler advocates restructuring of the Bundeswehr into a fully defensive force, and the replacement of flexible response with a purely defensive strategy. He supports the creation of a nuclear-free zone in Central Europe.

Relationships to other key figures

Eppler is a member of the SPD's extreme left wing.

Miscellany

Eppler's publications on security issues include *Wege aus der Gefahr* (1981) and *Die toedliche Utopie der Sicherheit* (1983).

Geissler, Heiner

Current positions

General secretary of CDU (1977–present); Member of Bundestag (1965–67; 1980–present)

Background

Birth date: 3 March 1930, in Oberndorf

Education: Studied philosophy and law at Universities of Munich and Tuebingen, LL.D.

Previous positions: Minister for Social Welfare, Health and Athletics, Rhineland-Palatinate (1967–77); Member of State Parliament, Rhineland-Palatinate (1971–79); Federal Minister for Youth, Family and Health (Oct. 1982–Sept. 1985)

Genscher, Hans-Dietrich (FDP)

Current position

Foreign Minister (1974–present)

Background

Birth Date: 21 March 1927, in Reideburg (GDR)

Education: Studied law at Universities of Halle and Leipzig

Previous positions: Managing Director of FDP (1957–65); Minister of Interior (1969–74); Member of FDP since 1952; Chairman of FDP.

Positions on security issues

Genscher is a strong proponent of arms control. He supported both tracks of the 1979 NATO decision to deploy INF. On other issues, Genscher favors a CTB, a global ban on chemical weapons, strict adherence to the ABM Treaty and continued observance of SALT II limits. He places increasing emphasis on a "European voice" in arms control, as a way to put pressure on the superpowers to conclude substantive arms control agreements. Genscher was instrumental in developing the terms of German participation in SDI; he opposed a state-to-state, military agreement, or governmental support for research.

Relationships to other key figures

Genscher is reported to be on fairly good working terms with Kohl, but clearly harbors an intense dislike of Strauss. The animosity between the two is long-standing. Genscher and the FDP played a central role in Strauss's ouster as defense minister during the *Spiegel* affair (1962).

Miscellany

Genscher is said to be cunning and prone to making decisions without consulting other FDP leaders. Guenter Verheugen, General Secretary of the FDP before the 1982 realignment, was highly critical of Genscher's role in engineering the change of coalition. Verheugen, along with others equally critical, subsequently left the party.

Haussmann, Helmut (FDP)

Current positions

Member of Bundestag (since 1976); General Secretary of FDP (June 1984–present)

Background

Birth date: 18 May 1943, in Tuebingen

Education: Studied economics and sociology; Ph.D. (political science)

Previous positions: Spokesman for Economic Policy, FDP Parliamentary Party Group; Member of FDP Executive Committee since 1978; Chairman of Working Group on Economic Policy, FDP Parliamentary Party Group.

Relationships to other key figures

Haussmann began his career in the left social-liberal wing of the party. In 1982, at the Baden-Wuerttemberg FDP party congress,

Haussmann opposed realignment with the CDU/CSU and called for Genscher's resignation. Haussmann changed his tune in 1982 after he was voted out of the party's executive committee. On economic policy, Haussmann allies with Lambsdorff. Haussmann also seems to enjoy the support of FDP state leaders, who played a role in his appointment as General Secretary.

Holik, Josef

Current positions

Ambassador, Federal Commissioner for Disarmament and Arms Control; Director of Division 2a, Foreign Office (Jan. 1987–present)

Background

Birth date: 20 April 1931, in Tetschen

Education: Studied law, administration, and political science at Wuerzburg, Speyer, and Colgate universities

Previous positions: Career foreign service officer. Posts: Madras (1963–65); Bonn (1965–67); NATO, Brussels (1967–71). Returned to Foreign Office to become Deputy Director of NATO desk (1974–77); Director of Desk 221 (1979–84); Deputy of Former Commissioner for Arms Control, Friedrich Ruth, since 1983; Head of MBFR Delegation (1984–86)

Horn, Erwin (SPD)

Current positions

Member of Bundestag (since 1969); Member of Bundestag Defense Committee; SPD Spokesman on committee; Member of SPD Commission on Security Policy; Chairman of North Atlantic Assembly's Military Committee

Background

Birth date: 2 May 1929, in Annerod

Education: Abitur 1948 at *Volks-* and *Aufbauschule*. Studied history, German, philosophy, politics

Previous position: Vice Chairman of Defense Committee (1980–83)

Positions on security issues

Horn was critical of von Buelow's security policy paper.

Kohl, Helmut

Current positions

Chancellor (1982–present); Chairman of the CDU, Member of Bundestag (1976–present)

Background

Birth date: 3 April 1930, in Ludwigshafen

Education: Studied law and history at Universities of Frankfurt and Heidelberg; D. phil.

Previous positions: Premier, Rhineland-Palatinate (1969–76); Chairman of CDU Bundestag Parliamentary Party Group (*Fraktion*) (until 1982)

Positions on security issues

Kohl belongs the ''Atlanticist'' faction on foreign policy issues. He believes that good relations with the United States are of primary importance and has hesitated to take any actions that would cause friction between the United States and the FRG.

Relationships to other key figures

Kohl's closest advisor on foreign policy in the Chancellor's Office is Horst Teltschick. Within the CDU parliamentary party group, he relies on the support of Volker Ruehe.

Lafontaine, Oskar (SPD)

Current positions

Premier of the Saar (1985–present); Deputy Chairman of SPD (1987–present)

Background

Birth date: 16 September 1943

Education: Degree in physics from University of Bonn

Previous positions: Mayor of Saarbruecken

Positions on security issues

Lafontaine was strongly opposed to INF deployment. He has also advocated a "loosening" of Germany's ties to NATO.

Relationships to other key figures

Lafontaine is associated with others in the left wing of the SPD.

Miscellany

Publications include *Angst vor den Freunden* (1981).

Lambsdorff, Otto Graf (FDP)

Current positions

Member of Bundestag (1972–present); Member of FDP Executive Committee (since 1972); Economics spokesman of FDP Parliamentary Party Group (1951–present)

Background

Birth date: 20 December 1926, in Aachen

Education: Studied law at University of Bonn, LL.D.

Previous positions: Minister of Economics (1978–84); Member of FDP (1951–present); State Treasurer, North Rhine-Westphalia (1968)

Relationships to other key figures

Lambsdorff seems to be loosely allied with Haussmann, Bangemann, and other FDP members who would like to see the FDP firmly tied to the CDU/CSU.

Moellemann, Juergen (FDP)

Current positions

Minister for Education and Science (March 1987–present); Member of FDP Executive Committee

Background

Birth date: 15 July 1945, in Augsburg

Education: Teacher's training

Previous positions: Chairman of FDP in North Rhine-Westphalia; Member of FDP since 1970; Parliamentary State Secretary, Foreign Office (1982–87)

Positions on security issues

Moellemann is a confirmed "Genscherist" (see below).

Relationships to other key figures

Moellemann was Genscher's assistant in the Foreign Office and supports Genscher's positions on security policy; he helped Genscher and Lambsdorff bring about the realignment of the FDP in 1982.

Miscellany

Spiegel reports that Moellemann is "too ambitious, too frivolous and too aimless" for many. Moellemann is reported to have hinted at ambitions for the Foreign Minister's post.

Rau, Johannes (SPD)

Current positions

> Premier of North Rhine-Westphalia (1978–present); Deputy Chairman SPD

Background

> Birth date: 16 January 1931, in Wuppertal
>
> Education: Gymnasium; Training as publisher's apprentice
>
> Previous positions: Member of State Parliament, North Rhine-Westphalia (1958–present); State Minister for Science and Research (1970–78); SPD Chancellor candidate 1987

Positions on security issues

> Rau belongs to the faction of SPD moderates on security policy. He has reaffirmed the party's commitment to NATO but opposes German participation in SDI. He opposed INF deployment as well.

Relationships to other key figures

> Rau is said to be on good terms with the Executive Committee parliamentarians in Bonn. His key aides in the Duesseldorf chancellery are Dr. Klaus Dieter Leister and Karl-Heinz Benteler.

Miscellany

> Rau categorically rejects coalition with the Greens at the national level.

Ruehe, Volker (CDU)

Current positions

> Member of Bundestag (1976–present); Deputy Chairman, CDU Parliamentary Party Group (responsible for foreign policy, security policy, inter-German and development policy)

Background

> Birth date: 25 September 1942, in Hamburg
>
> Education: Studied German and English at University of Hamburg
>
> Previous positions: Member of CDU since 1963; Member of City Parliament of Hamburg (1970–76)

Positions on security issues

> Ruehe is largely a "Genscherist" on foreign and security policy, and has been criticized by the Union's more conservative members for his policy stances. Ruehe supported the "walk-in-the-woods" formula for INF; he opposed participation in SDI, and supports adherence to the SALT II limits.

Relationships to other key figures

> Ruehe is a key figure in the CDU/CSU parliamentary group. When it comes to foreign and security policy issues, Ruehe plays a decisive role in securing a majority for any particular position. Ruehe is reported to have gotten involved in foreign policy after impressing Kohl during a trip to the United States. With Kohl's support, Ruehe campaigned for the position of Deputy Chairman of the parliamentarians' group, beating out an older, more conservative candidate from the Union's right wing. Ruehe has undoubtedly helped Kohl check the influence of the CDU/CSU's right wing.

Miscellany

> The *Frankfurter Allgemeine* describes Ruehe as extremely self-confident, a man who has won the respect if not the liking of his colleagues.

Ruehl, Lothar (CDU)

Current positions

> State Secretary, Ministry of Defense (1982–present)

Background

Birth date: 1927, in Cologne

Education: Studied law, and history at Universities of Bonn and Paris, Ph.D.

Previous positions: Journalist (1949–69) and Deputy Chief Editor (1969–73) of the conservative daily *Die Welt*; ZDF (German television) Correspondent (1973–79); ZDF Studio Director (1979–80)

Scheer, Hermann (SPD)

Current positions

Member of Bundestag (1980–present); Disarmament spokesman for SPD Parliamentary Party Group; Member of SPD's Security Policy Committee; Member of SPD Executive Committee in Baden-Wuerttemberg

Background

Birth date: 29 April 1944, in Wehrheim

Education: Abitur: Officer's training school in Hanover; studied economics and social sciences, Ph.D.

Previous positions: Office candidate and Lieutenant in Bundeswehr (1964–67); Member of SPD Advisory Committee since 1975

Positions on security issues

Scheer is part of the Brandt/Bahr group that advocates a more critical stance with regard to NATO. Scheer supports SPD proposals to restructure NATO for a nonprovocative defense. He has advocated the denuclearization of Central Europe and creation of a "conventional defense structure."

Schmude, Juergen (SPD)

Current positions

> President of Synod of Evangelical Church of Germany (1985–present); Member of Bundestag

Background

> Birth date: 9 June 1936, in Insterburg, East Prussia

> Education: Studied law at Universities of Goettingen, Berlin, and Bonn; LL.D.

> Previous positions: Parliamentary State Secretary, Ministry of the Interior (1974–78); Member of SPD since 1957

Relationships to other key figures

> Schmude is the SPD's specialist on inter-German policy.

Spaeth, Lothar (CDU)

Current position

> Premier of Baden-Wuerttemberg (1978–present)

Background

> Birth date: 16 November 1937, in Signaringen

> Education: State administration school (*staatliche Verwaltungsschule*)

> Previous positions: Member of state parliament, Baden-Wuerttemberg (1968–present)

Positions on security issues

> Spaeth is an Atlanticist and shares a consensus orientation similar to Kohl's.

Relationships to other key figures

> Spaeth is considered an up-and-coming leader in the CDU and a possible successor to Kohl.

Miscellany

> Spaeth has been praised for his promotion of high tech industry in Baden-Wuerttemberg.

Stobbe, Dietrich (SPD)

Current position

> Member of Bundestag (representative of Berlin) (1983–present)

Background

> Birth date: 25 March 1938, in Weepers, East Prussia

> Education: Studied at Free University of Berlin

> Previous positions: Mayor of Berlin (1977–81, resigned); Director of Friedrich-Ebert-Foundation, New York (1981–83); Member of SPD since 1960; Member of Executive Committee since 1977.

Positions on security issues

> Stobbe is a member of the moderate/conservative faction within the SPD.

Relationships to other key figures

> Stobbe belongs to the right wing of SPD, a member of the *"Seeheimer Kreis."*

Miscellany

> Stobbe was forced to resign from his position as Mayor of Berlin after the Flick construction scandal.

Stoltenberg, Gerhard (CDU)

Current position

Minister of Finance (October 1982–present)

Background

Birth date: 29 September 1928, in Kiel

Education: Ph.D., University of Kiel

Previous positions: Member of Schleswig-Holstein Parliament (1954–57; 1971–present); Minister for Scientific Research 1965–69; Premier of Schleswig-Holstein (1971–82)

Positions on security issues

Stoltenberg is a centrist on foreign policy issues, but his firm stance on economic policy — even after repeated pressure from the Americans — suggests that he might be a stronger advocate of German interests than Kohl.

Relationships to other key figures

Stoltenberg seems to enjoy the respect of many of his Union colleagues. Further, he is probably on good terms with Strauss. Stoltenberg campaigned for Strauss in Northern Germany during Strauss's bid for the chancellorship in 1980.

Miscellany

Spiegel has described Stoltenberg as "reserve Chancellor." He has been considered one of the most likely candidates to succeed Kohl as leader of the CDU, however his standing in the party suffered from a political scandal in 1987 in Schleswig-Holstein. There was even speculation that Stoltenberg would replace Kohl as the CDU/CSU's chancellor candidate. As Finance Minister, Stoltenberg is well placed to succeed Kohl; the ministry is considered one of the best springboard's to the Chancellor's office. Generally speaking, Stoltenberg is described as a "calculable conservative"; even his political opponents are said to praise his "confidentiality and reliability."

Strauss, Franz Josef (CSU)

Current positions

Premier of Bavaria; Chairman of the CSU; Member of State parliament, Bavaria (1978–present)

Background

Birth date: 6 September 1915, in Munich

Education: University of Munich, secondary school teaching examination in history and classical languages

Previous positions: Founding member of CSU; Minister of Defense (resignation in 1962 after *Spiegel* affair); Minister of Finance (1966–69)

Positions on security issues

Strauss has long been skeptical and critical of arms control. His opposition to arms control is long-standing: he opposed the Limited Test Ban Treaty, the Non-Proliferation Treaty, SALT, and the inclusion of ERW in arms control negotiations. More recently, he opposed the deployment/arms control link in the NATO dual-track decision, but favored the speedy conclusion of a state agreement paving the way for German participation in SDI research.

Relationships to other key figures

Strauss belongs to the "Gaullist" faction of the CDU/CSU, which puts him in alliance with Juergen Todenhoefer and Alfred Dregger.

Teltschik, Horst (CDU)

Current positions

Director of Division 2, Chancellery (since 1982)

Background

Birth date: 14 June 1940, Klantendorf, Sudetenland

Education: Studied political science, history, and international law at Free University of Berlin

Previous positions: Head of Group on Foreign and Inter-German Policy in CDU Party Office (1970); Advisor to Kohl, Mainz Chancellery (1972); Office Director for Kohl, during his tenure as Leader of CDU/CSU Parliamentary Group (1972–82)

Positions on security issues

Teltshik supported German participation in SDI research but has stressed the importance of continued conformity with the ABM treaty.

Relationships to other key figures

Teltschik is one of Kohl's oldest contacts, dating back to Mainz, where Teltschik spent four years as Kohl's speechwriter. He is Kohl's closest adviser on foreign policy and has even been called Kohl's "Henry Kissinger." Teltschik sees himself as a rival to Genscher.

Miscellany

Teltschik has published a number of essays on foreign policy. According to some reports, the Foreign Office and Genscher are contemptuous of Teltschik, calling him an amateur.

Todenhoefer, Juergen (CDU)

Current positions

Member of Bundestag (1972–present); Member of Bundestag Committee on Foreign Relations (1981–present) and Subcommittee on Disarmament and Arms Control

Background

Birth date: 12 November 1940, in Offenburg, Baden

Education: Studied law at Universities of Munich, Paris, Bonn, and Freiburg

Previous positions: Disarmament spokesman for CDU; Judge, State Court in Kaiserslautern (1972); Personal Advisor to CDU general secretary (1970–71)

Positions on security issues

Generally speaking, Todenhoefer believes that the critical factor in military security is stability, not the quantity of arms. He continues to stress the importance of strategic and security considerations over the process of negotiation.

Relationships to other key figures

Todenhoefer belongs to the "Gaullist" faction of the CDU/CSU and is allied with Dregger and Strauss.

Vogel, Hans-Jochen (SPD)

Current positions

Chairman of SPD; Chairman of SPD Parliamentary Party Group

Background

Birth date: 3 February 1926, in Goettingen

Education: Studied law at University of Marburg

Previous positions: Mayor of Munich (1960–72); Minister for Urban Planning, Construction and Justice (1972–81); SPD Chancellor candidate 1983

Positions on security issues

Vogel has opposed participation in SDI and calls for the demilitarization of space. He also supports reform of NATO strategy.

Relationships to other key figures

Vogel is a member of the SPD's moderate faction. He is a key player in the Bundestag and is the one responsible for putting together a majority on any specific position.

Miscellany

Vogel is said to be a quick and capable thinker, but also cold, distant, gloomy, and authoritarian.

Voigt, Karsten (SPD)

Current positions

Member of Bundestag (since 1976); Foreign Policy Spokesman for SPD Parliamentary Party Group; Chairman of SPD Executive Committee's Commission on Security Policy

Background

Birth date: 11 April 1941, in Elmshorn

Education: Studied history, German, Scandinavian at Universities of Hamburg, Copenhagen, and Frankfurt

Previous positions: Chairman of Young Socialists ("Jusos") (1969–72)

Positions on security issues

Voigt is a member of the Brandt/Bahr group on foreign and security policy issues. He opposed INF deployment and SDI participation. He has cautioned against undermining the ABM Treaty. Voigt has called for reform of NATO strategy and agreed-upon disarmament positions. He is also involved in negotiations between the SPD and East German SED.

Relationships to other key figures

Voigt works closely with Brandt and Bahr.

Miscellany

Voigt's publications on defense and security policy include *Wege zur Abruestung* (1981) and *Nuclear Weapons in Europe* (1983).

Wellershoff, Dieter

Current positions

Inspector General of the Bundeswehr (1987–present); Admiral, Navy

Background

Birth date: 16 March 1933, in Dortmund, Northrhine-Westphalia

Education: Scientific secondary school (Krefeld); Studied mechanical engineering at Aachen Technical University

Previous positions: Deputy Chief of Staff for Armament, Naval Staff, Federal Ministry of Defense (1977–81); Commandant, Federal Armed Forces Command and Staff College, Hamburg (1981–83); Chief of Staff, Navy (1985–86); Chief of Staff, Bundeswehr (1986–87)

Woerner, Manfred (CDU)

Current position

Secretary General of NATO

Background

Birth date: 24 September 1934, Stuttgart

Education: Abitur, studied law at Universities of Heidelberg, Paris, and Munich

Previous positions: Minister of Defense (October 1982–1988)

Positions on security issues

Woerner is probably one of the few Union leaders with some conception of the operational characteristics and technical aspects of weapons systems and arms control. Woerner's concern with arms control dates back to SALT I; he feared that the SALT process would decouple the United States from German security. Woerner viewed INF deployment as necessary to ensure the credibility of NATO strategy, and initially opposed the link between deployment and arms control negotiations. He favored German participation in SDI, but only if full access to technology was ensured. Woerner advocates a European land-based ATBM system.

INDEX

ABOUT THE AUTHORS

Barry M. Blechman is the president of Defense Forecasts Inc., a research and analysis enterprise in Washington, D.C. He has written extensively on U.S. defense policy and arms control, including the classic study of political/military operations, *Force Without War*. Dr. Blechman served as assistant director of the U.S. Arms Control and Disarmament Agency from 1977 to 1980. Before that, he directed the defense analysis program at the Brookings Institution. His previous Ballinger publications include *Rethinking the U.S. Strategic Posture* (1982) and *Toward a More Effective Defense* (1986).

Cathleen S. Fisher is a specialist in West German politics and security issues. She holds a M.A. from the School of Advanced International Studies of Johns Hopkins University and is a doctoral candidate at the University of Maryland. Ms. Fisher has been a Ford Fellow at the Center for International Affairs of Harvard University (1987–88) and a Fulbright Scholar in Bonn (1981–82). She is currently a fellow of the Free University of Berlin under the Social Science Research Council's Berlin Program for Advanced German and European Studies.

Jeffrey Boutwell is a defense policy analyst at the American Academy of Arts and Sciences. He has written extensively on German security affairs and domestic politics, including *Nuclear Weapons and the German Dilemma* (forthcoming). Dr. Boutwell is also the co-editor of *Weapons in Space* and *The Nuclear Confrontation in Europe*.

Clay Clemens teaches government at the College of William and Mary, where he specializes in European politics and security, with an emphasis on West German affairs. His publications include chapters in *The Greens* *of West Germany* and *Shattering Europe's Defense Consensus: The Antinuclear Protest Movement and the Future of NATO.*

Stephen F. Szabo is on the faculty of the National War College in Washington, D.C. and a professorial lecturer in European studies at the School for Advanced International Studies, Johns Hopkins University. Among many other publications, he is the editor of *The Successor Generation: International Perspectives of Postwar Europeans* and the author of *The Bundeswehr and Western Security* (forthcoming).